Praise for
TRAPPED WITHIN

Whatever impossible situation you are facing, *Trapped Within* will remind you that we have a God who makes all things possible. Kelly Denham's story provides two priceless commodities: hope and a reminder that you are not alone. Reading it will inspire you to move toward suffering, not away; and to believe that no matter how ill-equipped you feel, God can enable you to do the impossible. It's a celebration of a hero son and his warrior mom who refused to give up.

—**Meridith Foster**, radio host and host of *The Unfolding* podcast

This book is a sacred, front-row seat to what it looks like when a family says yes to faith, hope, and stubborn love, and then continues to say yes as everything else is stripped away. I sobbed as I read this book, I laughed as I read this book, and I felt the weight and beauty of this story change me. Make room on your shelf for *Trapped Within*, and then buy ten more copies for all the people you love. It is a tender, raw, powerful gift.

—**Kimberly Stuart**, author of *Sugar: A Novel* and *Heart Land*

God's unfailing love is a powerful force. (It) opens our minds and hearts to the possibility that He can and will transform certain defeat into resounding victory. It broke through the darkness and pain of TJ's circumstances, continually infusing Kelly, Travis and TJ with the strength to keep fighting and moving forward. TJ's pain is not in vain. His sweet example and testimony of faith through unimaginable suffering has changed many lives. It has changed mine. He *is* victorious.

—**Melinda Means**, author of
Invisible Wounds: Hope While You're Hurting

TRAPPED WITHIN

UNFAILING LOVE, UNIMAGINABLE SUFFERING

KELLY DENHAM

AUTHOR'S NOTE

This book is the true story of what my son, TJ, was compelled to endure as the result of a surgical procedure that went wrong and what my family and I learned from the experience. I have mentioned the medical facilities where TJ was treated, but the names of all doctors and other medical personnel who treated TJ have been omitted or fictionalized. Any similarities between the fictionalized names and the names of any real people is strictly coincidental.

The only exception is a rehabilitation physician named Dr. Landry, whose real name is mentioned in a story I tell about how my son's sense of humor remained lively even at the most challenging moments. You will see why I could not leave out his name.

I have written frankly and in detail about my son's experiences and how our family coped with his medical issues. However, my book is not meant to give medical advice, and the reader is urged to seek appropriate professional advice and care if a medical problem arises.

Copyright © 2020 Kelly Denham

All rights reserved. No part of this book may be reproduced or used in any manner without written permission of the copyright owner except for the use of quotations in a book review. For more information, please email contact@kellydenham.com.

All Scripture quotations, unless otherwise indicated, are taken from the The Holy Bible, New International Version®, NIV® Copyright © 1973, 1978, 1984, 2011 by Biblica, Inc.® Used by permission. All rights reserved worldwide.

Scripture quotations marked NKJV are taken from the New King James Version®. Copyright © 1982 by Thomas Nelson. Used by permission. All rights reserved.

Interior Formatting: MartinPublishingServices.com

DEDICATION

To my husband Travis:

When we said "I do" twenty-eight years ago, my hopes, dreams, and expectations were of a future filled with joy, laughter, and happiness. I have not been disappointed, as your quick sense of humor has kept me laughing our entire marriage. However, on this journey together, we have also experienced deep sadness, sorrow, and heartache. Through it all, I have seen you hold fast to your faith in Christ and grow into the godliest man I know. I am very proud of you, my dear husband, and I love you.

To "The Sisters,"
Ashley, Whitney, Courtney, and Chandler:

Your steadfast love for your brother has been apparent to everyone. You have lived through much sorrow and pain in your short years. Allow the troubles of this life to push you deeper into your relationship with Christ. He alone will meet all your needs and will never disappoint you. I love you.

To "Little Man," Aiden:

You have brought much joy to Nana and Papa's life. God held you during the hard years and has brought you into a place of abundance. Continue to walk in His ways, hiding His Word in your heart, and you will be blessed. I love you.

CONTENTS

A Special Message from Melinda Means xi
Preface xv

Chapter 1	Backstory	1
Chapter 2	She Likes Me	13
Chapter 3	The Diagnosis	19
Chapter 4	I Didn't Die	25
Chapter 5	Praise You in This Storm	39
Chapter 6	Mayo Clinic	47
Chapter 7	The Creepy Mustache	59
Chapter 8	The Darkest of Nights	73
Chapter 9	Training and Checklists	85
Chapter 10	Curveballs	109
Chapter 11	The Woman with the Box	123
Chapter 12	Dr. Laundry	143
Chapter 13	The Downward Spiral	159
Chapter 14	Jesus Walks Beside Me	173
Chapter 15	The Owl	191
Chapter 16	A Man Reborn	213
Chapter 17	Addicted to the Shindig	231
Chapter 18	A Morning in the Life of TJ	243
Chapter 19	Positive Vibes Only	253
Chapter 20	Full Circle	269

Epilogue 279
A Message from Kelly 291
Acknowledgements 299
Notes 301

A SPECIAL MESSAGE FROM

MELINDA MEANS

Author of *Invisible Wounds: Hope While You're Hurting*;
Unraveled Roots: Exposing the Hidden Causes of Damaging Behaviors;
and *Mothering from Scratch*

If truth be told, I never wanted to be Kelly's friend. Actually, I didn't even want to *talk* to Kelly. It was nothing personal. The day we met I didn't want to talk to *anyone*. The year was 2005. I was flying to my hometown in Iowa to attend a family member's funeral. Other events happening in my life at the time also had me completely spent and broken. As I boarded the plane, all I wanted to do was find my seat and be **left alone**.

God knew better.

Soon this lovely, kind-looking woman about my age sat down next to me. I forced a smile, but then promptly ignored her and tried to sleep. About halfway through the flight, she asked me a question. I don't even remember what it was. But we began to talk. We soon discovered that we had a crazy amount of things in common—we had both grown up in Iowa; she was also flying to a family member's funeral; and we even knew some of the same people! It quickly began to feel like a Divine appointment. We were both disappointed to discover that even though we were flying back on the same day, we were scheduled on different flights.

On the day of my departure, however, guess who was sitting at my gate? My new friend Kelly! Her plane had a mechanical problem, so she was bumped to *my flight*. Coincidence? I think not. She exchanged seats with another passenger, allowing us to chat the whole way back. A lifelong friendship was sealed.

Over the last 15 years, we have spent time with each other's families (my husband dubbed her "Airplane Kelly" and we still refer to her as that to this day), talked on the phone, met at Starbucks and Pizzeria Uno (halfway stops between her then-home a couple hours south of me). We have supported and prayed for each other through some of the most difficult times and seasons of our lives.

Our faith and shared experiences bonded us. Little did we know that we would eventually bond over a shared experience that neither of us would have ever chosen—watching our only sons battle through devastating, life-altering circumstances. I am so grateful we both know a Father who could understand the deep pain of watching an "only Son" suffer.

My son Micah's struggle began at birth. Now 20 years old, Micah was born with cystic fibrosis (CF). CF is a progressive, genetic disease that impacts the body's respiratory and digestive systems. At age 14, he was also diagnosed with CF-related diabetes (similar to Type 1 diabetes). Although our stories are very different and I am in no way equating the depth of our pain and difficulties, I can so closely relate to the cries of Kelly's "boy mama" heart through TJ's long, painful ordeal. Our struggles may be different, but the emotions we feel are often the same.

TJ and his family's story is full of dramatic and heart-wrenching ups and downs. Hope soared one moment only to be crushed the next. That kind of roller coaster journey is exhausting, agonizing and can easily become faith-draining. Yet, watching Kelly and Travis' faith in action often took my breath away or left me in tears. Their tireless devotion never wavered. As Kelly says throughout this book, the only way to persevere in the midst of such heartache is to cling to God and choose to believe the truth about Him—the truth that He is loving and good even when we don't understand (or like) His ways. It is an *act of the will* to choose to believe that God is working for our good even when we can't see how He possibly can be. We can't trust God's ways until we've learned to trust His heart.

I remember talking to Kelly shortly before TJ's hellish nightmare began. I vividly remember her saying to me at the time, "I don't know how you do it, Melinda. Watching Micah go through all he has to go through must be so hard." Kelly learned what I learned: God gives us what we need as we need it. He empowers us to do what we cannot do or face on our own—one moment, one step at a time. We've both experienced the painful paradox that His sweetness can often be felt most deeply in the midst of the struggle.

God's unfailing love is a powerful force. It gives us the comfort and strength to weather challenges that would otherwise crush us. God's love opens our minds and hearts to the possibility that He can and will transform certain defeat into resounding victory. It broke through the darkness and pain of TJ's circumstances, continually infusing Kelly, Travis and TJ with the strength to keep fighting and moving forward.

TJ's pain is not in vain. His sweet example and testimony of faith through unimaginable suffering has changed many lives. It has changed mine. He *is* victorious.

Through these pages, meet my friend Kelly and her son TJ. It may just be a Divine appointment.

PREFACE

He is trapped. Not trapped in the way one would imagine, such as within the wreckage of a car, a burning building, or a collapsed cavern, yet trapped all the same.

Year after year I watch him suffer as seemingly insurmountable barriers block his path to freedom. Worry lines form on my face, and tears streak my cheeks, while his unknown future looms over my head like a black cloud. Will he die a prisoner?

I'm exhausted from my attempts to free him. Every strategy has failed, but I keep trying. I can't give up hope that maybe one day my efforts will succeed.

Memories of his life play in my mind as if on a screen. Images scroll past of the blond-haired, little boy running in the sunshine, and I see that time is not my friend. The hourglass has been turned over, and the things I once thought were important, now seem so frivolous. As the sand plinks against the glass, I chide myself for not enjoying the little moments more.

I cry out to the Lord. Will this journey of suffering ever end? I am his voice now, and desperation consumes me while I wait for his rescue.

CHAPTER 1

BACKSTORY

I grew up in a small farm town in the Midwest. Van Meter, Iowa is located twenty miles west of our state's capital city, Des Moines. When I meet people outside of Iowa, they ask, "Don't you grow potatoes there?" To which I always reply, "No, that's Idaho. I live in Iowa. We grow corn and soybeans." In anticipation of their next question, I also add, "And we have bathrooms and running water in our homes, too."

I love Iowa. I think it's beautiful with its rolling hills, cornfields, and farms that dot the countryside. Iowa's nickname is *The Hawkeye State*, but it also could have been called The Green State. The grass and trees are the deepest shade of green from spring to fall. People in Iowa are welcoming, friendly, and helpful. There is no place I would rather live. I am an Iowan through and through.

Four generations of my family grew up in Van Meter. We were very ingrained in that tiny midwestern farm town. It's a community where everyone knows everyone. Sometimes that's good—and sometimes not so good.

After high school, I moved to Des Moines for college and graduated with a degree in court reporting. In 1992, I married my husband Travis and along with his three young daughters, Ashley, Whitney, and Courtney, we became a family. I quickly bonded with these sweet, blond-haired girls. They were funny, well behaved, and brought joy and laughter to my life.

Our first child together was a daughter, and we named her Chandler. She was born in April of 1993. I was overjoyed to be the mother of a new baby, and I rarely laid her down. She was a real beauty with light-brown hair, dark-brown eyes, and a fiery personality that kept me on my toes.

I loved being a mom and having a family, but I was inexperienced and was having a hard time adjusting to the blended family life. For the first few years of my marriage, we lived in the suburbs of Des Moines, but I longed to be back in that small town where my family lived. I felt safe there.

In 1996, after pleading with my city-born-and-bred husband, we moved to Van Meter. At the time, I was pregnant with our second child. During that pregnancy, Travis and I wanted to wait until delivery to learn the gender of our baby, but we so hoped it was a boy, especially Travis. He loved his four girls, but he really wanted a son. So, as a family, we prayed and hoped. In July of 1996, I gave birth to a son. We named him Travis Jordan and called him TJ. TJ looked just like his dad and had a gentle, happy, laid-back personality.

During the first year of TJ's life, I worked nights and Travis worked days so I could be home with Chandler and TJ while the older girls were in school. However, it wasn't long before we realized that arrangement wasn't working very well. We weren't getting any sleep, so I looked for a job that would allow me to work from home. After much prayer, I finally found a job doing medical transcription. I was thrilled to be home with my toddler and preschooler, but due to their young ages, working where we lived posed a significant challenge. We made it through but not without mishaps.

My desk was in the basement, and once Chandler went to preschool, TJ nearly always stayed beside me, playing with his toys while I worked. He was generally very well behaved and seldom got into things. However, when he was about two years old, while working at the computer, I suddenly stopped and thought, *It's too quiet in here.* I looked around the basement. He was nowhere to be found, so I went on the hunt for him. As I entered the kitchen, I immediately noticed him with the litter box in front of the refrigerator. He had dumped a gallon of milk and a carton of eggs into the litter and was mixing it with a wooden spoon. My mouth fell open, and I stared in disbelief as I watched the young chef stirring his stomach-churning concoction. Shaking my head, I wondered, *How on earth did he even think of that?* It didn't even occur to me to be angry because I was so impressed with his creativity. It was hilarious and really unlike him to be so mischievous.

As TJ grew older, we developed a special bond. Our personalities clicked because I understood him and the way he thought. He was sensitive, loving, and tender-hearted. He was my grocery-store boy. We loved going to the grocery store together in the middle of the day, and on the drive there, he would ask, "We're buddies, right, Mom?"

"Yep, you're my buddy," I told him, "and nobody loves you more than your mommy loves you."

One night when TJ was four years old, we were sitting on the couch snuggling, and we started talking about the Lord. I told him that God made him, loved him very much, and had sent His Son, Jesus, to be his Savior. We talked about heaven, and I told him that if he wanted to go there, he needed to accept Jesus into his heart. TJ said he wanted to go to heaven and wanted Jesus to be in his heart, so we prayed together.

"Okay, TJ," I said. "Repeat after me: Dear Jesus."

"Dear Jesus," he repeated.

"Please forgive me of my sins," I continued.

"Please forgive my sins."

"I love you very much, and I want to go to heaven and be with you when I die."

"I love you very much, and I wanna go to heaven, be with you when I die," he echoed.

"Please come into my heart."

"Please come into my heart!" he exclaimed.

TJ had done the most important thing he could ever do on this earth: acknowledging Jesus as Lord and Savior and his only way to heaven. If I did nothing else right as a parent his entire life, I knew I had at least done the most important thing I could ever do—pointing the way to eternal life.

In the fall of 2000, TJ went to preschool half days Monday through Thursday. It was during preschool when I started noticing that he marched to the beat of his own drum. It was Halloween, and the preschoolers were supposed to dress in their costumes for the class party—except he didn't want to wear a costume. *What kid doesn't want to wear a Halloween costume?* I wondered.

I tried and tried to coax him, but it didn't work, so I eventually surrendered and took him to school without a costume. We were holding hands as we walked into the building when we saw the other kids, all dressed up in their Halloween costumes. TJ began giggling.

"What's so funny?" I quizzed.

While pointing to the kids in front of us, he grinned and said, "Look at those kids, Mom."

"They look funny in their costumes, don't they?" I asked.

"Yep!" he said and giggled some more.

He didn't want to wear a costume, but he was very entertained by the other kids in their costumes. It never crossed his mind that he was the only one not participating.

The first day of his kindergarten year was both exciting and sad for me. My last child was going to school and my grocery-store boy was no longer available. His kindergarten teacher's name was Miss McClintock. He called her "Miss Clintock" and was very fond of her. She had a great influence on his thinking. Once, when his sisters were teasing him about his color preferences, he emphatically stated, "Miss Clintock says boys can like pink, too!"

While I was visiting his kindergarten classroom one afternoon, he excused himself to use the restroom, which was located inside the classroom. As he walked in and closed the door, I realized I had never forewarned Miss McClintock about his restroom habits. Whenever he used the restroom, he was there for a very long time. There was no medical reason for it. He just liked to take his time. He was never in a rush and didn't get anxious, even if he knew people were waiting on him. This particular day was no exception. I sat by myself with his class for a half an hour while he used the restroom. Periodically, Miss McClintock walked by the restroom, knocked on the door, and asked, "You still doing okay in there?"

After which she would hear a little voice say, "Yeah, I'm fine."

And then she walked away chuckling, saying that it was their daily routine.

Because TJ lived in a house with so many females, he had a sensitive side. His sisters adored him and sometimes made him up to look like their living doll. I often found him with barrettes in his hair and his fingernails painted. He didn't seem to mind at all and just let them do what they wanted, that is, until his dad saw it and commanded the girls to remove it.

Even though TJ allowed his sisters to do girly things to him, he also had a mischievous boy side. My husband grew up a sports guy. He played football, basketball, and loved watching all kinds of sports on TV. He grew up in the city and wasn't into hunting, fishing, or outdoorsy things. In fact, he said he could never kill an animal and wouldn't even put a worm on a fishhook. I, however, grew up with men who were hunters and fishermen. TJ took after my side of the family, and even though he'd never been around guns, he loved them. He turned everything into a gun: a clothes hanger, a ketchup bottle—you name it.

One afternoon when he was six years old, his oldest two sisters, Ashley and Whitney, were in their room with the door shut. I heard TJ yelling and went downstairs to see what was going on. I found him lying on his belly in the hallway outside their room with a Nerf gun pointed at the door. "Come out with your hands up!" he demanded. When the girls cracked open the door to see what was going on, they promptly got hit with a barrage of Nerf darts.

When TJ was in second grade, we moved to Naples, Florida. The summer before our move, we visited our family in Naples and discovered that this part of the country was beautiful with amazing weather. Travis was tired of the merciless Iowa winters and had always wanted to live in a warm place. When we returned home from our summer trip, we decided to embark on a new adventure.

While living in Iowa, Travis was a painter. Although he was good at it, he wasn't particularly thrilled with painting. It paid the bills but was boring, and he wanted a job that challenged him more. So, before moving, he accepted a job in Florida building houses. He was excited about the new opportunity and the change in career. We decided that since all the kids were in school now, it was time for me to get a job outside the home that paid better. I accepted a job at First Baptist Church Naples as a ministry assistant. We were all very upbeat about this new chapter in our lives. Everything was exciting and different.

TJ adjusted very quickly to his new school and environment. He made new friends easily, even though he wasn't the kind of kid who required a lot of friends. If he had one or two, he was happy. It also became apparent that he didn't care about being popular. He was a little bit on the nerdy side and fit in well with his group of friends. He was studious and cared about his grades. I never had to tell him to do his homework or ask him where his planner was so I could sign it at the end of the week. On Thursday nights, I always found his planner strategically placed on the kitchen counter where I could see it so I could sign it before he went to school the following morning. He was very responsible.

One sunny Florida afternoon, I chaperoned a field trip with TJ and his class to Marco Island. The plan was to use nets to strain water from the Gulf of Mexico to see what critters we could find. This activity wasn't my kind of thing, but I wanted to be involved with him and his school, so I agreed to chaperone. I was in charge of a small group of boys that included TJ and four of his friends. After riding a very noisy bus for a half hour, we arrived at our island destination, and excitement was in the air. The boys hurriedly jumped off the bus and wandered toward the Gulf. At the shore, they grabbed the net, waded into the ocean, and began straining water. I stayed back on the shore and shouted orders. However, I soon realized that all the other parents were in the water, and I would have to join them there. Reluctantly, I waded in and then felt a bit guilty for my princess attitude, especially after I realized how happy TJ was that I'd joined them. After straining for a while and finding all kinds of slimy creatures, I felt inordinately grateful and relieved when it was time for lunch.

After washing the slime off our hands, we walked to the picnic tables and handed out the sack lunches to many eager, hungry children. I sat down to eat lunch with TJ and his friends. After listening intently to the boys tell me story after story, I turned my attention to TJ, who was sitting quietly and beaming with pride that his mother was there. He was never embarrassed of his mom like some kids might have been.

On the bus ride home, his teacher, who was sitting a few rows ahead of us, turned around and asked, "What are you doing with this boy? He is so good!"

I answered, "Oh, thank you. He's a very good boy, but it's not because of me." I knew I couldn't take credit for how good he was. It was just the way God made him.

Like any working mother, I struggled to balance my work duties and my parenting responsibilities. While at First Baptist, I generally took my lunch break late in the afternoon so I could use that time to pick TJ up from school. After sitting for what seemed like hours in a car line outside Big Cypress Elementary, I finally made my way to the front of the line where the horde of children, all dressed in matching school uniforms, were waiting. Excited to see that I'd finally arrived,

TJ began running toward me. I always recognized him by the way he ran. It was sort of like a gallop and was almost painful to watch. I don't know why, but that boy just could not run.

After jumping in my car, inevitably, the first question out of his mouth was, "Can we get a snack?"

And, as always, I replied, "Sure."

Then we would drive off and make our usual pit stop at the gas station for a much needed after-school snack. He would usually choose a huge chili dog that looked more like a meal than a snack. Then I would take him back to the church for the remainder of my workday.

After arriving at the church, I instructed him to sit in one of the offices next to mine and do his homework. However, many times, he would disappear, and I later learned that he was going from office to office visiting with the pastors and their assistants.

He built many special relationships with some of my coworkers at First Baptist. One of his favorites was a pastor named Dr. Fisher. Dr. Fisher was from England and had a wonderful transatlantic accent. He was wise, godly, and loving. He was playful and liked to laugh and make others laugh. His favorite prank was to hide behind furniture in the church and jump out and scare someone walking by. Our whole family loved Dr. Fisher.

One evening while church was in session, I was across the courtyard in the Education Building getting ready for a *Bible and Life Group* that was meeting right after church. TJ was with me, but, as usual, he had disappeared. After preparing for a while, I heard a ruckus in the hallway and went to see what was going on. I looked down the hall and saw TJ running toward me at full speed while Dr. Fisher chased him. They were both laughing out loud. TJ ran past me, rushed around the corner, and disappeared. A few seconds later, I heard a teacher loudly scolding him for running in the hallway. Still in hot pursuit, Dr. Fisher rounded the corner. The teacher then realized that TJ had been running because a pastor was chasing him, and I heard her exclaim, "Dr. Fisher!" Both came back around the corner with sheepish grins on their faces, trying to stifle their giggles.

TJ was excited to be baptized by his partner in crime, Dr. Fisher. Beforehand, he had been very nervous about getting up in front of our massive congregation, but his fear dissipated with Dr. Fisher beside him. Everything went smoothly and it was a blessed time. Dr. Fisher later told me that his own heart was bursting with joy over the opportunity to baptize TJ. I was grateful that God had given him such godly role models in my co-workers who loved him.

After a few job changes, I became an assistant in the Evangelism Ministry. My boss was leading a program called *Faith Evangelism*. We had planned to use the program for adults but soon decided to include the teens as well. During that time, we took the high school and junior high kids on a retreat to Tampa, Florida, planning to teach the program in a teen-friendly environment. At that time, we had two daughters in the high school ministry, one in the junior high ministry, and TJ was in fifth grade. We took all four of them with us and set out on a weekend adventure with our church.

We stayed in cabins, and Travis and I were each cabin leaders for the students. I was in a cabin with some of the junior high girls, which didn't exactly thrill me. One, because the cabins were grimy and full of spiders. Two, because I needed to sleep in order to function the next day, and as you probably know, junior high girls like to stay up all night giggling.

One afternoon, during a break in the programming, TJ and some other boys his age were playing in a field. He came over to me and said the boys were leaving him out. I told him that he just needed to get in there and participate and that I was sure they would include him. So, he went back to playing. As I watched, I realized he was right; the boys were intentionally excluding him. He was running around trying to be included, and they were purposefully ignoring him. It was painful for a mother to watch. I knew he was different than the other boys and that they didn't appreciate his unique qualities. As I watched, I thought, *It's okay that he's different. God will do great things with TJ. Maybe one day he'll be a preacher standing on a stage telling hundreds of people about Jesus.*

CHAPTER 2

SHE LIKES ME

The summer of 2007 led us into TJ's sixth grade year. The housing market in Florida was crashing, and my husband kept losing his job. Housing businesses were either going bankrupt or closing their Florida offices, so we decided it was time to return home to Iowa. We packed up the kids and the house and moved. Even though the years we lived in Naples were a blessed time where we met wonderful people and grew in our faith, I was thrilled to be going home. I had been homesick the entire time we lived in Florida, and I missed Iowa terribly. I missed everything about it: the seasons, the friendly people, and the midwestern lifestyle. It was a happy day for me when the moving truck pulled out of the driveway and began the journey back to the heartland.

We bought a house in West Des Moines, and TJ started sixth grade at Fairmeadows Elementary School. Life quickly resumed where it left off four years earlier. TJ had a good teacher in sixth grade and was chosen by the teacher to be a class mediator. If two other classmates were having a disagreement, his responsibility was to mediate between them and help resolve their issues. Wherever he went, teachers noticed his maturity, and he excelled.

Throughout TJ's elementary years, we had him try all kinds of sports. He didn't really want to play, but we told him to give it a try because he might like them. Following our advice, he tried, but he was terrible at *all* of them. He didn't care. He didn't like it. So, after a while, we decided to put him—and us—out of our misery and told him that he didn't have to play sports anymore.

In late elementary school, we discovered that his passion was music. He became very excited when talking about musical instruments. After a few years of playing the tuba, he complained, "Mom, I really don't want to play the tuba anymore. All I do is go bom bom bom bom." So, we talked about it and decided he should try something else.

He really wanted to play the drums. We bought him a drum set, and he began taking lessons. He was quite talented. He loved to play in the youth group worship band and, once in a while, even played in the church band. You could see pure joy on his face as he played. We were very proud of him. As a mom, my dreams for TJ went beyond Des Moines, Iowa. I envisioned lights, cameras, and stardom for him as a future drummer in a Christian band.

During TJ's junior high years, we adopted one of our grandsons, Aiden. He was a toddler at the time and called us Nana and Papa. TJ and Aiden were very close, and whenever TJ walked through the door, the first thing out of his mouth was, "Hey, little man!" Since all four of our daughters were adults and living on their own, we were now a family with a majority of boys. We had taken a drastic turn from being a female majority family when our daughters were young, and I was now the odd (wo)man out.

For many years in Iowa, we had trouble finding a church we liked. We visited many, but either Travis and I were having trouble connecting with a class or TJ struggled to connect with his peers. Plus, none of them were First Baptist Church Naples. At the time, everything seemed to pale in comparison—until we finally decided to try a smaller Evangelical Free church. TJ immediately fit right into the youth group, quickly made lots of friends, and began growing in his faith. After years of searching, we had finally found our church home.

Not long after he began driving during his sophomore year, there was one evening when I couldn't find him. After repeatedly calling his cell phone with no answer, I started reaching out to his friends. No one knew where he was. At first, I was angry and thought that since he had gotten his license and newfound freedom, he had taken advantage of our trust and was out joyriding, even though it really wasn't like him to do something like that. As the night wore on and I still hadn't heard from him, I became increasingly worried, imagining that he was in a ditch somewhere and injured.

Finally, after what seemed like hours, the phone rang. "Mom, what's wrong? Why did you keep calling me?"

"TJ, where are you?!" I questioned.

Somewhat annoyed, he said, "Mom, it's Wednesday. I'm at church."

Oops! I'd never thought of that. I was embarrassed and felt bad for doubting him. I should have known better. Then I remembered the words Jesus spoke to his parents when they had been frantically searching for him: "Did you not know I had to be in my Father's house?"

Although he was a wonderful kid, he did have his faults. If he got mad at you, he didn't easily or quickly forgive. He was stubborn and would hold a grudge for weeks. He also had a lazy streak that drove his dad and me crazy. Case in point: It was TJ's job to mow the lawn. It was like pulling teeth to get him to do it. I overheard many arguments between him and Travis about it. Most days when he went outside to mow, after maybe ten minutes or so, he would stagger back inside as if he'd been lost for hours in the Sahara. Then he would stand at the kitchen sink drinking water, complaining about how tired he was and how hot it was outside. He then would ask if he could take a break, to which I would respond, "No, TJ! Seriously! We have a riding lawnmower! Get back out there!"

In his junior year of high school, he began making plans for his future education. He either wanted to be an engineer or study diseases. He also dreamed about being a sniper in the military, but I secretly prayed that plan would never come to fruition. At that time in his life, I could also feel him pulling away from me. He was spending a lot of time over at his friend Jason's house. I felt a little twinge of sadness that he was growing up and away, although I understood it to be the natural order of things.

Once in a while, though, he still liked to ask my opinion about things. Usually around 9 P.M., before his dad came to bed, while I was lying down watching a little bit of TV before falling asleep, he would come into my room in the mood to chat. One night he plopped down on my bed and asked, "Mom, how do you know when a girl likes you?"

He didn't usually talk about such things with me, so I sat up, feeling excited by the chance to discover what was going on in his life. "Who is the girl?" I inquired.

"Riley," he answered.

Riley was Jason's sister, and suddenly it became crystal clear why he'd been spending so much time with Jason. As we continued talking, I learned that TJ liked Riley. He was concerned that if he told her of his feelings and she didn't feel the same way, it might ruin their friendship. We went over a few different strategies he could try to determine if she felt the same way.

When the conversation was over and he was satisfied with the advice he'd been given, he got up smiling and disappeared down the hall. Oh, did I ever enjoy those conversations with him. A few nights later, about midnight, I heard my phone ding. It was a text message from TJ. I opened the text and it read, "She likes me!!"

CHAPTER 3

THE DIAGNOSIS

One evening in early 2013, I was sitting in a small Bible study at a friend's house with four other women. Quite surprisingly and unexpectedly, I shared a secret that I'd been keeping for many years—that I had always wanted to be a speaker. I kept that secret to myself all those years because I thought people would laugh at me. I wasn't qualified. I had no formal speaking or writing education, and I had no experience. Even so, the desire nagged at me and never went away. That night, as soon as I confessed my secret to the group, one of the women immediately began to pray over me asking God to fulfill my dream. The very last sentence of her prayer caught my attention, "…and Lord, please let it happen very soon." I'd been waiting for years for God to reveal His calling on my life. After her fervent prayer, I had the feeling that something was on the horizon.

In February of 2013, I began taking a Beth Moore Bible study titled *Believing God*. In the *Believing God* study, we learned that God is who He says He is; God can do what He says He can do; I am who God says I am; I can do all things through Christ; and God's Word is alive and active in me. (Moore 2004) I didn't realize it at the time, but later it became very apparent to me that what I learned in that study was vital biblical knowledge that I would need for the horrific trial that lay just around the corner.

In the middle of the night, in March of that same year, I awakened abruptly. TJ was sixteen years old at the time, and over the last few months, he had been complaining about his tailbone. Knowing that he was a hypochondriac, I didn't take his complaints seriously. Every time he fussed, I told him, "You're fine, Teej. You just bumped and bruised it. There isn't anything they can do about it anyway. The discomfort will heal and go away." But it hadn't gone away, and suddenly, out of the blue, I thought, *What if there really is something wrong? I'd better schedule an appointment.*

I took him to the doctor a few days later. At the beginning, the nurse practitioner checked his vitals: "Has anyone ever told you that he has a heart murmur?" she asked.

"No," I replied.

"Well, I think I'm hearing something," she continued. "You should probably go to a cardiologist and get it checked out."

Then she checked his tailbone and said she didn't feel any masses or fractures that caused concern. She didn't think there was anything wrong with it but said she needed to check the underside of the tailbone just to be sure there wasn't anything there either. She told him that she would leave the room so he could undress from the waist down.

I knew exactly what "check the underside of the tailbone" meant, but he was completely unaware of the internal exam that was about to occur. I decided not to tell him because I knew he would either refuse the exam or get off the table and run, so I excused myself to the waiting room and told him I would return when she finished. As I left the room, I hid my face so he couldn't see the smile I was trying to hide.

After the exam, I went back into the room. He was sitting on the table with huge eyes and a red face. He was extremely embarrassed and had a hard time making eye contact. I couldn't help but laugh when I told him, "Well, if nothing else, TJ, this will definitely cure you of your hypochondria!" He didn't think it was as funny as I did.

The nurse practitioner said that she had found no abnormalities. Before we left, she made an appointment for TJ with the cardiologist. When we got in the car, I told him not to worry about the upcoming appointment because doctors thought they heard a murmur in my heart when I was eighteen that turned out to be nothing and his would probably be nothing as well. I truly wasn't concerned, but I was oblivious to all that could go wrong.

A few days later, Travis took TJ to the appointment with Dr. Morris while I was at work. I was shocked when he began texting me, saying that something was wrong and they needed to do more testing. TJ's blood pressure was different in all four limbs. After the testing was finished, Travis called and said they discovered a heart defect: a coarctation or narrowing of his aorta. This type of defect is usually caught at birth. The cardiology team was perplexed as to how it was missed for so long. When they listened to his heart, it was very apparent. Dr. Morris then ordered a CT scan of his heart to determine whether the defect could be corrected by stents or would require surgery. I felt thankful for that nudge in the middle of the night prompting me to schedule the tailbone appointment. Left undetected and untreated, the heart defect would have killed TJ.

Travis brought home a diagram of a heart that showed where the defect was. Apparently, Dr. Morris had explained that if TJ was a candidate for it, Dr. Harmon would perform the surgery. In his opinion, Dr. Harmon was the best and only surgeon he would allow to operate on his pediatric patients.

Several days later, I took TJ for the CT scan, where I discovered that he was terrified of needles. In order to do the scan, he needed an IV. He was so upset and nearly in tears at the prospect. After much coaxing and explaining, the IV was finally in place, but I could tell that he was embarrassed that he put up such a fuss. I reassured him that it was okay and that needles were scary for lots of people.

When all the testing was completed, we went out for a mother-son lunch before I took him back to school. Like most teenage boys, TJ loved food, so I let him choose the restaurant. He chose *The Machine Shed* which is a down-home cooking, meat-and-potatoes restaurant with lots of charm and oodles of calories.

After the CT results came back, we learned that the heart defect, unfortunately, required surgery. The next step was to meet with Dr. Harmon. During our appointment, Dr. Harmon showed us TJ's CT scan, explained where the problems were, and discussed what he needed to do to correct them. Dr. Harmon explained that the surgery would take around six hours and TJ would be in the Pediatric Intensive Care Unit (PICU) for a few days before being discharged to go home. He would then need to stay home from school for a week because he wouldn't feel up to doing much. TJ's surgery was scheduled to be performed in three weeks.

After arriving home from the appointment, TJ immediately asked to go to his youth pastor's house. I was thankful that the first place he wanted to go was to God's people. I was also grateful that he had a church family and friends who would pray for him as he processed what he had just learned and prepared for the upcoming surgery.

A few days before surgery, TJ asked for the phone number of his old pal, Dr. Fisher. He hadn't spoken to Dr. Fisher since we left Florida six years earlier, but he had a sudden urge to have Dr. Fisher pray and encourage him with God's Word. He sat on the kitchen counter talking, and after he hung up, he told me he felt at peace. Confidently, he added, "Mom, if anything happens, I know where I'm going."

The day before surgery was a Sunday, and we went to church. Toward the end of the service, Pastor Gary asked TJ to come forward to tell the congregation what he was going to be facing the next day so the church could pray for him. As requested, he shared and did a fabulous job expressing himself:

Holding the mic, he said, "All right, so, about, you know, six weeks ago my tailbone was bothering me, and it had been bothering me for a while. So, we decided to go get it checked out, and when we went into the doctor's office, my nurse practitioner, Misty, heard a heart murmur. So, basically, they sent us to the cardiologist, and nobody really thought it was a big deal. But then after getting an EKG and CAT scan, we realized that I had a problem with my heart, and I'm about to have surgery. What it is, it's coarctation of the aorta which means—the aorta is the artery leading off your heart, and it's almost like it has a rubber band over it. Obviously not a rubber band because that would be impossible. But, yeah, surgery is tomorrow, and that's basically what's going on."

After he finished speaking, Pastor Gary said, "You're going to affect not only one person but many lives in this process. We look forward to hearing TJ's story after the fact."

In hindsight, I'm thankful that God gave him the opportunity to speak that day, that it was recorded, and that I caught a glimpse of his quirky sense of humor. He was a bit of a jokester and was always looking for a way to make people laugh. I treasure being able to hear his deep voice and see our confident, strong, and handsome son. The video was a precious gift from God to Travis and me, and we both cherish it. Months later, when Travis and I were reviewing the video, we recalled Pastor Gary's statement. We were amazed because that statement came true, and TJ's story did, indeed, affect many lives.

As we were leaving church, TJ raced me to the car. He always tried to get there before I did so he could sit in the front. Most of the time, even if he won, I still made him get in the back. On that day, because of the impending surgery, I let him have the front seat, and I sat in the back.

During the drive, TJ asked us several times if we thought he'd done a good job of speaking before the congregation. Each time, both his dad and I reassured him that he did an amazing job and we were very proud of him. And then he added, "I really like doing that. I really like speaking in front of people." Once again, I thought, *He will be on a stage one day speaking about Christ.*

CHAPTER 4

I DIDN'T DIE

The date was Monday, April 22, 2013. It's a day that will haunt me for as long as I live. It was my daughter Chandler's twentieth birthday and the day my only son became trapped in his body.

At 3:15 A.M., my cell phone alarm rang. It was early and I was exhausted. I was afraid of oversleeping and missing the surgery check-in time, so I tossed and turned all night and didn't sleep well. It was going to be a long day. I went downstairs to wake TJ, but upon entering his room, I noticed that he was already wide awake and sitting in front of the Xbox.

"Hi, Mom!" he said while grinning.

"TJ, did you even go to sleep last night?" I asked.

"No, I figured I would have plenty of time to sleep during the surgery," he answered, "so I stayed up all night playing Xbox."

"Oh, jeepers, TJ," I sighed, shaking my head. "Well, it's time to start getting ready. We need to leave in about an hour," I added, before turning and heading back upstairs to shower.

We arrived at the hospital early in the morning. Travis and TJ went over to the registration desk to check in while I sat in the waiting area. TJ was standing with his back to me, when I noticed that he had worn his blue Hurley shirt with his bright yellow Puma shorts. I watched them as they answered questions and filled out paperwork. At the time those details seemed insignificant, but because of what occurred later, they have since been seared into my memory.

After going through the check-in procedures, staff took us back to the pre-op room. One of the anesthesiologists came in and visited with us. "Don't worry, someone older, with much more experience than I have, will be taking care of him today," he assured. I appreciated his truthfulness. He listened to TJ's heart and then commented that he didn't know how the heart defect was missed all those years because he could really hear it.

After the anesthesiologist left, the nurse began asking routine questions. Sensing TJ's nervousness, she consoled, "You've got a great surgeon. Dr. Harmon is the best. You're in good hands."

TJ's youth pastor and kids from his youth group came back to the room to show their support. They briefly visited with him and then went to the OR waiting room for the long wait. Travis and I stayed with TJ until we were shooed out. As we were leaving the room, I turned around to take one last look at him. He was lying on the gurney making a silly face at me, so I snapped a picture. That would be the last time I ever saw my son whole.

As we walked down the hallway to the waiting room, fear suddenly overcame me. My mind ran the gamut of what ifs, and I burst into tears. Then I became upset with myself for being so dramatic and reassured myself, *They do this all the time. He's going to be fine. Get it together*. However, unbeknownst to us, our descent into hell had already begun.

Throughout the six-hour surgery, a nurse would go back to the OR and check on his status and then report to those of us who were waiting. At each check-in, she reported that everything was going well. Right before her very last check-in, she told us that this was the most critical part of the surgery. I continued to pray as I watched her leave the waiting room. When she came out to give us the last report, she said Dr. Harmon had given a thumbs-up. Whew! We were almost done.

Dr. Harmon came out after it was over, and the first thing he said was, "It was complicated."

I wasn't expecting that, and I caught my breath. I immediately asked, "But he's okay, right?"

He nodded. That was the first inkling I had that something was wrong, but Dr. Harmon affirmed that TJ was okay, so I quickly pushed the negative thoughts out of my mind.

Dr. Harmon told us we could go upstairs to see TJ, who was still asleep when I walked into his PICU room. He was covered in tubes and medical equipment, and upon first seeing him, a feeling of shock came over me. I'd never seen a person in that condition before. I nervously sat on the couch in his room and waited for him to rouse. Upon waking, the first thing he said was, "Mom, I didn't die." Relief washed over me.

As the afternoon went by, we noticed there was something wrong with his eyes. He couldn't open them very wide, and his pupils were pointed downward. He had to tilt his head way back in order to look at us. It wasn't long before he began to repeat, "I can't swallow! I can't swallow!"

Somewhat alarmed, but attempting to reassure myself that everything was okay, I calmed my fear with the reminder, *It's just from the anesthesia and the tubes that were running down his throat. He'll be back to normal soon.*

Before his surgery, we were told that he would be very thirsty after waking up but would not be able to drink for a period of time. Sure enough, he was thirsty and was continually asking for water. When the water was denied, the nurse took the brunt of his ire.

As the afternoon turned into evening, we noticed that he was becoming increasingly confused. Thinking it was a pitcher of water, he tipped an empty urinal over his head trying to drink from it. He was petting imaginary mice on the side of his bed. Pointing at the drainage tubes coming from his upper body, he exclaimed, "I have a miniature dragon growing in my chest!"

Repeatedly he asked, "Hey, what's going to happen in three weeks? There's something happening in three weeks. What is it?"

"You were going to have heart surgery in three weeks, honey," I replied.

"You just had it today, TJ. It already happened," Travis added.

"No, that's not it. You guys are stupid," he growled, clearly not himself.

He asked to use the restroom. When the nurse began helping him with the urinal, he chattered, "Wait. Wait. Wait. Can we talk about this? Let's talk about this. I don't even know you." Still thinking it was due to the anesthesia and that he would soon come out of it, it was hard not to laugh.

While still in his delusional state of mind, TJ jabbered, "Dad. Dad. Dad. That Dr. Harmon—he's the best. I want you to get to know Dr. Harmon. I don't want him to forget about me."

Travis, in mock sincerity, replied, "I will. We're going golfing next week," even though he doesn't golf. For a moment, TJ was satisfied with that answer and quieted.

About midnight, Travis left the room to go to sleep, and I stayed with TJ. His confusion and behaviors were escalating. He couldn't stop moving and talking and couldn't seem to calm down. He was aware that he was being difficult and would apologize afterward for keeping me awake. I reassured him that it was okay and not to worry about me because he was the one who had just been through heart surgery. However, as I lay down on the couch, I knew I wasn't going to get much sleep that night.

His confusion and agitation continued to worsen, and as the night wore on, it was becoming even more concerning. I was scared. At some point Travis came back into the room, sat beside him, and held his hand. TJ looked down at their hands clasped together and then leaned back on his pillow with a smile on his face.

Late in the night, TJ started ripping his IV out. After successfully removing it five times, security was called, and they tied his arms to the bed. In the early morning hours, unable to stay awake, I left his room to get some sleep while Travis stayed with him. After having slept for a couple of hours, I was feeling more hopeful and expected to walk into TJ's room to find my son recovered from the confusion he had been experiencing. Upon entering his room, my heart sank. I was confronted with TJ sitting in bed, head hanging, with his arms tied to the bed rails. My stomach churned when I heard him mumble, "It's so thick in here. I can't get through it. I need some scissors."

There was an all-glass wall that bordered the hallway in TJ's PICU room. Later in the morning, the surgeon was sitting outside the room. While exiting, I asked, "How long is this going to last?"

"I don't know," he answered.

"What's wrong with him?"

"He may have had a stroke," he replied.

"Oh, I never thought of that," I murmured, as I slowly walked away and tried to suppress the fear that was rising inside me.

The day after surgery was spent trying to keep TJ under control. His lips were bright red and chapped from wiping his mouth constantly with a towel because he couldn't swallow his saliva. They were cracking, peeling, and looked very sore.

On Wednesday, he finally calmed down a bit and was becoming more rational. The doctors informed us that it probably wasn't a reaction to the anesthesia causing the confusion because it wouldn't have lasted that long. They ordered an MRI to search for any damage in his brain. In my heart, I just knew that the MRI was going to be okay, and sure enough, his MRI looked pretty good. They did see a small area of oxygen loss in his brain, but the doctors said it wouldn't be causing the symptoms we were observing now. The doctors were going to continue testing. Dr. Morris explained that the MRI results were an encouraging sign. "We'll get your son back soon," he reassured. I began to feel hopeful again.

Thursday afternoon, while I was downstairs in the cafeteria, unbeknownst to me, the nurses got TJ up to walk to the waiting room. This was quite a distance from his PICU room. After I exited the elevator and turned the corner, I saw a shirtless, young man walking down the hall, pushing an IV pole. When I realized that the young man was TJ, I caught my breath. I was surprised to see him up and mobile. I accompanied him back to his room, and once he was settled back in his bed, he beamed, "Mom, I'm not going to lie. I'm pretty proud of myself."

By the end of the week, TJ was having trouble talking, and his voice had become no more than a whisper. I was very worried and confused about what was happening to him, and the doctors didn't seem to have answers. Even more alarming, he could no longer hold up his head. At times, his mouth started clamping shut, and he would try desperately to pry it open. He was biting his tongue and lips and then squealing in pain. He was also coughing and choking, and it went on for hours. We frantically tried to suction his airway, but because he couldn't open his mouth, removing the secretions was impossible. At one point, he murmured, "This is miserable."

Later that day, TJ whispered, "Mom, I can't breathe." Soon afterward, Dr. Harmon, the heart surgeon, entered the room, and I relayed TJ's respiratory concerns.

"TJ said he feels like he can't breathe," I informed him. Then added, "Oh, wait, you're not the doctor I'm supposed to…"

With a look of concern in his eyes, he said, "No, no. It's okay. We'll get a chest x-ray."

Later that day, a new neurologist was called in to consult. When he walked into the room and saw TJ's facial and neck muscle weakness, he said the symptoms resembled Myasthenia Gravis. Myasthenia Gravis (MG) is an autoimmune disease where muscles under a person's control quickly become very weak. Doctors thought stress from the surgery may have triggered the disease. New tests were run to determine the possibility of MG, and I felt hopeful that we would get answers regarding what was happening with our son.

Over the weekend, TJ was sitting in a chair in the corner of his room. The medical staff was running more tests, and he had electrodes on his head. We were taking turns helping him hold his head up. We encouraged him to try to hold his head up on his own, but he just couldn't. Then he whispered, "Duct tape."

While he was sitting in the chair, the nurse instructed him to not leave the chair without assistance. When he was finished with the testing, my motherly intuition told me that he was going to try to get up and walk to the bed on his own. I reminded him, "TJ, don't get up and walk on your own. You need to wait for the nurse to help." But he wasn't listening to me, and he *did* try to get up on his own. I scolded him and hurriedly walked over to stand in front of him in order to prevent him from walking.

He sat back down, and in an upset, whiny voice, whispered, "Why did you yell at me?"

Prior to TJ's surgery, I rarely had to raise my voice to him, and the unfamiliar firmness of my tone hurt his feelings. I was very perplexed by his behavior. It wasn't like him to blatantly disobey me.

Although his ability to talk was deteriorating and no one could understand him, he continued to try to communicate. After asking him to repeat himself several times, I noticed that it seemed like he wasn't strong enough to force air through his vocal cords. I told him to just say one word at a time and push the air hard through his vocal cords with each word. He became very upset and weakly muttered, "It won't be funny like that." My heart was breaking for him.

In an effort to help him communicate, we gave him a pen and paper to write on. At first, it worked, and we were relieved that he could convey his thoughts and have his needs met. However, later on, even writing was too hard. Once, when it was taking him an unusually long time to write out his thoughts, I looked to see how he was progressing. The paper was filled with lines of continuous circles.

At that point, he resorted to using hand signals. When asked how he was feeling, in an effort to make us laugh, using one hand turned sideways, he made the motion of a saw cutting a rib cage. Then with both hands, he motioned pulling the rib cage apart. Despite his worsening condition, he still kept his sense of humor.

Over the weekend, the medical staff began discussing discharging TJ to a brain injury rehab facility. If TJ was ready to transition, we weren't opposed to this move, as we had heard wonderful things about the facility. While there, he would receive therapy to regain his ability to swallow, talk, and restore control of his eye muscles, as well as strengthen his neck. I was full of anticipation as everyone seemed to be in agreement that it was a place where miracles happen. The hospital, rehab facility, and insurance company were coordinating efforts to have him transferred. We hoped to have him settled in the new environment by Monday—Tuesday at the latest.

Monday evening, a week after the surgery, TJ started having severe trouble breathing. I was feeding him ice chips to moisten his mouth. Since he couldn't swallow, he would swish the water around and spit it out. I felt sorry for him because he couldn't drink, so I gave him a bigger piece of ice than I should have. When I put it into his mouth, he started coughing and couldn't stop. He began to breathe extremely fast and hard, as if he couldn't get enough air into his lungs. They watched him closely and tried different strategies to bring his respirations back into an acceptable range, all to no avail.

It seemed like the high respiratory rate went on for hours. It was terrifying watching him struggle to breathe. Feeling panic stricken, terrified, and helpless, Travis asked the doctor how much longer they were going to allow him to suffer, and the doctor reassured him that it wouldn't be much longer. The respiratory therapist then came in and put a CPAP mask on TJ while they were waiting for someone to intubate him and put him on a ventilator. When she turned the machine on, the settings were too high, and the air pressure expanded his face and chest. A look of panic shot across her face, and the doctor told her to turn down the settings. The decision was then made to go ahead and intubate him themselves. Right before Travis left the room, he looked over at TJ, who was staring at him with pleading eyes that said, "Please help me."

At the time, I didn't understand what was happening. I was distraught, feeling that the ice chip might have caused his breathing problems, but I kept this concern to myself. I was so overwhelmed with fear that I couldn't think clearly. After intubation, the doctor advised us to go get some rest because there was nothing more that was going to be done that night. There was a Ronald McDonald House (RMH) area around the corner from the PICU, so we slept in one of the bedrooms for the night.

The next morning, I asked the doctor to explain what happened to TJ. She said it was respiratory failure. My heart sank, and I finally shared with her that I'd given him an ice chip that was probably too big and wondered if I had caused the whole problem. She answered, "Oh, no, ice chips didn't cause that." Relief flooded through me, releasing me from the feelings of guilt that had nearly overwhelmed me.

After intubation, TJ's upper body unexpectedly began swelling and filling up with air. Doctors thought that during the emergency intubation, his lung had been torn. The air that the ventilator was blowing into his lungs was now leaking into his chest and shoulders, and there was a crackling sensation under his skin. The excess air was putting pressure on his lungs and other organs. In order to remove the air that was accumulating, tubes were inserted between his ribs, one on each side.

One afternoon when Dr. Morris, TJ's cardiologist, was visiting with Travis and me, I asked, "Did that surgery go okay? Were you concerned about anything?"

Without hesitation, he replied, "No. It was textbook."

His answer calmed my fears.

On May 4th, twelve days after surgery, I started a CaringBridge page for TJ. CaringBridge is a website used to record a person's health journey. After his respiratory issues began, I debated whether I should start a CaringBridge because I thought he would soon recover and go home. However, I was receiving so many individual text messages asking for updates that I thought it would be easier to write a daily update than to respond to everyone individually.

May 4, 2013

CaringBridge
Written by Kelly

Yesterday TJ was extubated around ten-thirty in the morning. There were concerns that he would have to be put right back on the ventilator, but so far, he's been okay. Travis slept in his room last night and said he slept 4½ hours. They have begun some treatment for Myasthenia Gravis, and his eyes did open and were midline quite a number of times yesterday. We hadn't seen him open his eyes since he was intubated five days ago. They think he may have a tear in one of his lungs from the intubation, and it is leaking air into his chest and neck. His body is huge, and it's very uncomfortable for him. He's also having a difficult time with coughing. Because he is not able to swallow, his secretions build up, making it hard for him to breathe, and he doesn't have much energy to cough it up. His jaw is also locked, not sure why. We are seeing small steps of improvement, but there is also much to still be praying for.

After they took TJ off the ventilator, he coughed and choked continually for 2½ hours. He was miserable, and his breathing problems were terrifying. He was struggling as though he were drowning. His mouth was still clamped shut, so we were trying to use tiny suction catheters to stick between his teeth to remove secretions so he could breathe. However, we weren't very successful.

The neurologist arrived to assess TJ, and I asked how much longer it would be until the MG test results came back so we could treat him more aggressively. I told the doctor that he was miserable and that it was traumatic to watch him struggle. He agreed that it was awful, and he seemed genuinely disturbed by it. He said he expected the test results within a few days. I thought, *When the doctors, who have seen everything, are bothered by it, then it must be unusually bad.*

At times, the fear was overwhelming. I had never experienced that level of anxiety before. Once in a while, I needed to get away from the stress in TJ's room but still wanted to be close by, so I walked the hospital halls and prayed. Every time I passed his room, I poked my head in to see if Travis needed my help and to let TJ know I was still nearby.

Travis was so patient. I could see the pain in his eyes, but he stayed strong for both of us. He took over caregiving because by then, I was in shock and couldn't function. He stayed by TJ's side and repeatedly suctioned for hours. He adjusted pillows and helped him sit up so he could have more force behind his cough. He was a good caregiver. At one point our eyes met, and I read the exhaustion on his face. "I need a break," he said wearily. "I'm so tired."

I felt ashamed that I hadn't been helping more, but I was so afraid and would begin shaking every time I tried to help. I wasn't educated enough on how the catheters functioned, and I felt more comfortable having the nurses handle that part of his care. I was tormented by the thought of doing something wrong and potentially causing him even more suffering.

May 4, 2013 (Evening)

CaringBridge
Written by Kelly

Psalm 121:1–2: "I will lift up my eyes to the mountains—where does my help come from? My help comes from the Lord, the Maker of heaven and earth." (NIV)

This morning as I was walking, I heard the Lord whisper, "Don't go to the high places. Depend on Me and Me alone." The high places were where the Israelites built idols and worshiped false gods. What a temptation it has been to turn the doctors into idols. Psalm 121 reminds us that our help comes from the Lord, the Maker of heaven and earth—and doctors.

This afternoon TJ slept for five hours. So glad he is getting more sleep. During the first week he was here, he went a number of days without any sleep. Later in the afternoon today, he opened his eyes frequently. I did a little dance in the hall, and the nurses chuckled. He doesn't keep them open for long, but he is making progress. I believe the medicine is working. So good to see his eyes again.

We are getting him ready for bed now. We're hoping tomorrow will bring even more improvement.

CHAPTER 5

PRAISE YOU IN THIS STORM

Travis and I began taking turns staying with TJ. We loved him so much and didn't want to leave him alone. Not unexpectedly, our hearts were heavy watching him go through this. He was showing some signs of improvement, and the doctor was excited to see his progress. He was moving himself up in bed and keeping his eyes open for longer times than he had previously.

After extubation, he was placed on a CPAP machine—a machine that delivers a continuous flow of pressurized air to the lungs. He was on oxygen and doing better, but he still had many serious medical challenges. We were praying for his swallowing ability to return, the tear in his lungs to heal so chest tubes could be removed, for his neck to stop its severe spasming, for him to be able to hold his head up, that his jaw would unlock, and that his sight and speech would improve.

After a few signs of progress, things unexpectedly took a turn for the worse. After a long night of rapid breathing, he was intubated again. When the doctor asked us to leave the room, Travis and I went to the Ronald McDonald area. From the dining room window, we could see into TJ's room. Although we couldn't see exactly what was going on, it comforted us that we were somewhat present with him.

After the doctor had intubated him, he emerged from TJ's room and told us that right before TJ was intubated, he had been pointing to his throat. The doctor discovered that he had been coughing up secretions, but because his muscles were weak, they were getting stuck at the top of his throat. They hardened like concrete and were blocking his airway. It made me physically ill to realize that during the time that he was struggling to breathe, he knew what was wrong and was trying to communicate it, but they were unable to interpret what he was trying to tell them.

This second respiratory failure was devastating for us. It was terrifying to watch him struggle to breathe before his intubation, and it had to be just as frightening for him to endure it. I thanked God that each time he went into respiratory failure, he was in the hospital where he was being monitored. I shuddered to imagine what would have happened to him if he had been discharged to the rehab center where they have neither the equipment nor the training to handle it.

During TJ's admission, we had many visitors. Several visitors suggested having TJ transferred to Mayo Clinic in Rochester, Minnesota. We had never dealt with serious illness before, and we didn't know anything about hospital choices or what to do when faced with something like this. Upon the advice of those we trusted, we asked hospital staff for a transfer to Mayo Clinic. However, doctors decided we needed to stay put since he wasn't stable enough to handle the trip.

Dr. Harmon seemed unhappy about the request for transfer. Once, when I walked into TJ's room, he said, "I heard you want a *third* neurology opinion." The room was full of medical staff, and all of them turned to look at me. I was embarrassed and felt my face flush. *Are we doing the right thing?* I wondered. *Should we transfer TJ, or are we going overboard?* I was so confused.

Because Travis was the primary carrier of our health insurance, it was necessary for him to return to work. I was afraid to be without my husband, so I turned to God's Word and was comforted by Isaiah 41:10, "So do not fear, for I am with you; do not be dismayed, for I am your God; I will strengthen you and help you; I will uphold you with my righteous right hand." I clung to God's promise that He was by my side every step of the way and would help me get through this horrific trial. I decided that no matter what lay ahead, I wasn't going to blame Him but would remain faithful and trust Him.

Upon further testing, it was discovered that TJ had a blood clot in each lung as well as a collapsed lung. Because blood clots can be fatal, the medical staff had been careful to have TJ up and walking a good bit, at least until the first respiratory failure occurred. Upon learning these serious developments, the intensivist explained that it could take up to two months for him to recover.

TJ was miserable and very agitated during the day. He had a tube running down his throat as well as tubes in each nostril for feeding and removal of secretions. By then, he had a total of three chest tubes. We were taught that chest tubes are very painful because of the sensitive nerves between the ribs. As a result of the extreme discomfort this causes, they kept TJ sedated. A nurse commented, "You know the old saying, 'You never wake a sleeping baby?' Well, my new mantra is, 'You never wake a sleeping TJ.'"

One afternoon, the anesthesiologist for TJ's heart surgery stood in the doorway of TJ's room, checking on him. While he was standing there, I asked, "Did that surgery go okay? I mean, were you concerned about any blood loss? Oxygen loss? Anything?"

"No, we weren't concerned about anything. The surgery couldn't have gone any better," he replied.

Upon hearing his answer, I was relieved once again and decided that they would soon discover and treat whatever was wrong.

One of the PICU doctors called Mayo Clinic and spoke to three different neurology departments. They said TJ's condition was unusual, even for them, and that they didn't normally see a case that severe. They gave TJ's doctor a few more treatment options for MG and informed him that it wasn't unusual for a person to be intubated and extubated several times before things became stable. This information helped us feel a little more at ease.

May 8, 2013

CaringBridge
Written by Kelly

There is really no change in TJ today except he is having some trouble with his stomach. They thought he had a GI bleed, but as I was typing this, they came in and said there was no blood in the specimen. They're not sure what is causing the pain. They're going to run some more tests.

At times you can tell he's in pain, so they're adjusting his meds in an attempt to make him more comfortable. When they intubated him, they put him on powerful muscle relaxers. His neck is much better and his jaw is opening now. They think the jaw locking is due to the MG.

The doctor said this morning that he'll be on the vent a while and we have to be patient because this will take time. It's hard to be patient when your kid is miserable, but it's all about trusting God. There is work He is doing, and He'll turn down the fire as soon as it's accomplished.

This morning after reading my devotional, I concluded that I shouldn't be surprised by TJ's unexpected health issues because Jesus promised we would have trouble. I was reminded that I need to focus on Jesus and His promises, remembering that He has overcome the world, holds my right hand, and will give me the strength to get through this.

John 16:33

"I have told you these things, so that in Me you may have peace. In this world you will have trouble.
But take heart! I have overcome the world."

Isaiah 41:13

"For I am the LORD your God who takes hold of your right hand and says to you, 'Do not fear; I will help you.'"

Philippians 4:13

"I can do all this through Him who gives me strength."

Doctors had ordered three antibody tests for MG. We waited several days for those tests to come back and hoped and prayed that they would return positive so we could get a firm diagnosis and start TJ on a medication that would greatly improve his condition. However, they all came back negative. The doctor gave us no assurance that TJ was going to be okay. As a result, I spent a good portion of the day crying. The chaplain came in to encourage me. Even though he had kind intentions, his words felt empty. He was human and didn't have the answers I was searching for. I knew only God had the power to help our family. After the chaplain left, I opened my Bible to the Psalms and read whatever page it fell open to.

One verse in particular stood out, Psalm 32:10: "…but the LORD'S unfailing love surrounds the one who trusts in Him." God whispered to me, "Trust Me, and I will surround you with a love that never fails."

I was exhausted from the emotional roller coaster I was on. I lay down on TJ's couch and easily fell asleep. When I awoke, the lyrics to the song *Praise You in This Storm* by Casting Crowns were running through my head.

While staring at the floor, I envisioned myself standing in a downpour with dark skies, loud thunder, and lightning bolts overhead. Even though chaos was all around me, I was still. My arms were raised, and I was praising God.

Sixteen years ago, the Lord gave me a son. Was He taking him away now? Even though my heart was broken, I was scared and could barely breathe, I chose to continue praising Him because He is God and I am not. I trusted that He was by my side and would never leave me.

Shortly after, Neurology came in and informed us that they were now looking at Guillain-Barre syndrome (GBS), a rare disorder where the body's immune system attacks the nerves. They performed a spinal tap on TJ and said the results would be back in twenty-four hours. If we had to have a diagnosis, we preferred it to be Guillain-Barre syndrome. Unlike Myasthenia Gravis, Guillain-Barre syndrome can be treated so that healing occurs, while MG is a lifelong diagnosis. With new tests being run, hope sparked again!

While awaiting the results of the tests, I received a text message from a friend I hadn't connected with in weeks. She sent me a YouTube video link. I clicked on it, and it was the video for *Praise You in This Storm* by Casting Crowns.

My God had surrounded me with a love that never fails.

The next day, the spinal test results came back negative. TJ's diagnosis was not Guillain-Barre. Doctors then told us they were transferring TJ via Life Flight to Mayo Clinic. Because of the seriousness of his condition, TJ needed two Life Flight attendants, so, unfortunately, neither Travis nor I could fly with him to Rochester. The date was May 10, 2013, eighteen days after surgery.

CHAPTER 6

MAYO CLINIC

As nurses were getting TJ ready to board the helicopter, I once again walked the halls and prayed. I was alone in a section of the PICU that was not being used. Dr. Harmon's nurse saw me at the end of the hall and came to talk to me. In her sweet, soft-spoken voice, she said she had been praying for us and asking God to relieve the suffering of TJ and his mother. She also said that she wanted me to know that TJ was the first thing on Dr. Harmon's mind when he woke up in the morning and the last thing on his mind when he went to bed at night. I was surprised to hear that, but I felt thankful that TJ was so well cared for. I was also perplexed as to why Dr. Harmon would be so upset about TJ's condition if he believed it was caused by an autoimmune disorder over which he had no control.

While we waited for Mayo Clinic to send their helicopter to transport TJ, we reassured him that everything was going to be okay.

"Help is on the way, Bud," Travis comforted. "We're doing everything we can. We love you."

"We love you, Teej. We can't go in the helicopter with you, but we'll be right behind you, driving in the car. You're going to get there first, but we'll be there soon afterward," I explained.

He stared at us and gave a slow eye blink as if to say, "I understand and I love you."

The moment we received word that Mayo's helicopter had arrived, we hugged and kissed him and quickly said goodbye. We wanted to get a head start since we had a three-hour drive, while TJ only had an hour flight. Travis and I rode the elevator down to the lobby and exited the building. As we were walking across the parking lot, we kept our eyes on the roof of the hospital and watched the helicopter blades spin.

Thirty minutes later, while driving north on Interstate thirty-five, we heard the sound of the helicopter flying overhead. Leaning forward in the passenger seat, I cocked my head to watch them pass. I sank back into my seat and slowly exhaled. Feelings of hope and relief washed over me as I watched the helicopter fly into the distance. My son was going to one of the best hospitals in the world, and I was sure they would figure out what was causing his medical problems.

Mayo Clinic is comprised of many buildings that are scattered throughout the city. TJ was being admitted into the PICU at St. Mary's Hospital. Upon our arrival, I was overwhelmed at the sheer enormity of the hospital, and I felt like I was in a whole other world.

As we walked through the doorway of the PICU, we were staring straight into TJ's room. Although we couldn't see his face, we knew it was him by the huge feet sticking out from underneath the sheets. His feet did not look like the typical pediatric patient's feet.

TJ's lab work had already been completed, and nurses were preparing him for an extensive MRI. The MRI would evaluate the condition of his head, neck, spine, and blood vessels. They had also adjusted his medication. Even though we had just arrived, I immediately liked the place. They took action and things moved quickly.

"The doctors had trouble diagnosing TJ in Des Moines," I told the nurse, as I walked beside the gurney on the way to radiology.

"We'll figure him out. We're Mayo Clinic," she assured.

"We leave no stone unturned," the orderly pushing the gurney chimed in.

Travis suggested that I stay with TJ in Rochester while he returned home to continue working and taking care of our grandson, Aiden. I was very nervous about affording lodging in Minnesota since I had been away from work and had lost my income. We also had no idea what the future held or what medical expenses would be incurred. We needed to be wise and frugal with our money. I had been using the Family Medical Leave Act to excuse my absence, but I had a hunch I was going to run out of that benefit long before TJ would be healthy enough to transition back home.

During our marriage, Travis and I had always struggled financially. For over twenty years, our savings account had never grown to more than a few hundred dollars, but a couple of years before TJ's surgery, unexpectedly, money started rolling in. Our savings account had grown to a generous size. It was incredible. Now that TJ was hospitalized and very ill, I understood why God allowed the money to come in. We would need it to get through this journey. I was thankful that Travis and I were at a point in our lives where we had matured enough that we hadn't spent the money but had instead saved it for such a time as this.

Hospital staff told us about Ronald McDonald House down the

street from St. Mary's Hospital, but they warned us that it could be difficult to get a room as there is usually a waiting list. That news only increased my anxiety, so I prayed about my lodging and left it in God's hands, trusting that He would provide for me. A few hours later, I learned that a room had become available for me and I could move in that very day. God had answered my prayer and met my immediate need.

The first full day was spent meeting with neurologists, hematologists, intensivists, pulmonologists, and cardiologists. Adult Neurology believed TJ had the autoimmune disease MG. They said some people never test positive on the lab tests, so they were going to diagnose him clinically. The hospital in Des Moines had given TJ an Intravenous Immunoglobulin (IVIG) treatment for MG before we left. An IVIG is a therapy that helps people with weakened immune systems fight off infection. Mayo doctors were aware of that treatment and anticipated seeing marked improvement within a few days. They ran a few more labs and informed us that they would begin more aggressive treatment for MG once his lungs were in better condition. The goal was for him to be extubated in four days. It appeared to everyone involved that his lungs were getting stronger, and Adult Neurology even believed that he would once more regain all of his functions. That was exactly what a frightened mother needed to hear. The enormous weight I had been carrying for over two weeks suddenly felt lighter, and I could finally breathe easier.

Doctors then turned their attention to his brain, where two areas showed signs of a stroke. We knew about one area from the MRI performed in Des Moines, but the recent MRI performed at Mayo showed another area of stroke. Doctors believed the second area may have been caused by blood clots. However, they explained that they were not concerned because most heart patients have areas like this and that the locations in question couldn't be the cause of his current symptoms. The MRI performed on his spinal cord showed no signs of stroke. This surprised me because I wasn't aware that a spinal cord could even have a stroke.

May 12, 2013
CaringBridge
Written by Kelly

Today was a pretty quiet day, for the most part. We had one scare; TJ's heart rate started to go down very quickly. Because he's on a vent, they always have a nurse in the room with him. The nurse jumped up and started yelling, "TJ! TJ!" I had a freak-out mom moment and ran for the halls and started praying. They told me to come back and reassured me that everything was okay, that it was just due to the sedation meds he was on. One of them causes low heart rate, so they switched him to the Michael Jackson drug, which was oddly more comforting.

Tomorrow he is getting some kind of scope done to look at his lungs to see how the tear is healing. There is still air coming out of his right chest tube, so they are concerned the tear may be too big and he may need to have it surgically repaired. Hopefully not. He is supposed to get his left chest tube out tomorrow, which is another step in the right direction.

He seems to be getting much stronger. His cough is strong, and even though he is still on a ventilator, it is on low settings. They don't want to take him off yet until they look at the tear. It sounds like we may still be here a couple more weeks, but it also depends on what happens tomorrow. I told the doctor more than once that I don't want to take him home until he can swallow. She reassured me that they won't send him home until he is like he was before surgery.

Travis returned to Des Moines today. As he dropped me off at the hospital, we drove through a very large crowd. People of Asian descent lined the street, dressed in amazing cultural clothing. All eyes were on our car, and for a moment I felt very important. We later were told they were awaiting the arrival of the Dalai Lama who comes to Mayo once a year for his yearly exam. I'm sure they were disappointed when they saw me get out of the car, although they probably didn't think he would be arriving in a blue Chevy Malibu anyway.

Thank you for all of your guestbook entries. We really enjoy reading them. It's the high point of our day.

Matthew 11:28–30

"Come to me, all you who are weary and burdened, and I will give you rest. Take my yoke upon you and learn from me, for I am gentle and humble in heart, and you will find rest for your souls. For my yoke is easy and my burden is light."

The third day after TJ's arrival was a day of testing. The bronchoscopy was first. After scoping TJ's lungs, the pulmonologist said he didn't believe TJ even had a tear, so no surgery was required. They removed TJ's left chest tube and turned down his ventilator settings even more. Extubation was planned for the following morning. All of this was good news and things were looking up.

Pediatric Neurology came in next. With a skeptical look on his face, the neurologist said, "This is a very unusual way for MG to present."

"Well, Adult Neurology told me a couple of days ago that they think it's MG," I recounted.

"Well, MG doesn't usually present this way. This is very unusual," he reiterated. "I'm ordering a nerve conduction study."

Aww, come on, I thought. *Just say it. Just say you agree with Adult Neurology, that TJ has MG, and that he's going to be okay again.* But he didn't say it. Instead, he walked out of the room and left me standing beside TJ.

That evening, I walked back to my room at Ronald McDonald House. Like every day, TJ weighed heavy on my heart and was constantly in my thoughts. After tossing and turning, I drifted off to sleep and dreamt that when I arrived at the hospital the next morning, he was already up, off the ventilator, and outside playing football, which was probably a little overly optimistic since he didn't even like football.

The next morning, I pushed aside all my fears about his unknown condition. I concentrated on the fact that he was being extubated and would finally be breathing independently. I was hopeful that we were moving forward and positive change was finally in sight.

My devotional from *Jesus Calling* by Sarah Young that morning read:

"Thank me in the midst of the crucible. When things seem all wrong, look for growth opportunities…. Do you trust Me to orchestrate your life events as I choose…? If you keep trying to carry out your intentions while I am leading you in another direction, you deify your desires." (Young 2004, 140)

1 Peter 5:6–7: "Humble yourselves, therefore, under God's mighty hand, that He may lift you up in due time. Cast all your anxiety on Him because He cares for you."

1 Thessalonians 5:18: "Give thanks in all circumstances; for this is God's will for you in Christ Jesus."

On my walk to the hospital, I was so happy that I was practically skipping. *TJ will be well soon. It won't be long and we'll be heading home,* I thought. However, when I walked into TJ's room that morning, I soon discovered that God was leading us in another direction. TJ's nurse told me that he was not coming off the ventilator because he spiked a high fever in the night and was struggling to breathe on the lower ventilator setting.

Pediatric Neurology reported that his test results returned negative for MG. The resident could see the disappointment on my face and explained, "That's a good thing because you don't want that diagnosis."

After the negative MG test result, doctors began looking at damage to the brainstem or spinal cord. They said the brainstem can be hard to see on an MRI and that might be why the damage was not showing up. They also warned me that generally patients with brainstem strokes do not recover well. *But how can that be better than MG?* I thought. *A brainstem stroke is terrifying!*

After the doctors' morning rounds, I settled on the couch in TJ's room. Staring blindly out the window, my heart cried to God, "What do You want from me?" I asked. "Why won't You *do* something?" I wanted TJ to improve and for all his suffering to go away. I was beyond terrified, to say the least. It was a never-ending nightmare, and all of the unanswered questions about his health tormented me. This was not going the way I had planned!

I sat in TJ's room for a while and then excused myself. I just needed to get away for a minute. The restroom outside the PICU was becoming my favorite place in the hospital. It was a single-occupancy restroom, so I could lock the door and be alone. I went there often when things were too much. It was stressful being in his room, watching him suffer, and hearing more bad news than good. Sometimes I needed a break and alone time with God.

I thought back to my devotional earlier that morning. I was at a crossroads. Was I going to be thankful or angry? Was I going to trust God with TJ's life, or was I going to fight Him every step of the way? I wanted things *my* way. I wanted my son to recover and our lives to return to normal, but that was not the journey God had ordained. The battle between God's will and mine raged inside of me. I finally gave in and prayed, "Lord, thank you for the promise that You will never leave me. Thank you for the opportunity You've given me to glorify You as I walk this path. I don't understand this, but it's clear that Your ways are not my ways. I give this problem to You. May Your will be done." With God's help, I was able to surrender my will, but I would encounter many more battles in future days.

Upon my return to his room, with tears still rolling down my cheeks, I curled up in a ball and lay on the couch. I was so tired and bewildered. Upon seeing my distress, the nurse stated, "Kelly, you have to get up. You have to be strong for him." Irritated by her statement, I felt heavy with exhaustion and lay curled up a while longer. *I just need a minute to cry,* I thought. *Can't I just have a minute to cry?* Still undeterred, she then suggested I go for a walk or sit in the garden for a while. She told me that the time to get away from his room was while he was sedated because when he woke up, he was going to need me. "Take care of yourself first," she advised, "because if you aren't okay, then you won't be able to take care of him."

So, following the nurse's wise advice, I went outside and sat in the garden, but I couldn't relax. As soon as I was away from TJ, I had a strong desire to be close to him again. I felt guilty that I had the freedom and ability to go outside and enjoy the weather and the garden while he was lying in a hospital bed sick and suffering. As a result, I rarely left the PICU.

At some point, I began to feel like everyone was staring at me, but I didn't know why. No one said anything to me until one afternoon when I was sitting on the couch in TJ's room.

"We're having trouble getting medical records from the hospital in Des Moines," the nurse commented.

"Oh, just call the surgeon's nurse, and she'll make sure you get them," I responded. "She's really nice. She'll help you."

I saw the nurse raise his eyebrows as he slowly turned away, and I thought, *Something is wrong. Something is going on.*

Later, Dr. Steele, an intensivist, came into TJ's room and confirmed, "We're having trouble getting medical records from the other hospital."

"The nurse mentioned that to me. What does that mean?"

She sighed aloud. "It's a red flag that indicates there's something wrong."

I felt my body tense up, and my mind started racing. *No, that can't be it,* I thought. *There has to be another reason for it. Maybe there was a mix-up and it was just a coincidence that Mayo wasn't getting his records.* I quickly put it out of my mind.

A while later, a nurse told me a heart surgeon wanted to speak with me and pointed to where he was waiting in the walkway outside of TJ's room. After introducing himself, the surgeon shook my hand. He had the firmest handshake I had ever grasped, and I felt like my fingers would break. His demeanor was aggressive and direct. Frankly, he intimidated me. He asked me to give him the *Reader's Digest* version of the events leading up to TJ's surgery, so I gave him a brief recap.

After I finished, he stated, "I've never seen it done this way before. You can't do it this way. It's too much of an assault on the brain."

He seemed disgusted and irritated by the way the surgery had been performed.

Panic rose inside of me. "But everybody said he's a good surgeon," I quickly pointed out.

"Well, there are a lot of good surgeons out there," he replied, "but there are ten surgeons in this hospital (Mayo), and only two would perform this surgery because they work on the aortic arch all day long."

Fighting back tears, I quickly asked, "But is he going to be okay?"

"I don't know! It's been a month!" he snapped, seemingly irritated with my question. Then he simply walked away.

I was badly shaken by his words, but I desperately hoped that he was wrong. *There has to be a reason why the surgeon did what he did,* I thought. *I know that he's a good surgeon. Maybe this surgeon is wrong.*

A couple of days later, a cardiologist asked to meet with me in the waiting room outside the PICU. He introduced himself and motioned for me to sit down in one of the chairs. He handed me a yellow sticky note with three items written on it and told me they were TJ's heart surgery bypass times.

"Everyone is trying to be politically correct around here, but I'm going to tell you," he said. "We had trouble getting records from the other hospital, and when we finally received them, there were days missing."

I looked at the sticky note as he continued to explain that the item I needed to pay attention to was the circulatory arrest time. I noticed that it was fifty-two minutes.

"What *should* the time be?" I asked.

"No longer than thirty minutes," he responded.

I slowly exhaled and sank back into my chair. "I see what's wrong now," I murmured.

It was now clear that TJ was on the bypass machine for far too long and hadn't received adequate oxygen. He had a hypoxic brain injury. Memories flashed through my mind of Dr. Harmon stating, "It was complicated," when he came into the waiting room after TJ's surgery. I remembered the concerned look in Dr. Harmon's eyes and him sitting outside of TJ's PICU room when TJ's condition was deteriorating and he was confused. Was he watching TJ? Realization quickly began to set in that Dr. Harmon would have been well aware of TJ's bypass times! He knew TJ's circulatory arrest time was far too long! They all knew, and no one had the integrity to tell us. It was all starting to make sense.

I ran to Ronald McDonald House and flung myself onto the bed. I rolled back and forth and cried uncontrollably. I was sick to my stomach and felt incredibly guilty. *It's all our fault,* I thought. *TJ didn't even want to have the surgery, and we encouraged him to have it. We should have researched more. What have we done to our son?*

Even though TJ was still alive, it felt like we were experiencing a death. Our son would never again be the person he was before the brain injury. Doctors explained that his brain injury was in the area that controls motor function; however, the part of the brain that controlled his personality was uninjured. To put it in simpler terms, he was still mentally and emotionally sharp but was trapped in a body that no longer functioned properly. I called my husband and told him what I'd learned. He immediately shouted, "Don't listen to them! Don't listen to them!" We were two brokenhearted, petrified parents who felt deeply responsible for what TJ was going through. It was too painful to face the fact that our best intentions had failed him.

CHAPTER 7

THE CREEPY MUSTACHE

Dr. Steele said the doctors had been discussing the possibility of doing a tracheostomy on TJ, in order to facilitate the removal of secretions from his lungs. I confided in her that TJ's respiratory failures had been terribly traumatic for all of us, and she agreed that suffocating is one of the most terrifying sensations a person can have.

A tracheostomy is a surgically-placed opening in the neck that creates a pathway to the trachea, giving caregivers better access to the patient's airway. One would think I would be devastated at the prospect of my handsome son having a hole in his throat. However, because I was so horrified by his respiratory problems, I was comforted by anything that would help improve his breathing and prevent him from going into failure again.

The doctors and nurses at Mayo reassured me repeatedly that it wasn't our fault that this happened to TJ and that we made the best decision we could, with the information we had. We were told that we were "up against a wall" because the heart surgery had to be done or he wouldn't have lived past the age of thirty. Their reassurance was comforting and helped me work through the relentless guilt that gnawed at me.

The verse Jeremiah 29:11 became very important to me after TJ suffered a brain injury. I clung to this verse and recited it often in my mind, "'For I know the plans I have for you,' declares the Lord, 'plans to prosper you and not to harm you, plans to give you hope and a future.'"

During the *Believing God* study, I learned that the Christian life wasn't just about believing *in* God, but it was about believing what God says and taking Him at his Word. (Moore 2004) Even though Satan wanted it to look like God was harming TJ and must not love him, God's Word said differently. I made the choice to believe what God's Word says and not fall for Satan's lies. I chose to believe that God loved TJ and would give him hope and a future.

Six days after arriving at Mayo, I entered TJ's room while nurses were prepping him for trach surgery. After he was ready, he lay on a gurney outside of his room waiting for transport to take him down to the OR. I stood beside him, held him, and told him how much I loved him. As we hugged, we both had tears streaming down our faces. We were afraid of surgery because the last one hadn't gone well.

Transport wheeled him down to the OR, and I took my spot in the waiting room. After an agonizing wait, we learned the procedure was a success. When I first saw TJ after surgery, I was surprised to discover that he had a mustache under the ventilator mask that he'd been wearing for weeks! I'd never seen him with a mustache before.

The ENT doctor informed me that during the trach surgery, she discovered that TJ's left vocal cord was paralyzed from a nerve that had been damaged during TJ's heart surgery. This is often a complication from repairing an aortic arch.

May 17, 2013

CaringBridge
Written by Kelly

Gloomy, rainy day outside today, but the Son is shining in my heart. TJ had a very good night. The doctor said his lungs were sounding great and that they were looking at taking the right chest tube out. I have been concerned about his jaw clamping again. I saw it clamp down yesterday, and I became a little nervous. The nurses told me not to worry because it was purposeful.

The nurses said sometimes when they are going to suction, he will not open his mouth. Then they tell him they will have to go through his nose, and his mouth will fall open. He is becoming a feisty, little thing. Under different circumstances, I normally would get after him for that, but right now with what this kid has been through, he can pretty much do anything he wants and I won't say a word.

I have brief moments where fear will grip me and my thoughts run rampant, *What if he never gets better? What if he is like this for the rest of his life? What if he can't go to school again? What if he never gets married?* What ifs can drive you insane. Just when I am about to lose my mind, I will gently hear the word, "Surrender." God has told us in Romans 8:28: "And we know that in all things God works for the good of those who love him, who have been called according to his purpose."

Whether TJ recovers fully, recovers partially, or doesn't recover any more than he has, God will work this for TJ's good, and His glory.

In the following days, we noticed slight improvements in TJ. Since the ventilator was now connected to the trach, TJ no longer needed to be intubated and was gradually tapered off sedatives. He was awake a lot more often, and it was wonderful interacting with him again. However, reducing sedation also had its drawbacks. TJ went through intense periods of drug withdrawal, which made him very anxious. Doctors slowed down his tapering schedule so that it was not so taxing on his body all at once.

TJ's catheter and arterial line were removed, but unfortunately, his right chest tube was not ready to be taken out. It was still gurgling and sounded like a fish aquarium; however, I was hopeful that it would soon be removed.

Since arriving at Mayo, I had become very concerned about his left arm. During neurology examinations, TJ was able to squeeze his right hand and wiggle his toes on both feet, but doctors were unable to attain much of a response from his left hand. Now that he was less sedated, one morning during doctors' rounds, TJ didn't just squeeze his left hand; he picked his whole left arm up and moved it. A flood of relief washed over me when I saw his left arm move.

Travis told me later that he noticed the left side of TJ's mouth drooping at the time of his transfer to Mayo Clinic. In my state of shock, I hadn't noticed it, and Travis said he didn't point it out to me because he didn't want to frighten me anymore than I already was. To me, it looked like the symptoms of the left arm weakness and mouth drooping were a separate issue from the symptoms he presented within the first week after surgery.

The nurses began getting TJ out of bed and sitting him in a Medichair, a big, blue, very padded chair with an adjustable back. He hadn't been out of bed in a month, so sitting in it was very painful for him. He was terribly thin, and his back was curved and looked like he had scoliosis. I wondered how he would ever be able to sit up straight again. I wanted to tell the nurses to stop because it was too hard for him, but I resisted the temptation. I knew he was going to have to endure the pain in order to get better. Even though sitting in the chair was painful at first, he persevered and was able to sit up for two hours at a time. Gradually, the nurses increased the incline of his chair.

I was thankful TJ was awake and interacting more, but I was also incredibly sad and filled with grief over what had happened to him. One evening while sitting beside him, I became overwhelmed with sadness and turned my back to him so he couldn't see me crying. I leaned over the counter in his room trying to pull myself together. His nurse came over and put her arm around me, and I whispered, "He doesn't even seem like my son anymore."

"I can't even imagine what you are going through. I am so sorry," she consoled.

Because of the communication problems, meeting TJ's needs was very difficult. He didn't have enough control of his head and neck to nod, so we used a thumbs-up or down to communicate. He couldn't control his arms very well, and every time he tried to give a thumbs-up, his arm moved up the side of his body, went over his head, and then came back down to a resting position on his thigh with his thumb sticking up. It was really strange, and I didn't understand why he was doing that. Other times when he needed something, and I didn't ask the right question, he would understandably become very frustrated. As a result, communicating was terribly exasperating for both of us, and sometimes I felt like we were both going to go insane.

On Saturday, May 18th, Travis drove to Rochester to spend the weekend with us. When he walked into the room that morning, TJ was overjoyed to see his dad. While Travis was joking with him, in an effort to interact with his dad more, TJ moved his legs close to the edge of the bed, like he wanted to get up. For a minute, life felt normal again. Travis brought fun and laughter to the room, and the heaviness of the weekdays disappeared when he was present. I told TJ that while he was on the ventilator, he had grown a mustache. He then rubbed his index finger over the mustache, and a slight smile formed on his face. I secretly thought it was creepy looking.

Although doctors believed that TJ had a stroke in his brainstem, the MRI didn't actually show it. Doctors planned to perform another MRI where they would obtain "smaller cuts" of the brainstem since the brainstem can be hard to see on an MRI. At times, because the doctors had still not pinpointed the root cause of his health issues, they had differing opinions. It drove me crazy that we had no answers. At night when I lay in bed, I repeatedly reviewed the first week after surgery, trying to solve the mystery of what had happened. I was constantly doing research, trying to learn as much as I could about his condition in the hope of finding something that would help him.

On Monday, May 20th, Travis drove back home in the morning, and soon after he left, things began to rapidly deteriorate. Doctors had previously thought TJ's left lung was healing and had pulled out his left chest tube, but afterward, he struggled to breathe. They discovered the air around his left lung was back, and the area putting pressure on his lung was increasing in size. As a result, they inserted another chest tube in his left side to remove the air and relieve the pressure.

Dr. Steele sat on the couch next to me in TJ's room. In a serious tone, she told me that TJ might never again be able to breathe on his own. At the time, I didn't know Dr. Steele very well, and her bedside manner felt cold to me. What she was telling me may have been true, but hearing such devastating information from a stranger was very painful for me. I felt anger toward her and wondered, *Doesn't she care how much this is hurting me?* After hearing her opinion, I actually felt physical pain—like I had been kicked in the gut. I wanted her to tell me that my son was going to be okay, that he was going to go to college, get married, and have children just like I'd planned. But she didn't tell me that. In an effort to nudge her into telling me that TJ would be okay, I reminded her that he'd been walking and talking when he woke up from his heart surgery. In response she said, "He may have developed more blood clots during the transition here." Frustrated with her answer, I pushed back harder, but no matter how hard I pushed, she wouldn't tell me that everything was going to be okay.

Over the weekend, TJ's face had developed some intermittent, minor twitching, which we attributed to medication withdrawal. However, it wasn't long before it grew far more pronounced, making his entire head shake and his eyes blink rapidly. I was called by his nurse around midnight and asked to come to the PICU because she thought he was having a seizure. Before I left my room at RMH, I sat on the edge of the bed feeling deflated and thought, *We're not going home with the same TJ.*

Every time we took a step forward and thought we were making headway, we were hit with another issue and forced to pause and take two additional steps backward. I wondered if TJ would ever really get better or if he would just live the rest of his life in the hospital.

> **May 21, 2013**
>
> *CaringBridge*
> *Written by Kelly*
>
> Things looked bleak yesterday, but today is a new day. I am so thankful for my husband who refuses to give in and continues to fight and encourages me to keep going.
>
> In my morning reading, I learned that the feeling of my anxiety rising is really a sign that I am not trusting God. When I notice myself worrying, it is actually me attempting to take control of TJ's situation and make things go my way. The only way I can fix the problem is to stop focusing on TJ's health and to turn my focus to the Lord. He is for me and will hear me. I am waiting with hopefulness to see what He will do.
>
> **Romans 8:31–32**
>
> "What, then, shall we say in response to these things? If God is for us, who can be against us? He who did not spare His own Son, but gave Him up for us all—how will He not also, along with Him, graciously give us all things?"
>
> **Micah 7:7**
>
> "But as for me, I watch in hope for the LORD,
> I wait for God my Savior; my God will hear me."

Travis had just returned home after his weekend with us, but I was devastated after all the bad news I'd received. I called and begged him to come back to Rochester, which he did willingly.

After TJ's third MRI, one of the resident neurologists told us that they had seen nothing on it and didn't think he'd had a brainstem stroke. Travis and I were elated, and I did another dance in the hallway. Unfortunately, we still didn't have a diagnosis for TJ, and even though not knowing drove me crazy, it was better than thinking he had a brainstem stroke. We were hoping that an alternate diagnosis would mean he had a much better chance at recovery. The resident told us they were going to start "casting their nets wider now" and looking at "weird things." They also did an EEG on TJ and reported that the twitching and shaking we were seeing were not the result of seizures. That was more good news.

May 22, 2013

CaringBridge
Written by Travis

Hello from St. Mary's amusement park where the rides are free. On Monday night Kelly was told by the doctors that TJ would be on a ventilator the rest of his life, could not breathe on his own, and had a brainstem stroke. I could tell after talking to her that night that I needed to get back up here—fast! So, after Monday we were in need of some good news and got it Tuesday night. TJ had a third MRI that came back negative—nothing has changed!

We met with neurologists this morning, and everyone now agrees that the brain is off the table. The problem more than likely is neuromuscular. The plan is to get TJ drug free and off the ventilator. He is addicted to pain and sedation medicine—we did not realize he was a junkie too.

The lungs are the bigger issue for him right now. There cannot be any forward movement until they heal and he is off the ventilator. They have already started the tapering process and he gets his first dose of methadone tomorrow as they continue to cut back on the opiates. He is showing signs of withdrawal: sweaty, muscle spasms, tremors, anxiety, and much more agitated.

We were very excited and thankful that his brain was good—praise God! This also makes the likelihood of recovery much more attainable. There is a lot of work to be done on his part, but I think he'll be up to the challenge, especially if it gets him closer to hot wings and Dunkin' Donuts iced coffee.

Kelly has been by his side since day one. She is such a wonderful mother and wife! TJ's sisters have been here whenever possible, two of them coming from Texas. He loves having them here. The support we have received from our church Timberline, previous Bible study from First Federated, and friends has been overwhelming. We have never felt so loved and supported! I thank God every day for that! Posts from TJ's friends have been an encouragement to him. We read the CaringBridge comments to him regularly.

In light of all that has gone wrong, there is a lot to be thankful for. We still have our only son and hope of recovery. There are families who come here together and go home broken. We don't know God's plan for TJ or us as a family going forward. I do know that we have to trust Him for whatever outcome we have. We have no control here and are 100 percent dependent on our Heavenly Father.

> "Your most profound and intimate experiences of worship will likely be in your darkest days—when your heart is broken, when you feel abandoned, when you're out of options, when the pain is too great—and you turn to God alone."
>
> —Rick Warren (Warren 2012)

The first time TJ coughed and blew the ventilator connector off his trach, I screamed in fear as the nurses hurriedly reconnected the ventilator. They were unphased by the incident, and I later came to realize that it was a regular occurrence. However, at the time, TJ's respiratory problems continued to be absolutely terrifying to me, making me feel continually nauseated. As a result, I couldn't eat much and had lost a lot of weight.

The stress of the hospital environment was more intense than I'd ever anticipated. I constantly thought, *How can a body even live with this much stress?*

On the outside, however, I appeared calm, and one day a sweet nurse pulled me aside and said, "Kelly, you have to speak up. You're his advocate and his voice. If you don't like something, you need to tell us. Don't worry about hurting our feelings."

Although I appreciated her concern for us, I was confused by what she meant. They were amazing with TJ, and I was never worried about him while he was in their care.

Sometimes being in his room was entirely too stressful for me, but strange as it might seem, being away from his room was equally as stressful. The most comforting place I could find was sitting in a chair right outside his room. One afternoon when a resident walked by, I was reading my Bible. She commented, "I get it now," and walked away.

Some of the staff were very vocal and upset about what had happened to TJ, and I concluded by some of their comments that they were perplexed by my mild demeanor. I wondered if they expected intense anger and violent outbursts from me.

Although I appeared calm on the outside, a war raged inside of me between trusting God with TJ's life and caving in to fear. I was afraid that at any moment he would go into respiratory failure again and they wouldn't be able to pull him through it. The truth is that I really wanted to lose control and scream my head off but knew letting the fear overtake me would mean I had quit trusting God.

May 24, 2013

CaringBridge
Written by Kelly

TJ had such a good day yesterday. He sat up in a chair twice, clapped his hands, and crossed his legs. Every time I looked at him, he was lifting his legs or opening and closing his hands in an attempt to get them stronger. I felt peace yesterday and that everything was going to be okay.

This morning, however, was a different story. When I walked into his room, he was bleeding out of his trach and his mouth, and blood was running down his chin and throat. I asked the nurse what was wrong, and she said he's been bleeding and ENT will be up in thirty minutes to check his trach. Thirty minutes? Well, that just wouldn't do, so I ran down the walkway yelling, "He is bleeding and I want somebody up here right now!" Where had this crazy woman come from!? The ENT doctor then came up and was surprised by the quantity of blood. He packed it really well and stopped the heparin. Heparin is a blood thinner used to treat blood clots. All is calm for the time being.

TJ continues to twitch badly. It is very frustrating and exhausting for him. It started at the time they began tapering medications, but they don't think that's the cause.

On days like this, I am reminded of the story of Peter walking on the water. I think about that story often. In Matthew 14:22–33, Jesus made the disciples get into the boat and go on ahead of Him to the other side. Don't miss that word "made." Yes, sometimes He sends us into a storm.

When evening came, the boat was considerable distance from land buffeted by the waves. During the fourth watch of the night, Jesus went out to them walking on the lake, and they were terrified. Jesus said, "Take courage. It is I. Don't be afraid."

The Creepy Mustache

Peter said, "Lord, if it's you, tell me to come to you on the water." Jesus said, "Come," and Peter got down out of the boat, walked on the water and came toward Jesus. But when he saw the wind, he was afraid, and beginning to sink, cried out, "Lord save me!"

Immediately Jesus reached out his hand and caught him. "You of little faith," He said. "Why did you doubt?" They climbed into the boat and the wind died down. Then they worshiped him saying, "Truly you are the Son of God."

Many days I feel like I am on the water like Peter with waves crashing against me, darkness all around me, and the wind howling. With fear welling up inside of me, I imagine Jesus standing before me with the wind blowing His hair and white robe. Often it takes every ounce of energy I have to keep my eyes on His face and not on the chaos all around me. But when I do, the wind dies down, and I can hear my Savior speak, telling me to have faith and not to doubt.

Thank you for all of your prayers. The Bible teaches that we are to carry one another's burdens. We have never in our lives felt more supported and loved than we do at this time.

CHAPTER 8

THE DARKEST OF NIGHTS

Later in the day, two weeks after arriving at Mayo, the bleeding from TJ's trach started back up again, and they found blood in his lungs. They performed several different scopes and a CT scan of his heart to make sure the blood wasn't coming from there but were unable to find the source of the bleed. Later in the afternoon, doctors said the bleeding had stopped and now everything was okay. Still, I felt nervous about that answer. I couldn't help but wonder, *How can you fix something or prevent something from happening again when you don't know what caused it?*

That night as I was leaving to return to Ronald McDonald House, I had an uneasy feeling in my stomach that something wasn't right. Sure enough, around midnight my cell phone rang.

"Hello?" I answered.

"Kelly, this is TJ's nurse from the PICU at St. Mary's. TJ isn't doing well right now, and you need to come to the hospital immediately."

"Is he dying?" I asked.

"Well, we don't control that," she said, "but right now is a good time to come."

"Oh my gosh! I'm on my way!"

Panic set in as I jumped out of bed and hurriedly got dressed. My mind whirled. *Every time he goes into respiratory failure, the way they correct it is to put him on a ventilator. But he is already on a ventilator. What are they going to do now?*

I quickly called my husband who had just gotten off work and was already on his way to Rochester for the weekend. I told him that TJ wasn't doing well, that I was going to the hospital, and to meet me there when he got into town.

Aiden had been staying with me that week. I scooped him up, and we bolted out of the building. It was the middle of the night, and I was running up the sidewalk in Rochester, Minnesota carrying a three-year-old in my arms. I couldn't get to my dying son fast enough.

When I arrived at the hospital entrance I routinely used, the door was locked. With Aiden still in my arms, I frantically ran around the hospital checking every door. They were all locked. I was already in a state of panic and could feel the beginning of hysteria creeping in. I was terrified that he would die and I wouldn't be with him. I finally gained entry through the Emergency Room doors and rushed to his room.

When I entered the PICU, his room was full of people, and he was on a machine I had never seen before. It was pumping air into his lungs at a very fast rate of speed. It made a sound similar to quickly saying bah-bah-bah-bah-bah-bah. They told me it was an oscillatory ventilator, a machine used in a last-ditch effort to keep someone alive. They said TJ's lungs were hemorrhaging. The resident showed me the x-ray of his lungs. I wasn't sure exactly what I was looking at but thought I saw one lung completely collapsed and the other lung deflated with the exception of a softball-sized area.

After showing me the x-ray, they pulled a small table and chairs over to the area outside of the room so I could sit and watch what was happening inside his room. A nurse gently took Aiden from my arms. She said the activity in TJ's room was too traumatic for him to be watching. That hadn't even crossed my mind, and I was grateful the nurses were protective of Aiden.

After TJ's room began to clear out, I was allowed to go in and sit beside him. I asked his nurse what happened: "He was doing fine, and then all of a sudden, he started plummeting. He just turned on a dime." And then she confided, "I know what it feels like to lose a child. I had a son who died when he was young, and it never gets any easier."

Her choice of words sounded to me like death was inevitable, and I lost all hope. I sat on a stool beside TJ and told him over and over again that I was so sorry. The nurse walked over and put her arm around me and said that it wasn't my fault and I didn't need to apologize. However, I wasn't apologizing because I felt like it was my fault. I was apologizing because I was sorry that he wasn't going to live, that he would never get to grow up and do all the things he dreamed of.

An intensivist in the PICU, Dr. Tomar, asked, "If TJ's heart stops, do you want him resuscitated?" After a pause, he added, "I'm afraid he could have more brain damage."

At that moment, all I heard was "more brain damage," so I answered, "No, don't resuscitate him." I didn't want to keep him alive, to live in worse shape than he was already in, when I knew that a split second after his heart stopped, he would be whole and in the arms of Jesus.

I felt some stares and heard a respiratory therapist very loudly ask, "Is this really what we are doing?" I didn't understand why she would disagree with my decision, but because of all the disorder that was going on around me, I didn't put much more thought into it.

I sat outside of TJ's room for hours. At some point in the night, I went to my favorite spot, the restroom outside of the PICU. I was on my knees praying for God to save my son, and I didn't care how dirty the floor was. The only thought going through my mind was the story of Abraham's testing:

GENESIS 22:1–19

"Sometime later God tested Abraham. He said to him, 'Abraham!'

'Here I am,' he replied.

Then God said, 'Take your son, your only son, whom you love—Isaac—and go to the region of Moriah. Sacrifice him there as a burnt offering on a mountain I will show you.'

Early the next morning Abraham got up and loaded his donkey. He took with him two of his servants and his son Isaac. When he had cut enough wood for the burnt offering, he set out for the place God had told him about. On the third day Abraham looked up and saw the place in the distance. He said to his servants, 'Stay here with the donkey while I and the boy go over there. We will worship and then we will come back to you.'

Abraham took the wood for the burnt offering and placed it on his son Isaac, and he himself carried the fire and the knife. As the two of them went on together, Isaac spoke up and said to his father Abraham, 'Father?'

'Yes, my son?' Abraham replied.

'The fire and wood are here,' Isaac said, 'but where is the lamb for the burnt offering?'

Abraham answered, 'God himself will provide the lamb for the burnt offering, my son.'

And the two of them went on together.

When they reached the place God had told him about, Abraham built an altar there and arranged the wood on it. He bound his son Isaac and laid him on the altar, on top of the wood. Then he reached out his hand and took the knife to slay his son. But the angel of the Lord called out to him from heaven, 'Abraham! Abraham!'

'Here I am,' he replied.

'Do not lay a hand on the boy,' he said. 'Do not do anything to him. Now I know that you fear God, because you have not withheld from me your son, your only son.'

Abraham looked up and there in a thicket he saw a ram caught by its horns. He went over and took the ram and sacrificed it as a burnt offering instead of his son. So Abraham called that place The Lord Will Provide. And to this day it is said, 'On the mountain of the Lord it will be provided.'

The angel of the Lord called to Abraham from heaven a second time and said, 'I swear by myself, declares the Lord, that because you have done this and have not withheld your son, your only son, I will surely bless you and make your descendants as numerous as the stars in the sky and as the sand on the seashore. Your descendants will take possession of the cities of their enemies, and through your offspring all nations on earth will be blessed, because you have obeyed me.'

Then Abraham returned to his servants, and they set off together for Beersheba. And Abraham stayed in Beersheba."

As I prayed on my knees, I felt that God was asking me to willingly give Him my only son. *Do I love God more than I love my son?* I thought. *Will I still trust Him if He takes TJ home?* Although it was excruciatingly painful, I opened my arms and said to the Lord, "He is Your son first, Lord, so I am releasing my grasp and giving him back to You. But You're going to have to help me get through the rest of my life because his death will be unbearable."

Travis arrived at the hospital at 3 A.M. He rushed into TJ's room and stood over him with tears running down his cheeks and told him that he loved him. I noticed that TJ had tears in the corners of his eyes as well and asked the doctor if he could hear us.

"No, he's on way too many paralytics," Dr. Tomar answered.

But a short while later, TJ opened his eyes, and I yelled, "He's opening his eyes!" Medical staff quickly administered more medication and sedated him.

TJ battled all night. When morning came, miraculously his lungs reinflated, and he began to stabilize. After some investigation, doctors believed his lungs weren't actually hemorrhaging, as they previously thought, but that the blood from the trach surgery ran down into his lungs, dried, and closed his airway, causing his lungs to collapse. They believed that the aggressive suctioning done in the early morning hours successfully cleared his airway, enabling his lungs to reinflate. They said his lungs now looked even better than they had before. We were incredibly grateful for Dr. Tomar's expertise in getting TJ through our very dark night.

Well, I thought, *surely this must mean that TJ is meant to live because if God wanted him, He would have taken him last night. Surely, he is going to recover.*

May 25, 2013

CaringBridge
Written by Kelly

We met with doctors this morning, and things have become positive again. Healthwise he's pretty much right back to where he was before the incident last night. Last night we were talking about do-not-resuscitate orders and organ donation. Today he has turned around, and we have hope again.

One thing the doctors say is that he is a puzzle and they cannot figure him out. They said they will think it's one thing but then a couple of pieces don't fit. Then they'll think it's another, but yet again, a couple of pieces don't fit. Yesterday I was told he had a diffuse brain injury from lack of oxygen during the surgery. Horrible diagnosis. But today they said it doesn't fit because he woke up and was walking around and people who have that usually don't wake up at all. Every day for me is a rollercoaster.

> They believe there is something else driving this but they just can't put their finger on it. That's what we all need to be praying about, that whatever it is that's causing this will come to light.
>
> TJ is a strong kid. He keeps pushing through and fighting. Doctors advised us that he may have more of these critical incidents come up, and that if they do, there's always a chance that it might be his last, but until then, we are praying that he turns the corner and that the cause will be revealed.

Later that morning, an intensivist, with whom I wasn't familiar, pulled Travis and me into a small private waiting area. Upon entering the room, the first thing she said was, "Take that DNR order off TJ."

Because of my compliant, do-what-I'm-told personality, I immediately said, "Okay. Take it off." I could see that she wasn't happy with me about the DNR order, and it bothered me. I quickly began explaining what I was thinking the night before.

"Well, Dr. Tomar said if TJ's heart stopped, he could have more brain damage, so I told him not to resuscitate him."

In no uncertain terms, she responded, "Let *us* determine when it's been too long to resuscitate him."

My head was spinning. I didn't understand all the ins and outs of this new medical environment I had unexpectedly been thrown into. I wasn't aware that when the heart stops, there's a window of time to resuscitate before more brain damage occurs. I also didn't know that a DNR order was a standing order. I thought it was just for the event the night before.

Travis and I both agreed. "Yes, yes, take it off."

As we left the room, I felt horrible. *What if TJ finds out I put a DNR order on him?* I asked myself. *What if his heart had stopped? He would have died because of me.* (In that moment, I felt incredible guilt that he might have died because of my decision. However, today I know that's not true because Psalm 139:16 says, "Your eyes saw my unformed body; all the days ordained for me were written in your book before one of them came to be." I've since learned that it was never in my power to control the number of TJ's days. His days were determined by God before he was ever born.)

Pushing down the sick feeling I had in my stomach, Travis and I walked back to TJ's room. When I entered the room, I asked the nurse how he was doing.

"He's critical but stable," she answered.

I frowned. "He's critical?!"

Sounding annoyed, Travis said, "Yes, Kelly, he has been the whole time he's been here!"

I knew TJ was really sick but not *critical*. A "critical" label was something that happened to somebody else, not to *my* son.

I tried to laugh it off, but I knew there was something not quite right with me. On one occasion, while sitting in TJ's room, I looked down at the plugs in the outlet. One was labeled "Do Not Remove, Life Support," and I thought, *Oh my gosh! He's on life support!* I knew he'd been on a ventilator for weeks, but I wasn't connecting the dots that a ventilator and life support were the same thing. I think if he had been a stranger and not someone so emotionally connected, I would have been better able to process the truth. The term "life support" just sounded much more serious than the word "ventilator."

Sometimes during morning rounds, doctors used terms for TJ's medical issues that were different from what I'd been using in my head. They used phrases like "trach-dependent" as opposed to my phrase: "He has a trach." Their terminology sounded much scarier and far more permanent. Every time I heard that phrasing, panic and fear welled up inside me. I had to restrain myself from interrupting and asking, "But he's still going to get rid of the trach, right?"

Ordinarily, I'm an intelligent person, although it sure didn't seem that way at the time because I was in serious denial. Over time, I learned that denial is an interesting and necessary coping mechanism of trauma and not something to be ashamed of. When a person is in a distressing situation, the brain automatically goes into survival mode and only allows a little bit of information in at a time. I could feel it happening to me. Most of the time, I felt numb and empty, like a robot just going through the motions.

May 27, 2013

CaringBridge
Written by Ashley (TJ's sister)

Now that TJ is recovering from the other night, the doctors have started the process of tapering him off all the medications again, so he is going through withdrawal and is very uncomfortable, including much facial twitching and tremors in his arms. It's hard to see him struggling, but getting him off all these medications means he is traveling further down the road to recovery and we are one step closer to having our TJ back! Recently the doctors changed out his chest tubes and inserted some larger tubes that have been working so much better, and today a chest X-ray showed that the cavity of air around his lung was much improved. He has been on CPAP since nine this morning and is doing wonderful! This is the longest period of time in weeks that he's been successfully breathing on his own! On Wednesday all of his sisters will be here. I'm sure he can't wait to have us all in his face and lovin' on him. I'm almost afraid to say it because we have seen firsthand how quickly things can change, but it feels like we have finally turned the corner, and to God be the glory!

After TJ's close call, our four daughters made plans to gather in Rochester to see their brother. Because we lived in different states and one daughter lived in Germany, it had been nearly ten years since we had all been together. Since there could only be five people in the Ronald McDonald room at a time, lodging was a problem. Hotels were too expensive, so we prayed about it and left it in God's hands. Anna, another mother at Mayo, told me about a house that was made available, free of charge, to families staying at the hospital. We called and talked to the owners, and they said, "Yes, of course, your family can stay there." It was a beautiful home that sat on a peaceful, green, and well-maintained acreage on the edge of town. It was a gift from God and provided our family with a weekend of much-needed tranquility and solace.

In the morning when Travis and I walked into TJ's room, TJ, with the assistance of his therapist, was sitting on the edge of the bed. With his eyes open and a smile on his face, he was looking at his sister Whitney who had just arrived from Germany. Unbeknownst to us, she had chosen to go straight to the hospital. What a wonderful surprise that scene was!

After giving Whitney a big hug, I said, "TJ, tomorrow when I get here in the morning, I expect you to be up and outside playing football!"

May 31, 2013

CaringBridge
Written by Courtney (TJ's sister)

Today TJ sat up on the edge of the bed for five minutes with support from the nurses. That was the first time in weeks I've seen him sit up! His lungs are healing, and each day he breathes

> more and more on his own. His eye contact is also improving. He's in a little bit of pain still from the tapering of the drugs and the chest tubes, but hopefully that will soon pass. The music therapist came in today and asked TJ to copy her motion as she played a beat on the drum. He had no complication doing that! God is amazing! I'm very hopeful that he'll come out of this and be okay! TJ is a fighter, and he's here to stay. I want to personally thank everybody worldwide who is praying for my brother. The power of prayer is so amazing.

I saw the nurse who was with TJ the night he crashed. She shared with me that she was really surprised he made it through that night because she had expected a very different outcome. "I have seen miracles before, and this one was a miracle," she remarked.

"It was like we were in the middle of the storm," I said, "in the fourth watch of the night, and everything looked hopeless. And then Jesus showed up walking across the water and quieted the storm."

"That's exactly what it was!" she agreed.

We were so thankful TJ was alive.

CHAPTER 9

TRAINING AND CHECKLISTS

TJ was having trouble with sinus infections from the nasogastric (NG) tube placed in his nose the first week after surgery. An NG tube is a plastic tube that goes through the nose, past the throat, and down into the stomach. Liquid food is then pumped through the tube to provide nourishment to the body.

The first day of June, Dr. Alvarez, an intensivist in the PICU, sat down to visit with Travis and me. After updating us on TJ's status, it became obvious to us there was something else she wanted to say but was reluctant to say it.

"Okay, guys, I've got something I need to tell you, so I'm just going to say it. We need to put in a G-tube."

Travis and I immediately started laughing.

"We've been wondering why you guys haven't done that

yet!" I replied.

"That's fine," Travis added. "We knew it was coming,"

A gastrostomy tube (G-tube) is a tube that's inserted through the abdomen that delivers nutrition directly to the stomach. There were pros and cons to the G-tube. The pros were that it would alleviate his risk of sinus infections and it was more comfortable than a tube running through his nose. The cons were that it was another surgical procedure and TJ would have anesthesia a third time. The most concerning part for a parent was that a G-tube was more permanent than the temporary NG tube. Hope was fading that he would be able to eat and swallow on his own.

June 2, 2013

CaringBridge
Written by Kelly

When I walked into TJ's room yesterday, I felt the old fear, panic, and weariness creep into my heart. Just walking into this hospital does that to me. Most times in the past when I visited the hospital, it was to see a mother and newborn baby and was a joyous occasion. Hospitals seemed like busy and exciting places to me, but now I have seen them from a very different perspective. They're also places of desperation and are filled with pain and fear. Because of the state of mind I was in, I knew it was time to open my Bible for a much-needed word from the Lord.

Isaiah 40:27–31

"Why do you complain, Jacob? Why do you say, Israel, 'My way is hidden from the Lord; my cause is disregarded by my God?' Do you not know? Have you not heard? The

Lord is the everlasting God, the Creator of the ends of the earth. He will not grow tired or weary, and His understanding no one can fathom. He gives strength to the weary and increases the power of the weak. Even youths grow tired and weary, and young men stumble and fall; but those who hope in the Lord will renew their strength. They will soar on wings like eagles; they will run and not grow weary, they will walk and not be faint."

If I look at the chaos all around me, I grow weary and tired, but if I place my hope in the Lord, my strength is renewed. I decided to concentrate, not on what I see and how I feel, but on God's promises to me.

An hour later Neurology came in. Generally, when I see them coming, I try to disappear as fast as I can in an attempt to avoid any more bad news, but yesterday I found myself trapped in the room and unable to leave. It was a new doctor this time. She examined TJ and then said there was no reason from an MRI standpoint that he shouldn't recover. She explained that the tremors he is having are not a big concern, that they are not due to withdrawal but due to brain injury and will subside over time as his brain heals. Everything she said was very positive. God renewed my strength! Oh, how I love those moments when I feel God's presence.

TJ ended up having a fabulous day. He was very calm for most of the day. The surgeon came in and discussed putting the G-tube in and maybe surgically repairing the hole in TJ's right lung. (Although TJ didn't have a tear in his lungs, they did later find holes around the outside edges that happened during the first intubation when his lungs were overinflated. Even though his body filling up with air was disturbing, Dr. Alvarez informed me that overinflation of the lungs does happen sometimes when a person is in respiratory failure.) They have a couple of options to repair the holes, so they are discussing it with the team and will get back to us. We expect

> that to be repaired this week, and then those painful chest tubes can come out. Little by little, he is getting stronger. He is lifting his arms more; his grip is getting stronger; and he has even started moving his head on his own. We know we have to be patient because progress will be very slow and he has a long road ahead of him, but we do believe he is on the way. Late yesterday afternoon, for the first time on this journey, I thought, *I don't think I have to worry about death anymore.*

TJ's tremors were incredibly upsetting. We didn't know what brought them on or what stopped them. Sometimes his head shook back and forth from side to side. Other times, his eyes blinked and his eyebrows rose up and down rapidly. Once, when I asked him a question, he nodded slightly, but then a tremor took over, and he couldn't stop nodding his head. Sometimes I timed his tremors, and they would last for five or six minutes. I spent a lot of time massaging his neck and face in an attempt to stop them. Sometimes it worked and sometimes it didn't. It was painful for me to watch him in the state he was in, and I felt so sorry for him. He had no dignity. He drooled all over himself. He had no control of his body and wore a diaper. "Lord," I prayed, "is TJ going to be okay? Is he ever going to be his normal self again? Please make him okay, Lord. Please help him."

There was *some* good news: TJ's lungs were finally making progress. His left lung was healed, enabling the chest tube on that side to be removed. Since the right lung had a hole in it, they fused the lung to the chest wall to seal off the hole. Even though many times I felt horror at the events that were happening around me, I was also fascinated by the brilliance of the doctors.

TJ waved and smiled at every doctor who walked in. When I say smile, it may conjure up images of a person smiling from ear to ear, but his smile wasn't the same anymore. Because he couldn't open his mouth and couldn't move his eyes to make eye contact, smiling looked different.

Although he was weary at times, he maintained a cheerful attitude. We'd had six weeks during the time he was sedated to accept and adjust to his current condition. However, TJ was just waking up and coming to terms with his new normal. For him, the rehabilitation journey was just beginning. One of the nurses told me that even though he couldn't talk, she could tell he was a gentle kid. It was amazing to me that they could see someone's personality shining through, even in his condition.

Merriam-Webster defines the term "deficit" as: "A lack or impairment in an ability or functional capacity." (Webster 2003) The word "deficit" is often used in the medical community as a medical assessment. For some in the special-needs community, defining the abilities of a child with special needs with the term "deficit" is offensive and causes pain because children with special needs are wonderfully made by God exactly the way they are. They are valuable and not "less than" others. However, as the mother of a child who suffered a brain injury, the term "deficit" was not offensive to me. It simply defined an impairment in TJ's physical ability. Prior to his surgery, TJ had the ability to swallow. It was only after his brain was deprived of oxygen during surgery that he acquired an impairment in his swallowing ability (and many other abilities), and, therefore, had a swallowing deficit. His deficits were enormous, and as you can imagine, we grieved and struggled with their loss.

My biggest concern was TJ's swallowing deficit. I was trying not to worry about it and leave it in the Lord's hands, but fear and doubt crept in sometimes. And because TJ loved food, it broke my heart that he was no longer able to eat or drink. Every time I went to lunch, I felt guilty and tried to hide from him where I was going and what I was doing. I resolved to never eat or drink in his room. I wondered, *What is his life going to be like if he can't swallow his own saliva and is never able to eat again?* That would be such a radical change and loss for anyone let alone a teenage boy! I prayed continually for his swallowing ability to return.

We tried many different methods of communicating. Although they worked somewhat, they still left us both very frustrated. I did my best to meet any perceived needs that he had, but I often wondered if his needs were all being addressed.

One of TJ's nurses told me about a man with ALS whose deficits were very similar to TJ's. To help this man communicate, a caregiver slowly went through the alphabet, and the man would blink to choose the letter he wanted. He wrote an entire book using that method. Since it worked for him, I decided to give it a try with TJ.

One night, he squeezed my hand over and over, which signaled that he needed something. After asking every question I could think of but still not asking the correct one, I told him I wanted him to spell it to me. I was going to go through the alphabet slowly, and he was to squeeze my hand when I got to the letter he wanted. It took a long time and required a lot of patience, but the first word he spelled was "stay."

"Are you saying you want me to spend the night in the hospital with you?" I asked.

Squeeze, squeeze, squeeze.

Excitement was building inside of me. We could finally communicate!

I immediately said, "Yes! Of course, I'll stay!"

He continued squeezing my hand. I assumed he had more to say, so we started spelling the second word. That time he spelled "thirsty."

"Are you saying you're thirsty?" I asked.

He squeezed my hand several times, and tears rolled down his cheeks. My eyes filled with tears as relief spread across his face. I couldn't imagine how frustrating it was, and my heart broke for him.

"Lord, I know that you use suffering to refine us, but why does this have to be so miserable for him?" I prayed. "Can you please make this better for him?"

The nurse and I found a sponge, soaked it in apple juice, and rubbed it all over his mouth. A look of contentment formed on his face, and he stared at me intently with a beautiful look of gratitude in his eyes.

Nurses also taught us how to sign "I love you." The sign was made by putting a thumb, index finger, and pinkie finger up while keeping the ring finger and middle finger down. TJ used the sign frequently throughout the day, and it warmed my heart.

June 6, 2013

CaringBridge
Written by Kelly

Today TJ is still in a lot of pain from having site care completed on his right chest tube, and they have changed his vent settings and are making him take deeper breaths. He has gotten into the habit of taking shallow breaths, most likely due to pain from chest tubes and muscle weakness, so now they are forcing longer, deep breaths, and he isn't digging it. I finally had to leave the room because he looks at me with pleading eyes that say, "Please help me," but there is nothing I can do. The doctors know what's best for him.

> It looks like rehab will happen on Monday. The doctor said he was a little overly optimistic about TJ going tomorrow since he is having the G-tube put in this afternoon. I saw what the G-tube looks like, and it's no big deal. I think it's actually much better than a tube going through his nose. The right chest tube is still on schedule to be pulled out tomorrow. That's a big deal. He's been battling that right lung for six weeks now, and he is close to winning the battle.
>
> This morning as I was sitting and praying, the thought came to mind that God is in the process of forming TJ into a godly man. It reminded me of something our pastor in Florida said years ago, and I have never forgotten it:
>
> "God cannot use you greatly until He hurts you deeply."
>
> —Pastor Hayes Wicker

TJ went in for surgery for the insertion of his G-tube. After it was over, my cell phone rang. It was the nurse who told me that TJ's surgery had gone well. He was now in the recovery room but was very upset and agitated. Apparently, because of his inability to communicate, the nurse was struggling to understand what he wanted. She asked me to come to the recovery room to help with him.

Upon entering the room, a wave of shock came over me. I had been in recovery rooms before but none like this one. The room was much larger than I anticipated. There was row after row of patients lying on gurneys. Although I can only guess at the number of patients in the room, it seemed like there were 100. Some people had curtains pulled around their beds for privacy; however, many did not. The room was filled with noises of groggy, post-surgical patients moaning and groaning. An eerie feeling came over me, and I felt like a character in the scene of a science-fiction movie who suddenly stumbles into a strange room full of bodies in various stages of scientific experimentation.

After shaking off that strange feeling and finding TJ, I hugged and kissed him and pulled up a stool beside him. I held his hand hoping my presence would console and calm him. Instead, he was combative, and I wondered if the anesthesia was causing his confusion. I sat and struggled with him for about an hour and was relieved when the nurse said his vitals were normal and he could go back to the PICU. I was more than ready to be with the nurses who knew him best *and* to get out of that room.

A few weeks after being admitted to the PICU, a young man a couple of years older than TJ was admitted into the room next door to him. I had seen his mom coming and going, but we had never spoken. In fact, the nurses sometimes got confused because she and I looked so much alike.

One morning I walked into the PICU, and her son's room was full of people. I knew what that meant: He was not doing well. His mom was pacing and I tried not to stare. I made an intentional effort to mind my own business, but it was difficult. I knew what she was going through, and I desperately wanted to talk to her. After a couple of days, I finally struck up a conversation with her and learned that her name was Janet. Her son's name was Tom. They were from Wisconsin and were quite familiar with Mayo Clinic. Tom had Down Syndrome and had been a frequent patient at Mayo. He had surgery for a heart defect when he was younger, and he was now hospitalized for the treatment of leukemia.

Janet invited me into Tom's room and showed me the pictures on the walls. He was the youngest of three children and seemed to have a very full life with lots of friends, a girlfriend, and a family who loved him deeply. I hoped that Tom and TJ would have a chance to meet once they were both healthier.

Unfortunately, during our conversation, I learned that Tom was being moved to a different floor. Janet and I exchanged numbers and agreed to meet for coffee sometime at the Caribou Coffee shop across the street.

Since TJ's lungs were recovering, discharge from the PICU to the rehab unit was in sight. In order for him to be discharged, the PICU had a policy that parents must learn how to care for their child's medical condition. The medical staff taped a checklist of tasks to the wall that Travis and I must learn to perform. The list included performing three trach changes, cleaning the trach and G-tube twice a day, suctioning the trach, and taking CPR training.

I was overwhelmed at the prospect of taking care of his trach and learning CPR. Performing this kind of medical care wasn't like taking care of a cast or stitches in a wound. It was TJ's airway. If I didn't care for it properly, he would die. I was irritated with the medical staff for placing such incredibly high expectations on me and failing to understand my fear. I just wanted to be his mom, the one who would comfort and cheer him on and have *them* handle the trach care. In order to appease them, I attempted to learn—but only half-heartedly. When the nurses noticed my lackluster efforts, Dr. Steele showed up and had a stern talk with me: "You need to learn because he's not getting out of here until you do. You have it a lot easier than some of the other parents around here. They've got babies with trachs, and their trachs are tiny!" Her sternness irritated me even more. I wanted her to pat my back and sympathetically say, "You poor thing. I know this is really hard, and you've been through so much. We won't make you learn this." But she wouldn't give me a pass.

June 9, 2013

CaringBridge
Written by Kelly

It has been a few days since we have updated, so I'll give a brief rundown of each day. Thursday TJ had his G-tube put in, and the surgery went well. It was a quiet day.

On Friday TJ's right chest tube was removed. Finally, those painful tubes are completely gone! But he is still on the vent, and since the holes are healed and the tubes are gone, I'm not sure why they aren't taking him off the vent. I'll have to talk to the doctor about it.

Another big deal that happened on Friday—drumroll please— he stood up for the first time! His physical therapist, whom we also refer to as his "tormentor," said, "Okay, TJ, now on the count of three, I want you to stand." She'd barely said the word "one" when he stood. A few surgeons had come onto the floor and saw the activity going on in our room, so they came in to watch the event. Everyone had big smiles on their face and were really excited about his progress.

But, as usual, things turn quickly in the PICU, and toward the end of Friday, he started having a lot of pain; his stomach was killing him. He had developed a terrible sinus infection from the removal of the NG tube and was throwing up an enormous amount of drainage. It went on for hours, and I thought I was going to lose my mind. I had a bit of a breakdown, and TJ heard me and motioned me to come over to his bed. He reached out his hand to hold mine, and then he pulled me to him so he could hug me which made me breakdown more. :) What a precious moment. We are in this battle together, and I keep reassuring him that together we will get through this. I then called Travis, because he was in town, to see if he could come to the hospital earlier than planned. He was able to come and stay with TJ so I could get away and get some sleep. TJ was finally given some effective pain meds and was able to rest more comfortably.

Saturday was the best day we've had since this whole thing began. TJ was not in any pain, and he was playful and happy. His dad was standing by his bed saying ornery things to him like Travis does, and TJ slid his leg out and kicked him, smiled, and pointed his finger at him. For a moment, it felt like everything was somewhat normal again.

Today, Travis and I did our first trach change together. I admit that I have done everything I can to avoid learning anything about TJ's trach. I was hoping he wouldn't have it by the time he came home. But staff will not leave me alone about it and won't discharge him until I learn it, so I have finally started giving in. It's scary and intimidating, but it actually didn't go too badly. I am sure I will eventually be an old pro at trach changing.

Yesterday, the nurse and I talked to TJ about the Lord and His plan for TJ's life. TJ was listening so intently. I read to him from my daily devotional. We were reminded again that God is always with us. We learned that worrying about the future will prevent us from feeling God's presence in our lives and that when we begin to feel worried, we need to turn the situation back over to God. We are valuable to God, and He will meet our needs.

Luke 12:22–31

"Then Jesus said to His disciples: 'Therefore I tell you, do not worry about your life, what you will eat; or about your body, what you will wear. For life is more than food, and the body more than clothes. Consider the ravens: They do not sow or reap, they have no storeroom or barn; yet God feeds them. And how much more valuable you are than birds! Who of you by worrying can add a single hour to your life? Since you cannot do this very little thing, why do you worry about the rest?

'Consider how the wild flowers grow. They do not labor or spin. Yet I tell you, not even Solomon in all his splendor was dressed like one of these. If that is how God clothes the grass of the field, which is here today, and tomorrow is thrown into the fire, how much more will He clothe you—you of little faith! And do not set your heart on what you will eat or drink; do not worry about it. For the pagan world runs after all such things, and your Father knows that you need them. But seek His kingdom, and these things will be given to you as well.'"

John 16:33

"I have told you these things, so that in Me you may have peace.
In this world you will have trouble. But take heart!
I have overcome the world."

When I first learned that I had to acquire the skills needed to care for TJ's trach, I wondered how I would ever be able to handle it with my incredibly weak stomach. Amazingly, I overcame it. TJ was more important to me than my own comfort. It was indeed true that love conquers all. After I learned how to care for TJ, nothing gross bothered me anymore. I became so comfortable in my duties that I soon realized my filter was off. After sometimes giving too much detail and seeing the reaction on other people's faces, I learned to limit the graphic intricacies of his care when talking to other people.

I had been diligently working on checking off the boxes of my trach and G-tube checklist. After I completed them, I decided I was done and wasn't doing anymore. One morning when I walked into his room, after updating me on TJ's night, the nurse told me that I needed to do his morning site care. Site care involved cleaning around his trach and G-tube with Q-tips and changing the dressing. I had already checked off my three boxes for having done site care, and I felt that I knew how to adequately complete those tasks. Upon hearing her instruction, I immediately started bawling and exclaimed, "I've done my three times already and I can't do anymore! I'm tired! There are other things going on in my life right now that you don't know about!"

"Well, you still need to be doing them," she advised. "You can't just stop. You've got to keep practicing."

I turned my head away and looked out the window, and the room grew very quiet. What was going on? Well, I was grief stricken and heartbroken. My body was beyond exhausted. I wasn't getting much sleep. I tossed and turned every night wondering if my son was going to get better. I tried to imagine what kind of life he was going to have and how we were going to live that way. In my mind, I constantly replayed his decline that first week, trying to figure out what had gone wrong. Even doing five minutes of site care was too overwhelming for me. The nurse completed TJ's site care and gave me the break I needed. However, from that day on, it bothered me that she seldom made eye contact or spoke to me anymore.

Later that day, I mentioned to Dr. Alvarez that I thought TJ's respiratory failures were caused by an accumulation of secretions in his lungs. I'm assuming she thought I was in denial because at that point, she pulled me into a room and told me that TJ might go home with deficits, that things may not be as they once were, and that I needed to prepare myself for that. She said that he had central muscle weakness. I had heard this before but didn't truly believe it. Central muscle weakness is the result of brainstem injuries. She said that he was strong in his extremities but centrally his head, neck, trunk, and lungs were weak. This meant that his breathing muscles were weak and might not recover. As you can imagine, I was crushed and frightened—but I was also skeptical, remembering that I watched TJ walking and talking for a week after surgery in Des Moines. Combined with the fact that his MRI results showed no sign of a brainstem or hypoxic injury, I didn't truly believe that he had central muscle weakness.

After returning to TJ's room, I asked him to squeeze my hand if he thought he would regain the strength in his trunk. He squeezed yes. I asked him if he thought he'd be able to sit up by himself. Again, he squeezed yes and then began pulling himself up off the bed. He did it several times until he was just about sitting up straight. He was able to hold his head up as well. I whispered to him to do it again the next time the doctors came in.

Our system of communication was working well. It was tedious but worth it. TJ was able to express himself and get his needs met, which made him feel better. When he wanted to tell me something, he clapped his hands. I would pull my pen and paper out so we could start our hand squeezes through the alphabet.

TJ and I spent the days reading devotionals, verses from the Bible, and the story of Job. Even though the circumstances we were in were brutal, I was exhausted, and my heart was broken, I was determined to follow the Lord no matter what else came our way.

TJ, age two, & sister Courtney, 1998

TJ, age three, 1999

Training and Checklists

TJ, age eight, & Travis, 2004

TJ, age ten, & Dr. Fisher before TJ's baptism, 2006

Family picture, 2006
Back row: Whitney & TJ Front row: Chandler, Travis, Kelly & Courtney
(© Michael J. Barnes Photography, used with permission)

TJ, age thirteen, & sister Ashley, 2009

TJ, age fifteen, and Aiden, September 2011

TJ, age sixteen, summer 2012

TJ, age sixteen, summer 2012

TJ, age sixteen, junior picture, fall 2012

Training and Checklists

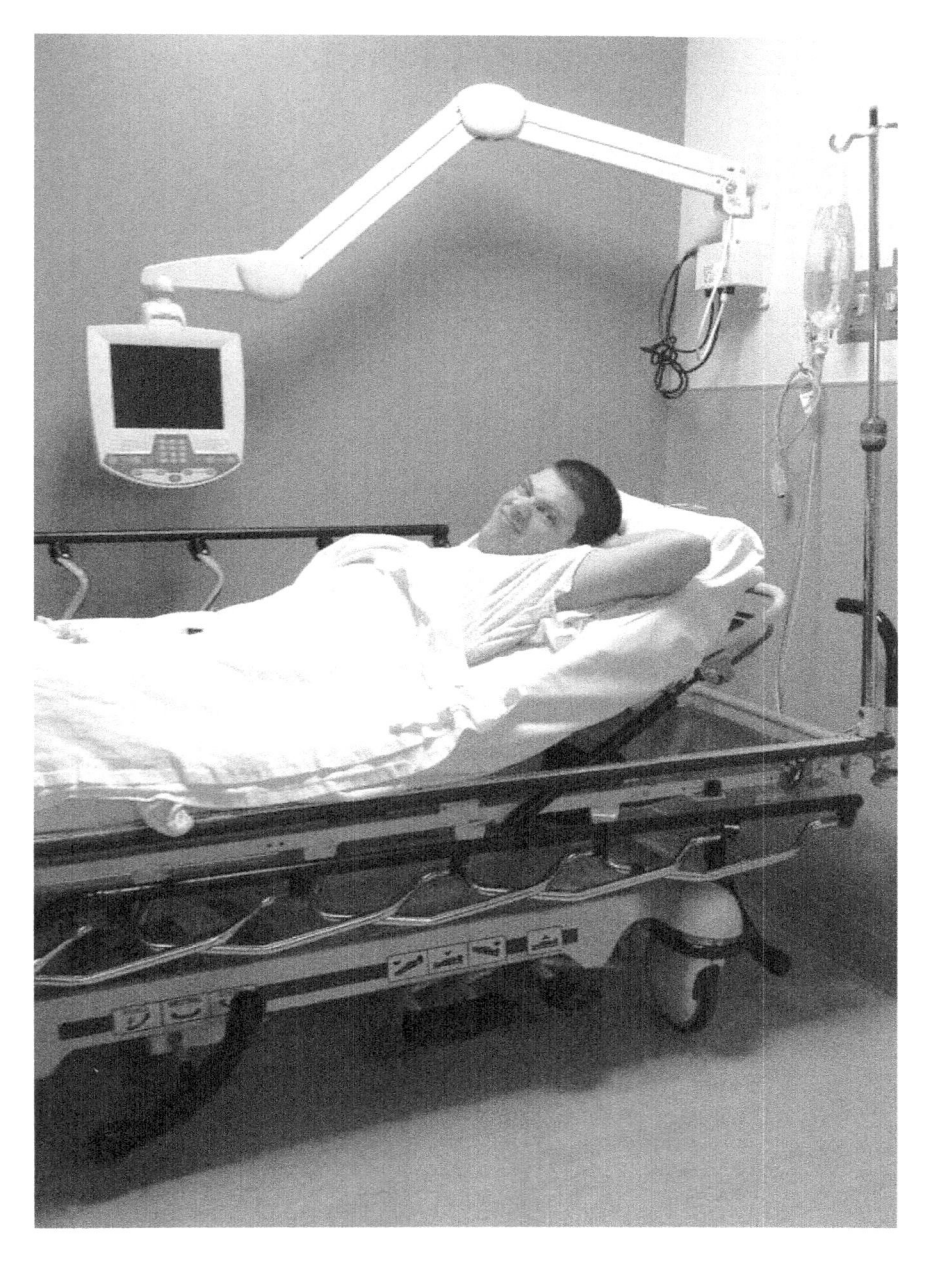

The last picture taken of TJ before heart surgery

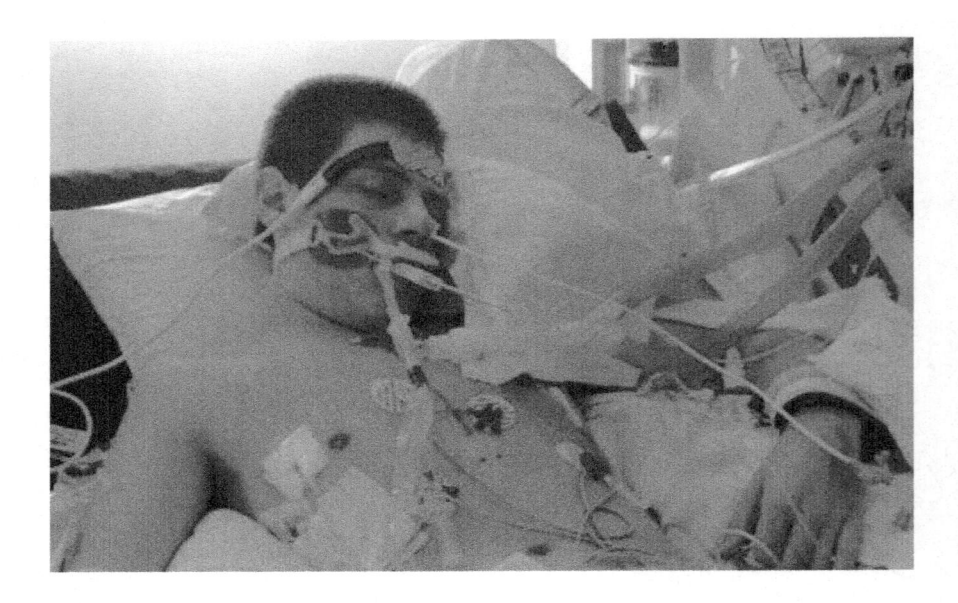

TJ's first respiratory failure, April 2013

TJ & Kelly, Mayo Clinic, 2013

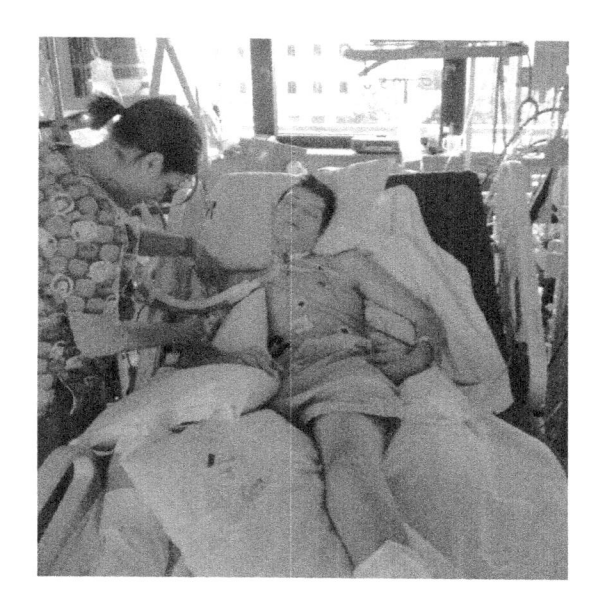

TJ in PICU, Mayo Clinic, 2013

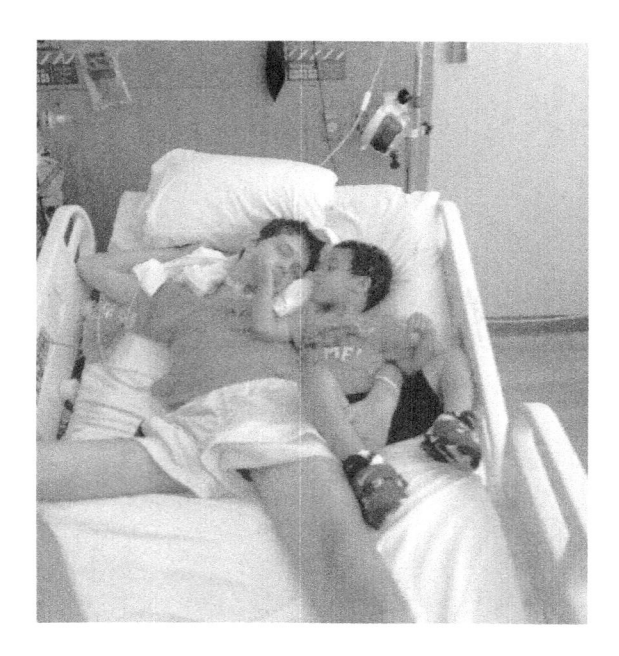

TJ & Aiden, Mayo Clinic, 2013

CHAPTER 10

CURVEBALLS

One evening, TJ told me several times to leave and go home because he knew I was tired. I was reluctant to leave and stayed a little longer. I was really glad I did because Dr. Tomar came in to do rounds. When TJ saw him, he started sitting up. Dr. Tomar's mouth fell open, and he exclaimed, "He's regaining strength!" My plan worked, and I was determined to never give up.

The next day, TJ would undergo a study of his diaphragm. When he breathed, there was a rumble that moved across his chest, so they decided to do some more diagnostic studies. They believed his diaphragm was either weak from the central muscle weakness that occurs during a brainstem stroke or that it was paralyzed. I was really dreading the results of the test.

The night before his diaphragm study, I was getting ready for bed, when it suddenly occurred to me that I needed to set the alarm on my cell phone so I could arrive at the hospital early the next morning for the test. I hadn't needed an alarm to wake up the entire time we had been at Mayo. It wasn't necessary to be at the hospital at any certain time, so whatever time I woke up and arrived there was fine. The truth was that I never slept well and often woke up very early anyway.

As I nestled into bed that night, I picked up my cell phone from the nightstand and pushed my clock app. The last alarm I set was for 3:15 A.M. on April 22, 2013. I exhaled a long sigh as I stared at the screen, and a ripple of sadness rolled over me. The last alert had been for the day of TJ's heart surgery. My eyes filled with tears as I remembered the activity and planning leading up to that fateful day. Prior to surgery, we were thankful TJ's heart defect had been found. There was laughter and hopefulness as we dreamed of his future, but so much had transpired since then: sadness, uncertainty, and pain. TJ wasn't the same anymore—and neither was I. After allowing myself to grieve for a while, I eventually fell asleep.

When the alarm sounded at 7 A.M. the next morning, I got up quickly and dressed. As I walked up the sidewalk to the hospital, I was a bundle of nerves as I thought about the upcoming diaphragm study. If they found that both sides of TJ's diaphragm were weak, he would likely be on a ventilator the rest of his life. *His quality of life will be terrible, and he'll never be whole again,* I thought.

Upon entering his room, I went straight to him. Following our normal morning routine, I put my face close to his and told him how much I loved him. He signed, "I love you," and I sat down to wait.

As the staff wheeled TJ down to the procedure room, I walked beside his bed. Down we went, deep into the basement of the hospital. It was dark there because it had no windows. I was terrified about the outcome of the test. I was shaking and my stomach hurt.

Under my breath I prayed, "Please let his diaphragm be okay,

Lord. Please let it be okay."

They wheeled TJ into the procedure room, and I took my place behind the glass with his nurse. I was so nervous that I was holding my breath and had to keep reminding myself to breathe. After taking a few minutes to prepare him for the procedure, they began the study. On the monitor, I saw something moving, and then there was a flurry of activity.

The nurse said, "It's the right side."

"Is this good? What does that mean? Is this good?" I asked.

"Yes, just the right side is paralyzed. The left side is working."

I breathed a sigh of relief, even though I still didn't fully understand what had just happened. After the procedure, Dr. Alvarez came in to talk to TJ and me. "The right side of your diaphragm is paralyzed, TJ," she said.

TJ began to wail loudly.

Then Dr. Alvarez hurried to say, "TJ, we can fix it! We can fix it!"

She went on to explain that the paralysis was most likely due to a nerve that had been moved and stretched. She said the diaphragm was paralyzed in an up position which was preventing his lung from fully expanding. They were going to do a surgery called a plication where they roll the diaphragm down to get it out of the lung's way so the lung can fully expand. Then they staple the diaphragm to the abdominal wall. If the procedure was successful, TJ would finally be able to live independent of the ventilator.

After the study, both TJ and I were emotional for most of the day. A paralyzed diaphragm? I'd never heard of that. He had so many medical issues, and they were all big ones. I wondered what TJ was thinking. I so wished we could talk, *really* talk. Spelling out one-word answers wasn't enough. I wanted to understand his fears and what was going on in his mind. I wanted to know what kind of conversations he had with God and what God was saying to him. I constantly reassured him that I loved him and that he was an amazing kid. I told him he would get through this, even as I wondered if it was true. I reminded him that God loved him, hadn't forgotten him, and still had a plan for his life.

Since TJ was experiencing many devastating changes, one of the doctors in the PICU felt that he would benefit from an antidepressant. As a result, psychiatry came in and visited with TJ about the recommended medications. TJ gave a thumbs-up that he would think about it. When she left, he clapped his hands indicating he wanted to tell me something and spelled out, "I do not want to take that pill." Smiling inwardly, I replied that it was his decision and that he could say no. I shared with him that sometimes when we feel sad, it's okay to feel the feelings and take the good times with the bad, trusting that God will see us through.

I relayed his answer back to the psychiatry doctors. Later, Dr. Tomar came in and mentioned that he'd heard that TJ didn't want to take the antidepressant. I affirmed, "Nope," and Dr. Tomar laughed.

TJ surprised the medical staff every day. Because he was still alive after all he had been through, he had earned the reputation for being a tough kid. A resident stood by his bed one afternoon and said, "This kid just amazes the heck out of me. He is so strong."

Dr. Alvarez then chimed in, "Well, look who he comes from."

Although Dr. Alvarez's comment made me feel good, it also caught me off guard because I didn't feel strong. I felt weak, exhausted, and worried about TJ's future.

Later that evening, nurses sat TJ in a chair. He was not very happy about being forced to sit up, but I knew he had reconciled himself to being there when all of a sudden, a pillow flew against my head. The fight was on. We spent the next two hours wrestling and tickling with TJ getting in an occasional kick. His hands had developed such strength that I wasn't able to pull my hands out of his grasp no matter how hard I tried. Laughing with my son and feeling his strength returning was a great way to end the day.

A few days after the diaphragm study, TJ was prepared for plication surgery to move the diaphragm that was preventing the expansion of his lung. This was his fourth surgery in approximately six weeks. One of the best surgeons in the country was scheduled to perform the surgery. We were praying that the procedure would be successful, give TJ much relief, and that most important of all, he would be able to breathe on his own.

Travis drove to Rochester so he could be there for the diaphragm surgery. Dr. Alvarez told Travis that both TJ and I were happier when he was there. There were days when we just needed his big shoulders.

The surgery took a few hours, and everything went well—until I received the dreaded call that the nurse needed help with TJ in the recovery room. I once again went to the recovery room and struggled with TJ until he was able to return to his room. Later in the day, I noticed that the movement in his chest looked much better than before. He seemed much more comfortable, but we still hadn't learned whether or not he could lose the vent.

When I walked into TJ's room one evening, Dr. Steele and Dr. Tomar were already in the room doing their rounds for the evening shift change. Dr. Steele was in her normal jovial mood and was throwing a ball back and forth with TJ. She was laughing, having a good time, and was in no hurry to move on to the next patient's room. It was obvious she was delighted to see his progress. I think she would have thrown the ball all night, but an exasperated Dr. Tomar finally tugged on her arm and in his thick Indian accent, exclaimed, "Come on! Let's go! I want to go home!"

Dr. Steele was an outstanding doctor, and she genuinely cared about the kids in the unit. She cared so much that after learning that TJ played the drums, she had her husband come in and play his guitar for him. Even though she was tough on me at times, I was growing very fond of her.

After learning that the original surgeon hadn't performed the traditional surgery on TJ's heart defect and that his circulatory arrest time was far too long, I'd been trying to sort out what I was told in Des Moines as opposed to what I was told at Mayo. Still holding onto hope that the Mayo doctors were wrong about their assessment of TJ's condition, I asked Dr. Steele if I could visit with her. By then, I had reached a point in TJ's illness where I was more accepting of his brain injury than I had been previously and could now talk about it without running away in fear.

"I'm confused about something," I said. "If both the cardiologist and anesthesiologist said TJ's surgery went well…"

"That would not be true," she stated, interrupting my question. "All of the doctors on TJ's team were shocked when we found out the times. TJ went a long time without enough oxygen."

At that point in TJ's journey, we still had no definitive diagnosis, and because all the tests came back negative, the doctors couldn't agree. Some still seemed to think his issues were brainstem related. After hearing the opinions of multiple doctors, I gathered from their assessments that TJ was unusual because he woke up walking and talking and then gradually lost his abilities during the first week after surgery. With a hypoxic injury, he should have woken up from surgery with those abilities already gone. It was also unusual that a hypoxic injury didn't show on an MRI. Even though TJ had to have lost oxygen because of the long bypass times, his presentation was unusual and complicated. Doctors never understood it.

I never blamed either TJ or the doctors who couldn't seem to diagnose him. I felt that God was responsible for TJ's unknown diagnosis. Mayo's doctors are amazing and brilliant, but they're also human and, therefore, have limitations. I knew that if they couldn't diagnose TJ, it was because God chose not to reveal that information to them.

June 16, 2013

CaringBridge
Written by Travis

I had a great day with TJ today. I spent most of the afternoon alone with him while Nana and Aiden burned off some energy. :) I accomplished my second trach change today, and he is still alive. He gets that deer-in-the-headlights look and his breathing goes crazy when I lower his bed.

Doctors are very pleased with the outcome of the surgery. He was on a trach collar for a few hours this morning and again this evening for a couple of hours. That means he is breathing without any help. They expect him to be fine and off the ventilator soon. Huge praise to God for lungs that work and for the best doctors in the world at figuring these little things out. :)

We are so thankful to be here and know TJ is getting the best care in the world. I cannot put into words how appreciative and fortunate we feel to have him at Mayo! If they can't do it, nobody can!

The short-term plan is to get him off the pain medicine, which is almost done; get him off the vent during the day and just use it at night, if needed; and then transition him into rehab hopefully mid to end of the week.

Long term he needs to get his strength back, swallow, eyes, tongue, talking, and jaw. We still don't know what has caused each of those deficits yet, but I think that will come after we get him going in therapy. They wanted to get his lungs conquered first.

I want to thank all of the prayer warriors who continue to hold TJ and our family up before the Lord. We are so thankful for our church that continues to support us in every way possible! Thank you to our families, friends, and people who we don't know that have helped support us. God is good all the time! Thank you!

Days like today are precious when you get time alone and he's feeling pretty good. I get to pick on him, and he gets to hit and kick dad. :) Sometimes it's not even about words, just getting to be with him is enough right now. I love my boy and look forward to the day when we can talk again. I have a feeling those conversations will be different. He is such a sweet boy! He takes after his momma. :) God bless.

I asked God for strength that I might achieve.
I was made weak that I might learn humbly to obey.
I asked for health that I might do greater things.
I was given infirmity that I might do better things.
I asked for riches that I might be happy.
I was given poverty that I might be wise.
I asked for power that I might have the praise of men.
I was given weakness that I might feel the need of God.
I asked for all things that I might enjoy life.
I was given life that I might enjoy all things.
I got nothing that I asked for, but everything that I hoped for.
Almost despite myself, my unspoken prayers were answered.
I am, among all men, most richly blessed.

— The Prayer of an Unknown Confederate Soldier

A few days later, TJ was completely off the ventilator, medically stable, and ready to be moved into the rehab unit. The nurses in the PICU conversed about how they were going to transport him to rehab. They discussed moving him in his bed, using a wheelchair, or calling for a gurney, but they ultimately decided on using a type of chair similar to a La-Z-Boy on wheels. They settled him in the seat and wheeled him down the hall to the rehab unit. I'm sure it wasn't the standard way of transporting a patient, but they sure made it fun for him. On the way there, he raised his arms and cheered the whole way. It was a fantastic day of celebration!

Rehab was a short distance from the PICU and was a newly-remodeled, beautiful facility. One of the first things TJ did after arriving on the rehab floor was take a shower. It had been two months since he had showered, and I can't imagine how good it felt. He also was able to perform most of the hygiene tasks by himself, which was also very encouraging.

The initial plan for length of stay in rehab was one month. The thirty-day goals established by TJ's rehab team were as follows: walking, navigating stairs, and swallowing. They said that his eye function would be the most difficult to restore and would take up to a year to recover. I was never as concerned about his eyes as I was about everything else. Of course, I wanted them to recover 100 percent, but his eye function didn't compound problems elsewhere like almost all of his other deficits did.

While in rehab, TJ regularly attended three therapies: physical therapy, occupational therapy, and speech therapy. He also took part in recreational therapy and music therapy, although those therapies were not as regular. Physical therapy concentrated mostly on leg movement, balance, and core strength. Occupational therapy involved working to strengthen the arms, hands, and fingers, helping him to eventually perform activities of daily living like brushing teeth, combing hair, and showering. The speech therapist worked on helping him open his mouth, move his tongue, swallow, and talk. We quickly learned that physical therapy was the easiest for him and speech therapy was the most challenging.

For one of his first combined occupational and physical therapy sessions, TJ was transferred to his wheelchair and pushed out to the courtyard. During OT, the therapist held small drums up high. While using drumsticks, TJ started banging on them. After doing that for a few minutes, he then started hitting them in one of his familiar drum rhythms. It was amazing. I think it even surprised the therapist. For PT he stood up three times and walked fifteen to twenty steps with Travis on one side and the therapist on the other. Another first! It was difficult and ungainly, but I was thrilled with his progress.

During speech therapy, his therapist gave him an ice chip and told him to move it around with his tongue, but he couldn't do it. He tried and tried, but as soon as she put the ice chip in his mouth, it immediately fell out. We often felt frustrated and discouraged when he finished speech therapy.

Shortly after arriving in rehab, TJ clapped his hands, which was the signal that he wanted to tell me something. He spelled: "I just accidentally swallowed." I wasn't sure what he meant when he said "accidentally." I was hoping that something in his throat was starting to wake up. In the previous two months in PICU, I would ask him if he could swallow, and the answer was always, "No." I tried not to get too excited about the first rehab swallow, but how could I not?

After therapy one day, he settled into bed and asked me questions about the night he almost died. We had never talked about that night with him and decided it was a story we would tell when he was further on the path to recovery and communication was easier. The night we were close to losing him, we were told he couldn't hear us because he was too heavily sedated, but he *did* hear us. As we reminisced, he spelled to me that he remembered his dad standing over him crying. I longed for it to be easier to communicate because I knew he needed to talk more about it.

One evening when I was staying overnight in TJ's room, I was dreaming that he was back to his prior self and was talking to me. I was startled awake by pounding on his bed. This was one of his signals that he needed something. I went over to his bedside. While he was lying there staring at me, his lips were moving like he was talking to me. I was shocked and wondered if I was still dreaming. I hadn't seen his lips move in weeks!

"Are you trying to talk to me?" I asked.

He gave me a slight nod. Then we hugged each other. I had no idea what he was trying to tell me. I think his reason for waking me up was that he wanted me to see that he could move his lips even if there was no sound coming out. I don't know why his facial movements turned on and off like that, but either way it was a precious moment. The next morning when I woke up, I asked TJ if it really happened or if I dreamed it. He gave me a thumbs-up that it really happened. I hoped and prayed that we would have more moments like that.

Many times, while TJ was in PICU, I heard doctors say that patients with brain injuries gain the most function during the first year after their brain injury. It had been two months since TJ's brain injury occurred, and I constantly felt the clock ticking. We were finally seeing progress when TJ became very sick after just a few days in rehab.

He had a fever and was having a great deal of pain in his abdomen. Doctors decided to send him back to PICU. As a result, I was very discouraged and wondered if he would ever be medically stable enough to continue with therapy.

After a couple of days in the PICU, we were transferred to the general pediatric floor because TJ wasn't critical. He had some sort of infection, and they were running tests to discover its source. The entire two months he had been at Mayo, he had struggled off and on with a fever and elevated white count, but they were unable to discover the reason. He also periodically had pain in his stomach, but they weren't sure why. The GI doctors had checked the G-tube several times but didn't think that was the cause of the issue.

After we were moved to the general pediatric floor, a team of new doctors with fresh eyes came in to take a look at TJ. One of the doctors pressed on TJ's stomach, and he doubled over in pain.

"Is it just anxiety that's causing his stomach problems?" I asked. I had anxiety and constantly felt that my stomach was in knots. I wondered if that might be causing his stomach pain, too.

With a concerned look on his face, the doctor said, "No, I think there's something else going on. We need to get a CT scan."

The medical staff told us we didn't need to be present while they did the scan. Since we had down time, Travis and I drove to Target to buy some groceries for my fridge at Ronald McDonald House. While we were on our way back, the doctor called.

"We have taken TJ into surgery, and I need a verbal consent. It's his appendix. He needs an emergency appendectomy."

"What?! Are you kidding me?" I asked. "Yes, of course, you have permission. Oh, my gosh! We'll be there shortly."

I couldn't believe it, and I felt terrible that we hadn't been there. I rarely ever left the hospital. It was the first time I hadn't been present for a scan, and as it turned out, it had been important for me to be there.

We raced back to the hospital and went straight to the OR waiting room. The surgery was completed quickly and had gone well. After helping with TJ in the recovery room, we went up to TJ's room and talked to one of the surgeons in the hallway. He told us that there were no abscesses on the appendix and it had not ruptured.

"I just can't believe he had appendicitis," I told the surgeon.

The surgeon sighed aloud. "Who gets appendicitis while they're in the hospital for a brain injury? This kid throws curveballs at us!"

Travis nodded. "Only TJ would get appendicitis while in the hospital."

After the appendectomy, TJ was pain free and like a different kid. Still, it haunted me. I felt terrible that he had to endure all of that pain and wasn't able to tell anyone. I knew he had abdominal pain, and I scolded myself for not taking it more seriously. I should have been more vocal to the doctors about it. Because of occurrences like this, I constantly felt like I was failing him.

Since TJ was feeling better, he regained his sense of humor and developed a routine for breaking in new nurses. Often, the nurses were young. Upon seeing their fresh, new faces, a little smile would break out across TJ's lips, and instantly I knew what was coming. While the new nurse was being given his bedside report during the shift change, TJ would pretend he was going into respiratory failure and start thrashing around on his bed. Then when the new nurse became wide-eyed and nervous, he would finally stop his antics and begin laughing.

Even though I'd been upset that we had to leave rehab to return to PICU, I now was very thankful that it happened the way it did because the appendix problem was discovered and resolved. God always has a plan. You'd think I would have learned to trust Him better when those setbacks occurred, but they still sent me into a downward spiral. I was still a work in progress.

CHAPTER 11

THE WOMAN WITH THE BOX

After TJ's appendectomy, he stayed on the general pediatric floor for a few days. This area was in a completely different part of the hospital than the PICU and rehab. The pediatric floor was housed in the Francis Building, which was one of the very old, historic-type buildings that comprised St. Mary's Hospital. Because the building had heavy woodwork and small windows, it had a dark and dungeon-like feel to it, comparable to a hospital setting in a scary movie. Mayo is one of the leading hospitals in our country, and people from all over the world travel there to receive medical care. Knowing that, I had imagined a fancy, modern medical center. I was afraid that this once small-town girl would feel that she was way out of her league. However, St. Mary's Hospital was anything but fancy and modern, but that didn't matter to me. What was most important to me was that their medical care was outstanding. When your child is sick, you don't care how nice the building is; you just want great medical care.

The general pediatric floor had a policy that patients as compromised as TJ were never to be left alone, so TJ had a nurse with him at all times. If his nurse was leaving to take a break, another nurse came to fill in for him or her. He was so well taken care of at Mayo Clinic that I was able to just be TJ's mom. Since then, I've learned that it's rare when a hospital is able to provide that level of care.

The environment on the general pediatric floor was much different than in the PICU. Because the PICU deals with life and death, the atmosphere is very serious. The nurses are "all business," so you don't get to know them very well. We rarely heard the sound of laughter because, most of the time, we were surrounded by other worried, tired, stressed-out parents. The general pediatric floor, however, had a more relaxed and lighthearted atmosphere. It was a welcome change, and we felt like we could relax a bit.

The staff in the PICU had been frustrated by my lack of initiative regarding learning TJ's care, but now that he was no longer critical, I was starting to adjust to the new TJ and the hospital way of life. With the heaviness of the PICU days behind us, I finally decided it was time to jump into the trenches with TJ's team and provide care to TJ instead of just being a mom standing on the sidelines.

One evening, I demonstrated to the nurses on the general pediatric floor how best to suction TJ's trach. Immediately, one of the nurses praised me, saying, "This mom is ON IT!" His praise made me feel good because I knew how far I had come.

While on the general pediatric floor, TJ began to show signs of improvement. One night he opened his mouth wide. I was very shocked to see it, and it took a little while for it to sink in. He opened it five or six more times. Finally, I had to tell him to stop because sometimes his mouth didn't close correctly. We could hear his teeth grinding and maybe even chipping. It sounded awful. It took a few minutes for the muscles to calm down, and after they calmed, he clapped his hands and spelled, "I am going to need dental work."

In an attempt to find a faster way to communicate, I began brainstorming other methods of communication. Sign language came to mind. He didn't have great control of his arms, but I was curious if he could at least sign the letters of the alphabet with his fingers. I started teaching him the sign language alphabet. Trying not to overwhelm him, the first couple of days I taught him just five new letters a day. He quickly became frustrated with me because he wanted to learn them faster, so I began teaching him more. He had the whole alphabet learned in a few days. While I held his wrist for support, he would finger-spell each word. It worked great! It was much faster than our old method, and he was able to spell longer sentences.

One afternoon while I was sitting in the room with TJ, he signaled that he wanted to ask me something. I grabbed a pen and paper, and I held his hand while he finger-spelled, "Can I still get a mini fridge?"

In 2012, the summer before TJ's heart surgery, we had remodeled TJ's basement bedroom and promised to buy him a mini fridge. After his renewed request, I felt awkward and unsure how to answer. I didn't want to remind him of his inability to swallow. Afraid of squelching any shred of hope he had, I answered, "Sure, of course, you can still get a mini fridge." After answering, I immediately felt terrible that maybe I had just given him false hope that his swallowing ability would return.

Later in the day, the pediatric psychiatrist and a resident came by.

Their role was to talk with the patients and offer counseling. Since TJ couldn't talk, they usually ended up visiting with me. We were standing in the hallway just outside TJ's door when the doctor asked how TJ was doing. I responded, "Well, this morning he asked for a mini fridge for his bedroom at home." And then I added, "But I don't know what he thinks he's going to put in it because he can't swallow anything." The moment those words left my lips, I realized how ludicrous the whole scene was and began to laugh. My son, who was still cognitively intact but couldn't swallow, open his mouth, hold his head up or sit up, had minimal control of his arms and was in a wheelchair, wanted a *mini fridge* for his bedroom. A tangled mess of emotions had been swirling inside me for months. I was heartbroken that he was injured, thankful he was alive, terrified of the future, hopeful for recovery, yet simultaneously grief stricken beyond belief. The complexity of my varied emotions had been like an overfilled balloon, stretched to capacity. It had just exploded.

As I stood there laughing uncontrollably, the psychiatrist and the resident stared at me with straight faces and never once cracked a smile. I imagined they were either thinking that I was behaving inappropriately, laughing at my son's condition or that I was having a mental breakdown and needed to be confined to the nearest padded room. Either way, their refusal to join in my laughter only made me laugh harder. In my exasperation about TJ's condition, I had come to a place in time where my emotions found much needed relief in the form of laughter.

After a few days on the general pediatric floor, TJ went back to rehab for a second time, but a few days later, he began coughing uncontrollably. His heart and respiratory rates became dangerously high, and he was once again having severe stomach pain. He was moved back to the PICU where doctors discovered he had pneumonia and some kind of infection in his stomach called pneumatosis. We were disheartened from another failed attempt at rehab. Every time we thought things were getting better and that there might finally be a light at the end of the tunnel, TJ would become ill and be transferred again.

Even though he was very sick, his physical therapist didn't want him to lose what he had gained, so she had him stand up next to his bed. I was standing nearby, and after he stood, he reached over and wrapped his arms around me and hugged me real tight. Then he grabbed my hand and led me in a slow dance. My heart melted and tears filled my eyes. When he was a little boy and I was making dinner, he and I would dance in the kitchen together, but after he grew up, he wouldn't dance with me anymore. I frequently teased him that he was too cool to dance with his mom now. He may have been physically changed from his brain injury, but he was still the same sweet TJ that he had always been.

Before the transfer, doctors had scheduled a procedure to inject Botox into TJ's salivary glands to reduce their activity and decrease the amount of saliva produced. They informed us there was no guarantee it would work, but Travis and I were hoping and praying it would considerably improve his quality of life. We were relieved to learn that even though he had been moved to the PICU, doctors were still moving forward with the procedure.

Most of the time the nurses took care of TJ, but once in a while, I jumped in to help. It was good for me to stay hands-on so I wouldn't forget what I learned. During this particular bout of pneumonia, TJ had very heavy secretions, and I was constantly suctioning his trach. I was taught by medical staff that when I suctioned, I needed to use a new sterile catheter each time. I was suctioning so often that the nurse let me lay the catheter on the bed when I was done because in just a few minutes, I would be picking it up to repeat the process. It was absolutely miserable for him and for me. *How are we ever going to live like this?* I wondered.

During this illness, my stepmom, Connie, stopped by the hospital for a short visit. She stood beside the bed quiet and wide-eyed as I suctioned. Years later, I asked her what she was thinking and feeling when she saw TJ's condition: "I was sorry for all of you to be experiencing this profound and sustained pain. I felt guilt and inadequacy because I didn't know how to help. I was impressed that you were doing something vitally important which you had resisted doing and now were doing competently and with love. I felt a little like an intruder and observer rather than the helper that I wanted to be, and I felt profound dismay because this shouldn't have happened to TJ and being there made it very, very real."

One evening Dr. Alvarez was walking by TJ's room and saw me crying. "What's wrong?" she asked.

"He's just so sick. I'm really afraid that one of these lung infections is going to kill him," I answered.

"Follow me," she prompted. She took me back to her office. It was small and located behind the nurses' station. We sat down and I began unloading my fears.

"Several weeks ago, one of the nurses told me that if TJ can't protect his airway, he's going to keep getting lung infections. If he keeps getting these lung infections, are they eventually going to kill him?" I questioned.

"TJ will make it," she reassured, "but he may not be the same TJ that he was. Don't give up hope. The pneumonia isn't a big deal. You don't need to worry. We can treat the pneumonia. However, the pneumatosis is more concerning."

"Okay, so I don't have to worry about the pneumonia, but I *do* need to be concerned about the pneumatosis. I don't even know what that is!" I exclaimed.

"It's unusual for a person TJ's age (sixteen) to have a pneumatosis diagnosis, as generally it's seen in babies," she explained. "Pneumatosis happens when gas gets trapped in the intestinal wall. He may need to have surgery to remove that area of the bowel."

I shook my head in frustration. "Oh, geez. He can't get a break. He's sick and in pain all the time. I just don't want him to live a life of suffering."

"Don't give up hope. It's not going to be easy, but give it a year," she encouraged.

"How do you do this job?" I asked. "How do you deal with seeing sick and dying kids, day after day?"

She responded, "People often ask me why I care so much. I ask them what if there was somebody working here who *didn't* care as much as I did?"

Dr. Alvarez had the kindest eyes. She was gentle, and I felt deeply cared for. Over time, I grew very fond of the PICU doctors at Mayo. I knew they were cheering for TJ and wanted him to improve. In the beginning, when we first arrived at Mayo, their demeanor felt cold to me, and they told me things I didn't want to hear. I was often angry at them but eventually began to understand that what I perceived as coldness was really an emotional protection put in place enabling them to make clear and focused decisions on behalf of their patients. In order to go home at the end of the day and be emotionally available to their families, they couldn't take on the tragedies they saw day after day. From that new perspective, I began to admire them because I couldn't imagine how difficult it would be to deliver terrible news to parents or how it would feel to work tirelessly trying to save a child only to have him die. I found them to be caring, compassionate, and brilliant. They were my heroes.

Thankfully, after several days in the PICU, the antibiotics treated the pneumatosis, and TJ did not require surgery.

As the weeks passed, I struggled with increasing exhaustion and weariness but was determined to trust in the Lord and not get angry or turn away from Him because of what *seemed* like His lack of intervention. I remembered the verse Mark 8:34–36: "Then He called the crowd to Him along with His disciples and said: 'Whoever wants to be My disciple must deny themselves and take up their cross and follow Me. For whoever wants to save their life will lose it, but whoever loses their life for Me and for the gospel will save it. What good is it for someone to gain the whole world, yet forfeit their soul?'"

I heard a great number of testimonials from people about how our CaringBridge posts were touching their lives for Christ. Through CaringBridge, God gave us an opportunity to share our faith with others while we were walking through our tragedy. Jesus said that just as He suffered, so shall we suffer, so it was really no surprise that suffering had come upon us.

I often thought of the disciples who suffered when carrying the gospel forward after Jesus' death. It didn't matter what evil happened to them, they stayed determined and true to their Lord—even to death. Wherever God's Word is moving and making headway, Satan attacks. Many times, throughout TJ's illness, I wondered, *If we stopped glorifying Christ, would TJ get better?* Not honoring God during our suffering might have eased Satan's attacks, but we chose to obey and kept pressing on for Christ despite our suffering. After TJ's brain injury, the things of this world that once were important to me had lost their appeal. I had a greater understanding of what Ecclesiastes 1:14 meant: "I have seen all the things that are done under the sun; all of them are meaningless, a chasing after the wind." What mattered most was honoring God, telling others about Christ, and fixing my eyes on eternity.

July 16, 2013

CaringBridge
Written by Kelly

TJ's birthday is today, but he mostly slept through it. He did have some very welcomed visitors from church who drove up to see him on his special day. I know he was looking forward to seeing them, but he had a hard time staying awake. Hospital staff came in and sang happy birthday to him. He got up a few times for OT and PT to walk and bang on the drums a little, but then he quickly fell back to sleep. All of this sleep is good and helps his brain heal.

A friend of mine from church drove up here to be with me today. She brought a devotional with her from another friend. It was bookmarked for today—TJ's birthday. A Bible verse was at the top of the page.

Genesis 22:16–18

"…because you have done this and have not withheld your son, your only son, I will surely bless you and make your descendants as numerous as the stars in the sky and as the sand on the seashore. Your descendants will take possession of the cities of their enemies, and through your offspring all nations on earth will be blessed, because you have obeyed me."

When I opened the book, I was utterly shocked to read that Genesis 22:16–18 was the verse used for the devotion on July 16th. The Lord was speaking directly to me. Genesis Chapter 22 is the story of Abraham's testing, the very story I was thinking of when I was on my knees in the bathroom the night TJ almost died. Only the Lord and I knew the thoughts that were running through my mind that dreadful night.

After reading the devotional, I felt the Lord telling me that although at the moment we were going through the garden of Gethsemane, the tomb, and the cross, after a short time, we would experience the power of the resurrection and ascension of Jesus. Just as the Lord multiplied Abraham's blessing when he obeyed by not withholding his only son, He would also multiply my blessing because I obeyed by not withholding my only son. I desperately wanted TJ healed, and just as Isaac was spared, I prayed and hoped God was telling me that our son would also be spared. I did know for certain that the Lord was with me and was walking right beside me. I felt surrounded by His unfailing love and knew that He was pleased with me because I had obeyed.

During this phase of TJ's hospitalization, we bounced around the hospital a lot. We were constantly being moved from rehab to the general pediatric floor to the PICU. It was exhausting, and I felt like it would never end. I knew it was one of Satan's tactics. If he could successfully discourage us and tell us there was no hope, then we would stop trusting the Lord and take matters into our own hands. I had to remind myself and TJ repeatedly that this trial wouldn't last forever and that God hadn't forgotten us.

One afternoon, TJ and I went downstairs for scheduled imaging studies. After the staff moved TJ onto the table and got him situated for the studies to begin, one of the attendants began talking to me.

"Are you his mom?" she inquired.

"Yeah, I'm his mom."

"We remember when he first came in. He came in at night," she said.

"Yeah, that's right. His MRI was done at night."

I was totally amazed that the staff in radiology remembered TJ. It had been months since that very first night he was flown to Mayo. The imaging staff had to have seen dozens of patients since then. I wondered what it was about TJ that made him so memorable. Was it his age? Was it the severity of his injuries—the devastating circumstances that *caused* his injuries that left that lasting impression? My curiosity was piqued as to why TJ was so memorable to them, but I never did ask why.

July 21, 2013

CaringBridge
Written by Travis

I came up Saturday morning for my weekend visit. I stay with TJ while Nana gets away from the hospital and spends time with Aiden. The Botox is working great, and TJ is pretty much dried up now and has decided he needs to catch up on the sleep he's missed. He seems so much more relaxed now that he doesn't have to be suctioned constantly, and his body can and wants to rest.

He was pretty drowsy most of the day Saturday. They did get him up in the morning and worked a little. The minute they tell him to go, he starts throwing his legs out of the bed, ready or not. He slept for most of the day Friday, and they think he's getting his days turned around.

Today during his first therapy, he got dressed, and we walked through the hallway by his room. He took a quick look out of the window, walked down three stairs and then a ramp. While he gets a lot of help during these walks, it is nice to see him up and moving. It's also a reminder of not only how far he's come, but how far he has to go! There is a lot of work for him to do to even be back to his previous self.

Still praying for eyes, swallowing, talking, weight gain, and strength. We're thankful for how far he has come! He is pretty stable medically, and they're in the process of taking him off all his medications.

I want to thank everyone for all the help and support we have received, like mowing our lawn, watching Aiden for a few hours in the afternoon, providing meals, gift cards, and the prayers. No words can explain how much it's appreciated!

Below is a beautiful poem titled *Bike Secrets* I found years ago that describes a life with Christ:

> At first, I saw God as my observer, my judge,
> keeping track of things I did wrong
> so as to know if I merited heaven or hell when I die.
>
> He was out there, sort of like a President.
> I recognized His picture when I saw it,
> but I really didn't know Him.
>
> But later when I met Christ,
> it seemed as though life was rather like a bike ride,
> but it was a tandem bike, and I noticed that
> Christ was in the back
> helping me to pedal.
>
> I don't know just when it was that
> He suggested we change places,
> but life has never been the same since.

The Woman with the Box

When I had control, I knew the way,
   but it was rather boring and predictable.
It was the shortest distance between two points.
   But when He took the lead,
   He knew delightful long cuts,
up mountains, and through rocky places,
   at breakneck speeds.
   It was all I could do to hang on!
Even though it looked like madness,
   He said, "Pedal."
I worried and was anxious and asked,
   "Where are you taking me?"
   He laughed and didn't answer.
And I started to learn to trust.
   I forgot my boring life
   and entered into the adventure.
   And when I'd say, "I'm scared,"
   He'd lean back and touch my hand.
He took me to people with gifts that I needed.
   Gifts of healing, acceptance, and joy.
   He said, "Give the gifts away;
   they're extra baggage, too much weight."
So I did. I gave them to the people we met,
   and I found that in giving I received,
   and still our burden was light.
I did not trust Him, at first, in control of my life.
   I thought He'd wreck it,
   but He knows bike secrets,
knows how to make it bend to take sharp corners,
   knows how to jump to clear high rocks,
   knows how to fly to shorten scary passages.

> And I am learning to shut up
> and pedal in the strangest places,
> and I'm beginning to enjoy the view
> and the cool breeze on my face with my delightful constant companion, Jesus Christ.
>
> And when I'm sure I just can't do any more,
> He just smiles and says, "Pedal."
>
> (Unknown Author)

Janet, the mom I met in the PICU, and I were becoming great friends. We often met for lunch or coffee. One afternoon during lunch time, I walked to Ronald McDonald House to check my mail, as I often did. As I was walking back to the hospital, I walked by the *Canadian Honker,* a restaurant located across the street from the hospital, where I often ate. Janet was sitting outdoors eating lunch, so I pulled up a chair. Rochester was beginning to feel like home.

As Janet and I visited with each other, we caught up on how the boys were doing and, of course, shared our tears and fears. Since she'd already been through many hospitalizations, she gave great advice.

"After Tom's last hospitalization, I had a really difficult time integrating back into society."

I was perplexed by her words, but I took her word for it and never asked for details.

"TJ was such a neat kid," I lamented. "You would have really liked him if you had known him before his heart surgery. I wish you could have met him."

"He's still a cool kid, Kelly," she consoled. "Even if he can't talk."

"I just don't know what his life is going to be like if he can't talk."

The world of special needs was completely new and unfamiliar to me. I was glad God provided me a friend I could learn from who understood what it was like having a child with special needs.

July 25, 2013

CaringBridge
Written by Kelly

TJ continues to have headaches, which started when they began tapering him off methadone, so they believe they are due to that. They upped the dose of his methadone in hopes it would alleviate the headaches, but so far, he's still continuing to have them. The plan is to take the taper slower. I have been dreading tapering off the rest of these drugs. It's miserable. But on the flip side, I've noticed his eyes don't look so hazy. Please pray for the headaches to subside. I have spent the last three days in a cave. His room is freezing because he's hot-blooded and dark because light hurts his eyes, so I guess you'd better pray for me as well.

His right shoulder is also hurting now. He's gotten into the habit of keeping his arms above his head, and he doesn't have enough muscle there anymore to hold his shoulder in place. His shoulder has started popping and partially dislocating, which is causing him a lot of pain. Please pray for the shoulder.

TJ is swallowing more and more. He said he swallowed twenty-five times yesterday, and he finger-spelled to me to get him some Smartwater. I looked over at the nurse whose eyes were big and saw that he was shaking his head no, so I told TJ not today. Today he said he was craving juice of any kind, so the nurse asked the doctor if we could put a sponge of grape juice in his mouth. I squeezed just a little out, and I saw his throat move. I asked him if he swallowed it, and he squeezed my hand several times. He laid his head back on the pillow with a smile on his face. Just what he needed in order to keep him going! God is answering our prayers!

He is opening his mouth a lot more and has better control over it. It isn't snapping shut like it used to. Today he was able to keep it open when I asked and shut it when I told him to. I am hoping that if it continues to improve, he'll be able to talk soon. I miss hearing his voice.

It sounds like there won't be any problem with us going back to rehab when he is medically stable, so I anticipate we will be home mid to late September. A big prayer request for me is he will lose the trach before he comes home. I have a love-hate relationship with that thing. I love it because it keeps him alive, but I hate it because it's scary and a lot of work. We cannot even leave his room without a bag of emergency trach supplies, oxygen, and a suction machine. It takes three of us to get him to the gym for PT in the morning.

I will close with a poem I recently read:

> Is it raining, little flower?
> Be glad of rain;
> Too much sun would wither one; It will shine again.
> The clouds are very dark, it's true;
> But just behind them shines the blue.
> Are you weary, tender heart?
> Be glad of pain;
> In sorrow, sweetest virtues grow, as flowers in rain.
> God watches, and you will have sun,
> when clouds their perfect work have done.
>
> (Lucy Larcom)

It was late July. A wave of heat hit me as I exited the doors of Ronald McDonald House on my morning walk to the hospital.

Summers in this part of Minnesota were milder and shorter than in Iowa, but we still got the taste of a good heat wave for a few weeks late in the summer. The hospital was always so cold that I didn't mind a little heat. With my head down, I meandered through the parking lot to the sidewalk just beyond. I was in deep thought about the coffee I would soon be purchasing at the Caribou Coffee shop across the street. Pleasing thoughts of mochas and lattes danced in my head. I quickened my pace in eager anticipation of enjoying my treat.

I glanced up to gauge how far away from the hospital I was when I noticed a rather peculiar sight. There was a young woman ahead of me carrying a large box. Even though I was still quite a distance from her, I could see that she was really struggling with it. It held my attention for a while because I wondered why she would be taking such a large box to the hospital. Unable to come up with a reasonable explanation, I went back to walking with my head down. The next time I looked up, I was surprised to see that she had yet to reach the hospital doors. It appeared that she had given up and was, by then, sitting on top of the box, beside the sidewalk. *Hmm—that's not something you see every day,* I thought.

As I approached her, I realized she was crying. Concerned, I stopped and inquired, "Are you okay? Can I help you carry the box?"

She nodded, and together, we picked the box up and started out again for the hospital. As we walked, she began to open up about what was troubling her. "I'm from North Dakota, and my baby is having heart surgery. I have three other kids at home with my husband. He's angry with me, so he only sent me half the money he was supposed to. I need to ship this box, and I don't have enough money to ship it."

My heart sank. Living in the hospital environment was so hard. Everywhere I looked there were sick children and grief-stricken parents. For most families, financial difficulties loomed large, and fear regarding their child's sickness hung over their heads like a black cloud. It was no wonder she and her husband were struggling. One very sick child was a state away with one parent, and three other young children were at home with the other. That family had to be stressed to the max. As we walked, I listened and offered what encouragement I could.

After arriving at the hospital, we came to my elevators just inside the Francis Building. "These are my elevators. How much farther do you still need to go?" I queried.

"Not much farther. I can take it the rest of the way by myself. Thank you for helping me."

I then stopped, set the box down, pulled out my wallet, and handed her $60.

She shook her head. "Oh, I can't accept this."

"No, please take it," I coaxed. "It's not my money anyway. People sent it to me."

During my stay in Rochester, I was amazed at the amount of money I was receiving in the mail. I couldn't believe how kind people were. Some of them were people I didn't even know. A few weeks after TJ's surgery, when we realized his medical problems were not going to end any time soon, I quit my job to stay with him. Since we lost an entire income, my goal was to use the money I received in the mail to live on so I wouldn't have to dip into our already tight finances back home. Up to that point in our stay in Rochester, I always had everything I needed.

So, after once again encouraging the woman to take the money, she finally relented and accepted it, and we went our separate ways. I pushed the "Up" arrow for the elevator, and when the elevator doors opened, I was happy to see that I would be riding the elevator alone because I had some praying to do. As I rode to TJ's floor, I prayed, "Lord, I gave that woman almost everything I had, but I know it's what You wanted me to do. I'm low on money now, so You're going to have to help me."

Then I walked off the elevator and pushed aside my concerns about money because I trusted that God would take care of me. I really didn't have time to worry about money anyway. I had to stay focused because there were more important things going on.

Over the next few days, I limited all unnecessary spending. There were no more mochas or lattes from Caribou, and I ate simple meals prepared in the kitchenette in my room at Ronald McDonald House. About three days after the box incident, during a short lunch break, I walked to Ronald McDonald House to check the mail. I was excited to see that my mail cubby held a card from a good friend named Carole. I always loved getting mail from home. After opening the envelope and reading the front of the card, I noticed there was a check inside for $60—the exact amount I gave the woman with the box. God had met the needs of the woman carrying the box as well as my own.

I learned a powerful lesson that week. I learned that if I hold on tight to everything I have because I'm afraid I won't have enough, then I'm not really trusting that God will provide for my needs. But if I take a step of faith and believe that God will meet all my needs as He promises, I will confidently release my grip on material possessions and allow Him to use me as a conduit to meet the needs of others. The Lord says in Matthew 6 that just as He feeds the birds of the air and clothes the grass of the field, He will also feed and clothe His children. All He requires of us is to trust Him and take Him at His Word. If we do that, then we will be enormously blessed by watching how the great hand of God moves into action to provide for His children.

August 2, 2013

CaringBridge
Written by Kelly

Another great day yesterday. He is continuing to improve every day, and his strength is increasing. Doctors have gotten his headaches under control, and he didn't complain of any pain yesterday. His shoulder is also doing better. The plan is for us to be transferred back to rehab on Monday. We appreciate your prayers that this time in rehab will be successful.

Travis was in a bad car accident early this morning when he got off work at 12:30 A.M. He was hit by a drunk driver at an intersection of a cross street where the speed limit is fifty-five. The driver ran the light and hit the passenger side of our car flipping the car over. It skidded down the street and then hit the curb and flipped back over. He's okay and didn't need to go to the hospital, but his neck is killing him and our Malibu is totaled. He would appreciate your prayers as well right now.

CHAPTER 12

DR. LAUNDRY

Dr. Davis, one of TJ's rehab doctors, was very concerned that our insurance company wouldn't approve TJ's admittance into rehab a third time. She said no one in the past had ever needed readmission that many times, so she had no idea what insurance would do. Upon hearing her concerns, I felt a twinge of fear, but after all of the ups and downs we'd been through since surgery in April, I decided not to worry because if rehab was denied, God would provide another option. When we received the news from rehab staff that TJ was accepted a third time, I was elated. We hoped this admission would be the new beginning we'd been praying for.

Doctors expected TJ to be in rehab three to four weeks and asked again about our goals. Of course, trach removal was first and foremost on our list. TJ's attempts at swallowing were so difficult that doctors were hesitant to say he would ever swallow again. When we asked about this particular part of his recovery, their answer was, "Well, we'll certainly try." I could tell they were doubtful, and their answer filled me with fear. I desperately wanted to hear the words: "He will swallow again."

Physical therapy consisted mostly of TJ walking the halls. In the beginning of rehab, he used an upright walker, a tall walker that allows users to walk in an upright position. He had been lying in a bed for four months, and his torso was very weak. The upright walker provided more support while he strengthened his trunk muscles. While he walked, his therapist, Lynne, faced him and walked backward while holding the front of the walker. As he walked with his therapist, I walked behind him pushing the wheelchair in case he tired and needed to rest. After a couple of weeks, he graduated to a standard walker that provided less support.

He pedaled a NuStep, a rehab recumbent bike, almost every day and often climbed up and down stairs. He also used the Zero Gravity machine, a walking system with a harness that hangs from the ceiling. He was safe from falling while in the harness. The therapist could lessen the amount of support required and allow him more control, which helped improve his balance. He liked using the harness and oftentimes tried running while in it, much to his therapist's dismay. Quite often, that ornery teenage boy made an appearance in therapy.

One day in particular, while using the Zero Gravity machine, he looked natural, balanced, and his arms were swinging by his side. TJ's speech therapist, Sharon, entered the gym, and while watching TJ walk with Lynne, she exclaimed, "A month ago, did you ever think you would be seeing this?!"

From my perspective, it looked like his walking was rapidly improving, but sometimes I didn't trust my judgment. The next day I asked Lynne her opinion while TJ was walking the halls in physical therapy.

"His walking is *very* good," Lynne agreed.

I asked, "Do you think he'll walk on his own again?"

"Oh, yes!" she assured me.

In prior months, whenever doctors discussed TJ's grim condition, I never believed he was as bad as they said he was because I'd seen him walking in Des Moines a week after surgery. After spending weeks in a bed, I was glad to see his walking had improved. However, I had a nagging fear that something would happen to halt his progress. If I thought about it too much, the fear became overwhelming. I told myself to ignore the negativity and focus on enjoying the improvement I was seeing in TJ.

One morning when I arrived at the hospital, TJ was in the shower. Maggie, his occupational therapist, was standing outside the curtain keeping an eye on him and giving him directions. I heard Maggie say sternly, "Tee Jaaay!"

"What's wrong? What's he doing?" I asked. I walked to the bathroom, and as I entered the room, I saw water spraying over the top of the shower curtain.

"He's trying to spray me with water," Maggie replied.

"TJ, stop it!" I scolded. "She's working and can't go home to change. Quit spraying her. Hurry up and finish your shower!"

However, hiding beneath my disapproval was a giggle. If he knew I thought his antics were humorous, he would spray her again, so I squelched my laughter. Although he was being a stinker, it *was* funny. I was thrilled that he was feeling better and could be a teenage boy again.

TJ also worked on handwriting in occupational therapy. I was shocked one morning when Maggie handed me TJ's handwritten paper. She had asked him what he liked to be called, and he wrote, "TJ, Teej, or Travis (when my dad is not around). I sadly was named after my dad." It was amazing to hear his thoughts. Oh, how I missed talking to him and hearing his voice. But he was writing again! I immediately felt hopeful that even if he never talked, at least he could write and communicate.

A few nights later, TJ pointed to his writing podium, pen, and paper. I set the podium on his legs and then handed him the pen and paper. I was eager to see what he had to say, but he didn't write anything and just sat for the longest time staring at the paper. I could tell he wanted to write but couldn't get started. He then became upset and frustrated. After giving him a pep talk, I told him to sign the first two letters to me and I would help him write them. He finger-spelled M - O. I held his hand and helped him write "M," and then something clicked. He wrote the rest of the sentence by himself: "Mom, we need to get one of those silver dogs." (The day before, one of the nurses brought her silver lab puppy to visit him.)

I smiled, "Of course, we can get one," although the truth was that I truly didn't want a dog and secretly hoped that he would forget.

August 10, 2013

CaringBridge
Written by Kelly

TJ spoke for the first time today. He has been wearing the speaking valve on his trach, but even so, he still has never talked. Today he was lying on the couch in his room, and Travis was teasing him. Nearing the end of his patience, TJ yelled, "Shut up!" It sounded like him but maybe just a little hoarse. The room erupted with excitement and cheering, and his nurse, who was in the hallway watching through the window, was celebrating as well. What a happy moment that was! I was grinning from ear to ear, and I think TJ was surprised also.

I'm thrilled and relieved those things are coming back. God has been good to us. A few weeks ago, I taught TJ the sign language alphabet. We now use it constantly, and it's much faster than our old method. But not everyone knows sign language so that, unfortunately, keeps him dependent on me to translate. They're talking to us about a communication device so he can use that to communicate when I'm not around.

Otherwise, he was pretty quiet today. He slept a lot. We had family visit, but he had a hard time staying awake. He worked really hard yesterday in therapy, and he just needed a lazy day.

From the shoulders down, TJ was quickly improving but physically wasn't the same as he was before the brain injury. He was weak and had balance problems. His arms moved awkwardly. He couldn't sit straight in a chair for very long, and while sitting, he was sometimes compelled to raise his arm over his head. But even with all those problems, we could still see potential for a good recovery. His head, however, was a whole different story. Nothing worked. As I watched him struggle through therapy, I wondered if his eyes would ever move correctly, if he would ever open his mouth in a regular manner, or if he would ever swallow or talk again. I held on to every iota of positive improvement I could see.

Sharon, TJ's speech therapist, worked on his eyes, speech, mouth opening, and tongue movement. For therapy she spread large playing cards on the table and asked him to pick a certain card out to work his eyes. After picking the card, he was to count up to that number. He was able to say most of the numbers, but his voice was very faint. He also sang the happy birthday song, and we could hear about a third of the words. Sharon's birthday was coming up. Our homework was to work on the happy birthday song so he could sing it to her on her birthday. I loved seeing the changes with his speech, however small they were!

Another time during speech therapy, he ate orange sherbet. He chose to feed himself, and his mouth flew open as soon as the spoon was near it. He had a hard time swallowing it and became frustrated. We had to stop and encourage him because, previously, he hadn't even been able to open his mouth. He once again tried an ice chip, and this time we heard a crunch. He was making progress! After the sherbet and ice chip, we suctioned his trach to see if there was anything orange in it. There was not, which meant he was able to control what was in his mouth and not let it run down into his lungs. He did give a thumbs-up that he was able to swallow a little bit, although his speech therapist was skeptical.

Some days during therapy, his mouth would open and his eyes would move or he would say a few words. But other days, he couldn't do any of the exercises. His success was very sporadic. Most of the time, when I asked him to open his mouth, he couldn't do it. If I put ice on a spoon, and he fed it to himself, his mouth would open. Sometimes if I needed him to open his mouth and he couldn't, I would tell him to think about yawning. After a few seconds, his mouth would open. The brain is an amazing, complicated organ. We were always trying to think of ways to trick it into cooperating.

After a while, I stopped going to therapy sessions with TJ because the therapists wanted him to gain independence. I used that time to walk around the city and explore the shops in downtown Rochester. I also went for long walks in the neighborhood behind Ronald McDonald House called "Pill Hill," which got its name because so many doctors lived there. It was a beautiful area that reminded me of my favorite neighborhood in Des Moines called "South of Grand." A feeling of normalcy was starting to come over me. I no longer felt the constant fear, panic, and heaviness that I had felt for so many, long months.

Tom, the young man admitted into the room next to TJ's PICU room, was in rehab at the same time as TJ. He was in a room just down the hall from us. Some nights I wheeled TJ down the hall for a movie night with Tom and Janet. It felt like we were staying in a big hotel with friends. Tom was improving, TJ was improving, and Janet and I were once again very happy.

Now that it was August, the subject of school was coming up. The staff felt he wasn't ready to start the first semester of school, so we were looking at alternative options for him, hoping he would be well enough to attend the second semester. I was heartbroken. It was his senior year. Every parent looks forward to the senior year. Senior pictures, homecoming, college visits. But he wasn't going to get to do any of that—I wasn't going to get to do any of that. More than likely, he wasn't even going to graduate with his class. Our life had been altered drastically. I dreaded telling him that he wasn't going back to school right away. However, after telling him, to my surprise, he seemed okay and gave a thumbs-up. He was a smart kid. I'm sure he already suspected that school plans had changed.

Our plan after rehab was for TJ to live at home and attend outpatient therapy. Dr. Davis was concerned that caring for TJ at home would be too much for us, but there were many reasons why we felt

TJ should be at home instead of in a facility. We wanted TJ to come home, and he desperately wanted to come home. The thought of putting him in a facility made us feel terribly guilty. We just couldn't do it. He was still a child who had been through a terrible tragedy, and we wanted him surrounded by people who loved him. His doctors said they saw no reason why he wouldn't continue to improve. We reasoned that even though it might be hard at first, he would improve and it would get easier. Medical staff said that patients generally recover better at home. The social worker at Mayo encouraged us to apply for the brain-injury waiver because it would give us additional services not covered by Medicaid. The wait for acceptance was two years, but because TJ was already institutionalized, we were moved to the top of the list. We were hoping we would be approved around the time of discharge.

August 14, 2013

CaringBridge
Written by Kelly

TJ has another respiratory infection, and he isn't feeling well. I started noticing a slight increase in secretions in the late evening yesterday, and then this morning when I arrived, it was really bad. I've spent most of my day by his bedside suctioning every fifteen minutes. He just got his first dose of antibiotic. They're giving him a stronger one than last time. He struggled with therapy today. With the exception of his morning therapy, all of the other therapies were done in his bed, and he worked on strengthening exercises. Please pray for him that these infections will stop. He is so dry now, so I don't understand why he continues to get them. I am afraid we'll get sent back into the hospital again.

This morning before I got to the hospital, TJ got up from bed with help from his nurse, who wasn't quite sure what he was up to. He shuffled over to the white board that listed the names of all of the doctors and therapists on his team. He erased Dr. Landry's name and wrote "Dr. Laundry" in its place. When asked if he had been planning that for a while, he smiled and nodded his head. He still has a wonderful sense of humor.

The next morning when I walked into TJ's room, he was in a great mood and feeling much better. Doctors thought the last infection hadn't completely resolved. I was relieved to hear that it wasn't something new and we weren't going to be moved. They gave him something stronger and said that should take care of it.

Dr. Landry, one of TJ's rehab doctors, said we were still on schedule to be discharged on September 3rd and that everyone on the floor was talking about how well TJ was doing. We were both ready to go home. God had been so good to us and had seen us through the most difficult trial we'd ever faced. The truth was that we still had a long way to go, but the worst was over. I opened my Bible to the Psalms and read praises to TJ.

Psalm 66:8–12

"Praise our God, O peoples, let the sound of His praise be heard; He has preserved our lives and kept our feet from slipping. For You, God, tested us; You refined us like silver. You brought us into prison and laid burdens on our backs. You let men ride over our heads; we went through fire and water but You brought us to a place of abundance."

The news of TJ's mischief spread across the rehab floor, and much to Dr. Landry's chagrin, medical staff also began referring to him as "Dr. Laundry." A few days later when Dr. Landry entered TJ's room for morning rounds, TJ was in the bathroom with his nurse. When he heard Dr. Landry's voice, he picked up the dirty laundry from his bathroom floor, and with his nurse in tow, walked out of the bathroom and threw the dirty laundry at Dr. Landry.

The battle was on.

Days afterward, when TJ was walking down the hallway with Lynne for afternoon therapy, Dr. Landry, walking a short distance ahead of him, suddenly turned around and began shooting TJ with a Nerf gun leaving TJ ducking, dodging, and to his therapist's dismay, trying to chase down Dr. Landry.

Rehab was a wonderfully encouraging experience. It was a time of excitement, laughter, and happiness. It left us with a lot of fond memories. TJ was improving, and we were hopeful about the future.

Pulmonology informed me that TJ was having his trach removed before we were discharged from rehab. They said he didn't need it anymore and that it was more of a hindrance than a benefit, so the next day his trach was capped. Capping the trach involves keeping the trach but placing a plastic cap on it. If the patient is able to manage secretions while capped for a few days, then it's safe to remove the trach entirely.

After TJ's trach was capped, he started coughing, which was the signal that he needed to be suctioned. Because it was capped, he either had to spit or swallow on his own. As I watched him struggling, I began to panic—experiencing a moment of PTSD. I wanted the trach out, but flashbacks of respiratory failures plagued me. The respiratory therapist reassured me that his trach was still there and we could assist him if he was unable to help himself, so I settled down and watched to see what he could do. TJ leaned forward and held a towel to his mouth for a while. Then, he gave a thumbs-up that he had cleared it. I reminded him that he was in control of whether or not the trach was removed. I asked him if he thought he could handle clearing the secretions without the trach. He squeezed my hand for a "yes," but I was still skeptical and afraid.

Although Pulmonology said he could have the trach removed, a few days later, ENT said he could not. They said he wasn't ready, so it wasn't safe to remove it just yet. However, they didn't think he would have the trach much longer. The thought of his airway becoming occluded with secretions terrified me more than taking care of the trach, so I was satisfied with their decision. Their decision didn't seem to bother TJ in the least.

One morning upon entering TJ's room, the nurse told me that TJ had behaved unexpectedly before I arrived. TJ and the nurse were standing at the sink in the bathroom while he was brushing his teeth. TJ waited until the nurse had turned his back for a split second and then dove down under the running water and began drinking. I'm sure he missed water terribly. I can't even imagine what it would be like to not be able to drink, but even so, he was becoming a real pistol. Thankfully, he had no ill effects after that little stunt.

A couple of days before TJ was discharged from rehab to home, I saw Dr. Steele sitting at a desk outside of TJ's room. I was excited to see her and went out to talk to her.

I got right to the point. "You used to make me so mad."

"Why? What did I do?" she asked.

"You told me the truth and I didn't like it!" She laughed, and I continued, "When I asked you a question and didn't like your answer, I walked away muttering, 'She doesn't know everything.'" With that, she jumped off her chair and hugged me.

Toward the end of rehab, TJ, Travis, and I used our first pass and went out into the community. We decided to take TJ to a movie. I was excited for him to get out of the hospital and do something that teenagers enjoy. Unfortunately, it didn't go as well as I had hoped. His wheelchair presented a dilemma. Because of the lack of strength in his trunk and his inability to sit unassisted, he really needed a tilt-in-space wheelchair that reclined. The rehab doctors said if he used a tilt-in-space wheelchair, his trunk muscles would never get stronger. So, we had to tough it out and use the standard wheelchair. Since he couldn't sit for long periods of time and was so uncomfortable during the movie, we laid him down across the chairs in the theater. He was nervous, which caused his secretions to increase, so we were suctioning often during the movie. The suction machine was loud. We were concerned that we were annoying other movie-goers, so we left early.

During our pass, we learned that reintegrating into society was difficult. People stared at TJ everywhere we went, but I hoped he didn't notice. While riding in the elevator, a woman began talking to TJ. I was happy she noticed him and included him in the conversation, even though he couldn't talk. But then she looked at Travis and me and said, "I'm a special-ed teacher." My heart sank. It was the first time we heard the words "special-ed" as applied to our son. I wondered how TJ felt, being included in a category that was foreign to him. What she didn't know was that TJ had been a typical kid his entire life and had just recently acquired a brain injury. The "special-ed" label was painful at the time because it was a new identity and happened while we were still grieving the loss of his old identity.

August 31, 2013

CaringBridge
Written by Kelly

We've had such a busy week. I've been at the hospital most days by 8 or 9 A.M. and stayed until 10 P.M. I've been doing a lot of training to get us ready to go home.

Tuesday, we had a Care Conference with his school. It was an unexpectedly emotional day for both of us. When the doctors described TJ's injuries and what he has gone through, he cried. When they discussed his subsequent deficits and termed him a "severe" brain injury, a word I had never heard before, I cried, and it continued for the rest of the day. Some days I just need to cry.

We both have mixed emotions about going home. We are happy to go home and see friends and family that we love and miss, but we're sad to leave the friends we've made here at Mayo. Past doctors have been stopping by to say goodbye and some have brought gifts for TJ. The life that we have been living the past few months no one would describe as an abundant life, but this week, I realized that the abundant life is exactly what this is. Every moment now is just a little sweeter than it used to be before we began this journey. Jesus didn't lie when He said in John 10:10 that He came to give us life and to give it more abundantly. (NKJV) He always does things in the most unexpected ways. Below are three of our abundant life highlights from the week:

- Earlier in the week, we visited the PICU. Dr. Steele (my favorite doctor) told TJ that she wanted him to come back and visit but not until he could walk through the doors. Last week he graduated to a standard walker, so off we went to the PICU. When he walked in, Dr. Steele was across the room, and her mouth fell open. She and the nurses came running to see him. He got lots of hugs. I'm sure it must make them feel good to see the difference they've made in someone's life.

- As I mentioned before, TJ and Tom were neighbors in the PICU, and now they are both in rehab. Sometimes they are both in the gym at the same time for PT, and it is such a blessing to watch them. Tom will be yelling at TJ to encourage him, and TJ will give Tom the thumbs-up to keep going. Then Tom will walk to him, and they'll try to give each other a high five, but they miss each other's hands because they're weak and TJ has trouble judging distance. It's hard not to chuckle. Then Tom will say, "May the force be with you!"

- We're putting a bed in our room for TJ for a while. Travis had been teasing him that he was going to put pink sheets on it. The other night I had Travis on the phone on speaker and asked if he had TJ's bed ready, and TJ said as clear as a bell, "Pink!" I'm sure what he meant was *not* pink. But, of course, Travis went out and bought hot pink sheets for him, so he'll have a surprise when he gets home. I treasure every word he says.

I've been discussing with TJ's therapists and doctors what his future is going to look like. Most believe that he will talk and eat again. He does have coordination and balance problems and will likely struggle with those the rest of his life, but they will be to a lesser extent than he has now. He has poor impulse control. If he wants something, he'll stand up and go get it and won't wait for help, so safety is a big issue. That is right now the hardest deficit for me to deal with because he's big and hard to control. They've said it should get better with time. Doctors have told me repeatedly that he won't be the same. However, in the future, they think he'll be able to do most things he wants to do with accommodation.

John 10:10 (NKJV)

"The thief does not come except to steal, and to kill, and to destroy; I have come that they may have life, and that they may have it more abundantly."

I knew TJ wasn't going to be the exact same person he had been before his heart surgery, and although I was still heartbroken and hadn't fully accepted it yet, I was much more accepting of it than I had been. I struggled between wanting my son back and trusting that God would still do amazing things with TJ's life. I believed that even with his deficits, God could still give him a good life. We would eventually adjust to the new person he'd become. This terrifying journey was now a part of TJ's life story. I knew his career path would probably change, but I reasoned that detours in life are how God directs our paths. I imagined God using TJ's powerful story to speak to others about His unfailing love that broke through unimaginable suffering and to point others to a relationship with Christ. I believed God would use TJ's loss of physical ability for His glory.

SEPTEMBER 3, 2013

CaringBridge
Written by Kelly

Headin' home…

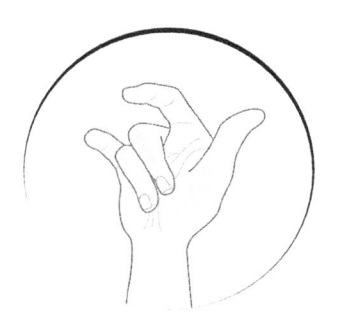

CHAPTER 13

THE DOWNWARD SPIRAL

I was excited, but also a bundle of nerves, as we wheeled TJ out of the rehab unit that afternoon. Many questions ran through my mind. *What if I forget to give him his medications? What if his trach gets clogged and I can't get it unclogged? What if I hurt him? Will I have help? What will I do if I get tired and it's too much? What if I forget something?*

After stopping at the pharmacy on the first floor of the hospital to pick up prescriptions, we wheeled TJ out to the car and transferred him quickly into the front seat. Since he couldn't sit up straight for very long, we laid the seat back as far as we could. I sat in the back and suctioned his trach when needed while Travis drove the three hours home.

After arriving home, a small group of friends and family had gathered to greet us. After four months in the hospital, TJ was overjoyed to be home and couldn't wait to get inside. Upon entering the house, there was a great deal of excitement in the air; however, I became upset when I saw the arrangement of the family room furniture. It was *tight*. I didn't know how I would get TJ's wheelchair into the room. I immediately started rearranging the furniture. Everyone then became uncomfortable and the room got very quiet. Then I sat down and started crying, which made everyone even *more* uncomfortable. *What is wrong with me?* I thought. Deep down I knew it really wasn't about the arrangement of the furniture. The truth was, I was frightened and overwhelmed. My child's medical needs were daunting. I had no control over anything, and at that moment, the placement of the family room furniture was the only thing I could control. After I pulled myself together, I managed to put a smile on my face, but inside I felt terrible and embarrassed that I ruined TJ's homecoming.

A couple of days after getting home, we had an appointment with a pediatrician in Des Moines, Dr. Howell, who treats children with special needs. We were happy to see that we already knew the doctor. He lived in Van Meter when we did, and our kids grew up together. Even though I was fearful of what lay ahead, it was clear the hand of God was providing for us and guiding us during our transition back home.

After the initial excitement of TJ's homecoming, daily life began. I quickly discovered that Dr. Davis was right. It was a very difficult task to take care of TJ at home. Travis took the first week off work to help me adjust to our new routine, but even with both of us tending to TJ's needs, it was still overwhelming. Neither of us had yet adjusted to the relentless demands of caregiving.

Our home is a four-level split with stairs everywhere. It wasn't the best setup for a person recovering from a brain injury and using a wheelchair. Prior to his injury, TJ's room had been in the basement. Doctors felt that it wouldn't be long before TJ would be walking on his own again and able to sleep in his room in the basement. However, for the time being, he was going to sleep in our room on a makeshift cot with a comfy padded mattress wrapped in hot pink sheets. Even though he was only an arm's length away from me at night, I still couldn't sleep. Just like when he was a newborn baby sleeping in a bassinet next to me, my mind simply would not turn off. I was always listening, always watching to see if he was breathing.

We talked to the Department of Human Services about the status of acceptance on the brain-injury waiver. They said it could take up to two months before we would receive any help and even then, it was minimal. At that point, we were discouraged and constantly in prayer.

Soon after arriving home, we began noticing changes in TJ's physical condition. His walking was deteriorating. As Travis walked TJ around our cul-de-sac, he noticed that TJ was needing more support than before and that his feet were slapping the pavement. When sitting, his arms were always over his head, and he would fall over to the side. He tried crawling, but he couldn't coordinate his arms and kept falling on his face. One of his hands was tight and continually squeezing. Something was happening to him but we didn't know what. Once again, I could feel the old, familiar panic and fear rising up inside of me.

A few days after arriving home, we attended our first outpatient therapy session in Des Moines. We learned TJ had been scheduled for every Friday at 8 A.M. Once Travis went back to work, I didn't know how I was going to get TJ to therapy by myself that early, especially with Aiden in tow. I broke down and began to cry in the waiting room.

The speech therapist met with TJ, and after about ten minutes of therapy, she stopped and asked us why he'd been discharged to home. She felt that he should be in a transitional care facility and that outpatient therapy was not going to work for him at this stage in his recovery. The therapist gave us names of two transitional care facilities. We were happy to learn that Dr. Howell visited one of those facilities each week.

After arriving home from therapy, I called the facility right away, mostly because I was very concerned about the physical changes we were seeing in TJ. The facility told us to bring him right over. As we were getting ready to leave the house, I asked Travis if we should call the insurance company to ask if TJ would even be approved for admittance. He simply said, "No, let's just go."

Incredibly, as we were walking out the door, the phone rang. It was the insurance representative checking in to see how things were going. We informed her about the outpatient therapist's concerns and the decline we were seeing in TJ, and she instructed us to take TJ to the transitional care facility.

When we arrived, we were greeted at the door by a high-school friend of mine whom I didn't know was employed at the facility. I was comforted by her presence and believed it was God's guidance. Although TJ wasn't happy about the move, Travis and I were initially very pleased with the facility. I felt terribly guilty that he couldn't be at home with us just yet but knew he needed to keep progressing in his recovery to enable us to care for him at home. Pending insurance approval, they expected him to be there three to six weeks.

After struggling with insurance for over a week because the transitional facility was out of network, TJ was finally admitted. It felt like a huge weight had been lifted off our shoulders. We anticipated that he would get the therapy he needed to keep improving, which would also make it more manageable for us to care for him at home.

We were pleased to see that TJ's room was big and comfortable.

Although the facility had a policy that parents could not stay overnight with their children due to safety issues with other children staying in the unit, they let me stay with TJ for a few nights to get him settled in. TJ would be receiving physical, occupational, and speech therapy while there. It would be similar to the rehab at Mayo. TJ's speech therapist was anxious to get started with him. She had never seen anyone who couldn't open his mouth and looked forward to the challenge of working with him. I was hopeful that her enthusiasm would help him improve.

Three days after his admission to the transitional care unit, TJ's stomach began bothering him. To me, his pain looked similar to when he had pneumatosis. When we arrived at the ER, I told the doctor I thought it was pneumatosis. She looked at me strangely and then left the room, probably thinking, *"Pneumatosis? What does she know?"* When she returned, her eyes were wide open, and she said, "He *does* have pneumatosis." TJ was admitted to the general pediatric floor and placed on antibiotics. We were told that he would need surgery if he didn't respond to the antibiotics.

Insurance coverage determined which hospital we could use, so we went back to the same hospital where TJ's heart surgery took place. There were many bad memories there, and I found myself consumed with anxiety. Every time I entered the hospital, I would glance over to the reception desk. The image of TJ standing at the desk the morning of surgery in his blue Hurley shirt and bright yellow Puma shorts would flash through my mind and leave me feeling very sad.

The children's floor had been newly remodeled not long before TJ had surgery and had that new material smell to it. Upon walking into the unit, the scent would overwhelm me, and my stress level would rise, once more triggering memories of those dreadful couple of weeks after surgery. Seeing familiar faces around the hospital was sometimes more than I could handle and ultimately increased my anxiety.

Since being home, I was overwhelmed with grief and sadness as I remembered TJ before surgery. Everywhere I looked I saw reminders of the abilities he used to have and all the things he was missing out on, while day after day we sat in a hospital and battled his brain injury. Many days I laid my head on his chest and cried, and true to TJ's nature, he lovingly patted me on the back. He was much stronger than I was.

Some days I struggled, trying to understand why God wouldn't step in and save the day. *Had He forgotten us?* I had to ask. *Does He even love us? Doesn't He know how weak and exhausted we are?* Deep down I already knew that the answer to those questions was a big *yes*. I continually prayed for God to give us strength to keep trusting Him as we continued this seemingly endless journey.

TJ's body continued to deteriorate while he was in the hospital. His balance was so bad that it was difficult for even two people to keep him upright as he tried to walk. His arms looked like they were twisting. His hands were turning outward making sign language too difficult for his hands and fingers to manage. I showed the therapists at the hospital videos of TJ walking just a few weeks before, while he was at Mayo. They couldn't believe how well he was doing then compared to what they saw now. I was frightened and didn't understand what was happening to my son. They asked neurology for a consult and to possibly do another MRI of his brain.

My stress level was enormous because of TJ's condition and the environment we were in. One day I hit the limit of what I could tolerate and lost my temper with a nurse. For days TJ had been getting an IV drip of medication. On a day that TJ had gone downstairs for some testing, the nurse disconnected him from his IV drip and instructed me to call her if he needed it and she would bring it down.

During his stay at Mayo, I noticed that he seemed to be very sensitive to medications, so after he'd been disconnected from his IV medication much longer than anticipated, I became worried that he would have adverse effects if he didn't get his required dosage. After three calls, the nurse finally brought the IV pole down. When she walked into the room, she said nothing, but I could tell she was irritated.

After the testing was finished, and TJ was back in his room with Travis and me, the tension became palpable when that same nurse entered the room. Travis picked up on it and asked what had happened to cause the increased tension between us. I explained the details and made an effort to forget the whole thing, figuring she would also get over it eventually.

Just as I feared, TJ had a horrible night—even worse than I'd expected. His body became severely twisted and wouldn't stop moving. He was miserable, twisted and turned into strange positions. It was terribly painful for TJ and horrifying for us to watch. Nobody slept at all that night. The next morning, TJ had the same nurse again. She was sitting in the hallway outside of his room, and my friend Diane overheard her say, "TJ would be better off if she wasn't here all the time, questioning our every move."

When my friend shared with me the insensitive things the nurse had said, I became furious. The next time the nurse walked into the room, I lost control. Lack of sleep, stress, and anxiety overpowered what little self-control I had left. Everything I had been holding in, came out. I was raw and unfiltered, and this nurse caught the brunt of it when I said, "You have no idea what I have been through the last six months! Do you see what my kid looks like?! This hospital did this to him! I asked you three times yesterday to bring TJ's medication to him because I knew this was going to happen. Did you sleep well last night? Did you enjoy your family last night? Because we didn't! This is what we went through all night!" I turned to the other nurses who had walked in to inquire about the scene and demanded, "Get her out of here! I don't want her here. Get her *out*!"

Afterward, I sat down on TJ's couch with my friend Marcy, completely exhausted from my tirade and scolded myself for losing my composure. I was disgusted and disappointed with myself. Even during my worst days, I'd never had a meltdown of that magnitude. I was hanging on by a thread.

"I can't believe I just acted like that," I said to Marcy. "How can I call myself a Christian and point people to Christ if I act like a screaming lunatic?"

"Everyone makes mistakes," Marcy comforted. "You need to forgive yourself, put it out of your mind, and move forward."

A doctor told me that TJ could've had a seizure after going without his medication for so long. Even though my anger was justified, none of the nurses on that floor wanted to work with us anymore. So, they brought in a PICU nurse to care for TJ. I was pleased to see it was the nurse TJ had the very first night after heart surgery. She was an excellent nurse, and we all liked her. She was happy to see us and had a big smile on her face when she walked into the room. I was thrilled with the positive change in nursing staff and promised the nurse I would be on my best behavior.

TJ's muscle contractions lasted for several days. His suffering was severe. I began to fear that it might never end and he would be like this for the rest of his life. No one could live that way. It was so uncomfortable for him that there were times when I begged and pleaded with God to heal him. Then there were other times when I begged God to take him home. After confiding in friends through tear-filled eyes about the content of my prayers, I read the look of shock on their faces and heard the condemnation on their lips. I felt all alone. They didn't understand that when a mother is praying for her child to die, it's only because she would do anything to see his suffering end.

To make matters worse, our insurance company would not allow TJ back into the transitional care facility since they were out of network. Instead, we were told that he needed to go to a brain injury rehab facility. When the brain injury rehab facility reps came to visit TJ at the hospital, after seeing first-hand the severity of his condition, they told the social worker they couldn't accept him because his needs were greater than they could handle. Insurance then allowed TJ re-admittance into his original transitional care facility.

October 5, 2013

CaringBridge
Written by Kelly

TJ's MRI came back with no changes from the previous MRI, so that's good news. His body continues to twist, but it is now better controlled with only short breakthroughs of agitation. They plan to watch him through the weekend to monitor his meds, and if all goes well, he'll be discharged to the transitional care facility Monday morning. The neurologist here said the spasming and twisting in his arms and hands is called dystonia. Some of the doctors wanted to add more medication to stop the twisting, but the neurologist's recommendation was to get him off the medications because they were poisoning him, instead of adding more, and do physical therapy.

Before TJ found out about his heart condition, he had thoughts of going into the military. He loves guns and shooting and had dreams of being a sniper. After he learned the military wasn't going to be an option because of his heart defect, he was very sad and disappointed. The other day I came across a quote from Charles Spurgeon that talked about being a soldier in battle. I knew this was something TJ needed to hear:

> "See you not, then, that God may take away your comforts and your privileges to make you the better Christians? Why, the Lord always trains His soldiers, not by letting them lie on feather beds, but by turning them out and using them to forced marches and hard service. He makes them ford through streams, and swim through rivers, and climb mountains, and walk many a long march with heavy knapsacks of sorrow on their backs. This is the way in which He makes soldiers—not by dressing them up in fine uniforms, to swagger at the barrack gates, and to be fine gentlemen in the eyes of the loungers in the park. God knows that soldiers are only to be made in battle; they are not to be grown in peaceful times. We may grow the stuff of which soldiers are made, but warriors are really educated by the smell of powder, in the midst of whizzing bullets, and roaring cannonades—not in soft and peaceful times.
>
> "Well, Christian, may not this account for it all? Is not thy Lord bringing out thy graces and making them grow? This is the reason why He is contending with you."
>
> —Charles H. Spurgeon

I told TJ that even though he will never be in the military, God is still turning him into a courageous soldier. He has become a fighting warrior in God's army, and instead of killing people, he is being used to save people and turn hearts toward God.

Initially upon discharge back to the transitional care facility, TJ was stable, but shortly after arriving, he again quickly declined. We were struggling with tapering him off medications as the doctor advised. At times he was unable to stop moving and his legs and joints ached. He was no longer able to walk and squeezed my hand when I asked him if he was weak and dizzy. The Botox was wearing off. His tongue was in constant tremors, and his secretions were terrible. We were once again suctioning nonstop. I was having trouble convincing the medical staff that he needed more frequent suctioning at such times to prevent another respiratory distress crisis. I'd seen it happen several times, even at Mayo.

At times he was twisted like a pretzel. His shoulder and wrist were sometimes partially dislocating. Sometimes his back was arching so much that it looked like his trach was pressing into the trachea wall, causing him to struggle to breathe. Once, I panicked and told his nurse that he couldn't breathe. She responded, "Well, maybe that's a good way for him to learn to stop arching his back." I was shocked that a healthcare worker would imply that TJ was intentionally arching his back and that the ensuing breathing difficulty would teach him a lesson. He could not control the dystonic movements, and the resulting airway obstruction needed attention immediately. I was quickly starting to realize that I would never be able to leave him unattended when he was in the care facility because he wasn't safe.

After observing my distress, my friend Rhonda, who is a registered nurse, graciously offered to stay the night with TJ so I could rest. To my surprise, the facility allowed her to sleep over, but due to facility policy, they would not allow her to suction his trach. Early the next morning, Rhonda called to inform me that TJ seemed to be in respiratory distress. After learning of the inadequate suctioning he was receiving from staff, I called his nurse. After arguing back and forth with her for several minutes, she hung up on me.

When I arrived at the facility that morning, five or six staff members suddenly surrounded me. I explained my concerns regarding TJ's respiratory issues. I also added that TJ was rapidly losing weight and that I was very concerned. I asked for daily weights because that was the standard of care at Mayo. No one seemed to be as concerned as I was, and one staff member rolled her eyes at me. In desperation, I finally said, "I just want to take him to the hospital. He just needs to go to the hospital."

A short while later, the supervisor marched into TJ's room and was clearly very agitated when she told me that they would call an ambulance to transport him to the hospital. And though the policy was that they would send a nurse with the patient, they refused to send one. I assume it was because I had argued with his nurse earlier that morning. I told her that if he was admitted, I was going to ask for a transfer to Mayo. She shot back, "Do you know how expensive that is? They're never going to do that." By then, I was crying, frustrated that in the midst of one crisis after another, I couldn't get anyone to listen to me—the one who knew my son best. I had no choice but to let the difference of opinion go and was just relieved that TJ was going to the hospital.

When we arrived at the ER, after seeing TJ's rapidly-deteriorating condition, the ER staff became very concerned about his respiratory issues. When I learned they were planning on admitting him, I asked if he could be transferred back to Mayo. The doctor agreed. "Yes, that's where he needs to be because they know him best."

Because of his trouble breathing, which I knew was due to lack of suctioning, the ER staff placed him on a ventilator. He was loaded onto a helicopter and flown back up to Mayo that morning. I was relieved to be returning to Mayo where I knew he would receive exceptional care. However, the entire six weeks at home left me traumatized. I felt, for the most part, that we had been abandoned, left to fend for ourselves.

CHAPTER 14

JESUS WALKS BESIDE ME

As Travis and I exited the freeway in Rochester and turned right toward the hospital, a calm feeling came over me. The words "I'm home" echoed through my mind. I had spent so much time in Rochester in the previous months that it now felt like home. It was October 21, 2013, six months after surgery. My plan was to stay at Ronald McDonald House again, but Travis and I checked into a hotel by the hospital for the time being. Once TJ was back in the PICU, I felt safe again.

Since TJ was on a ventilator, he was heavily sedated and calm. Dr. Steele told me that when they received the call that TJ was coming in on a ventilator, knowing it couldn't be his lungs, she told the other doctors, "Something else is going on." She was right. Once aggressively suctioned, TJ came off the ventilator quickly, and some of the nurses seemed confused as to the reason for the transfer.

The next morning, however, it became very apparent to medical staff why I asked for the transfer. Once TJ woke up, the twisting started, and TJ's nurse told me he could see why I was so concerned.

Dr. Steele entered TJ's room and was standing next to me. As she watched TJ twisting and turning, I asked, "Have you ever seen anything like this before?"

She leaned into me, and out of the side of her mouth said, "Only in the movies." Her humor lightened my mood. It was so good to be back.

As I reacclimated myself to the PICU, I noticed that some areas had undergone remodeling while we were gone. The waiting room and halls had been reconfigured. My favorite restroom was now larger and updated. Although it was modern and clean, I felt a twinge of sadness that my prayer room wasn't the same anymore.

Since TJ's lungs were doing well, PICU doctors said he wasn't critical and moved him to the general pediatric floor to address the dystonia.

October 22, 2013

CaringBridge
Written by Kelly

TJ was moved to the general peds floor this morning. He is back in his old room with his familiar nurse. We were very happy to see her, and she was shocked at how much he has declined. He has lost 15 lbs. since the discharge on September 3rd and is down to 128 pounds. The doctor was shocked at how low his calorie intake was because when muscles are tight and contracting, they burn more calories. They switched him to a different formula and are ramping up the volume. He is already scheduled for Botox to his jaw and salivary glands on Thursday. Woo hoo! Neurology has been consulted for treatment of his dystonia, and the pain team is working together to adjust his medications. PT and OT start tomorrow. They don't waste any time around here. It's an enormous weight off my shoulders. I'm also thankful for hair dye because I think I'm completely gray now.

I have a room at Ronald McDonald House again. Last night we stayed in a hotel right across the street from the hospital. I couldn't sleep, so I sneaked across the street at 4 A.M. to sit with TJ while he slept. It was nice and peaceful.

Doctors educated us regarding the source of his uncontrolled movements: TJ's brain was sending signals to his muscles to contract, contract, contract, so he was started on a drug called Artane, which blocks the signals between the brain and muscles. We were told it would take two weeks before we would notice any improvement and six weeks before it reached peak effectiveness.

Dr. Davis, TJ's rehab doctor, heard about his decline and said she never imagined something like this would happen when we left just six weeks earlier. She asked what our plans were going forward. Travis and I had been discussing TJ and I living in Rochester long-term to be close to the hospital and outpatient rehab. TJ's case was so complicated that we felt he needed to be near a hospital where they treated patients with complex medical problems. Dr. Davis was pleased to hear of our plans but also felt that if the medication failed to work, I wouldn't be able to handle him by myself and he would need to be in a facility. It stung to hear her thoughts on the matter, although I knew she was right. I prayed that the medication would help him so that he could come home. He would be so unhappy in a nursing home. I just couldn't bear the thought of placing my seventeen-year-old son there.

Doctors informed me that if TJ's dystonia was controlled with medications, it was possible that he could once again walk on his own. However, the medications used to treat dystonia would make TJ very weak, so he would need a wheelchair for times when he was walking longer distances.

The part of the brain that controls movements is called the basal ganglia. TJ presented as someone with cerebral palsy, but with cerebral palsy patients, damage to the basal ganglia is usually visible on an MRI. In this case, TJ's basal ganglia appeared to have no visible abnormalities.

The next morning when I entered TJ's room, I learned that he was downstairs in X-ray because his left shoulder popped out of place. His body was horribly twisted in positions that didn't even look possible. His therapists and doctors from rehab stopped by. They were stunned when they saw him lying in bed all twisted up.

Neurology was very helpful. The neurologist said it was not uncommon for these kinds of movement disorders to show up months after the initial brain injury. I asked if the movements could be a side effect of the medications he was on. He said that was a good question but they didn't think medications had anything to do with it. I also asked about the "normal" MRI. They said it happens sometimes when the lesions are microscopic and that just because the brain appears normal on MRI doesn't mean it's functioning as it should. They also believed that dystonia was responsible for the symptoms TJ had been experiencing all along, including both motor issues and difficulty opening his mouth. They informed me that there were many options to treat it and that they could even insert a deep brain stimulator. The neurostimulator would send electrical impulses to specific targets in the brain. I was thankful to be at Mayo.

After the medication took effect, he was no longer in pain or discomfort, so therapy resumed. His therapists from rehab came to the pediatric floor. Recovering from a brain injury is a long and arduous battle, but patients can regain many of their abilities with diligent therapy. And even though therapists gave TJ no rest, they were good to him. TJ had a special bond with them.

He also had a great relationship with his nurses, and one was beside him at all times. Since TJ's hands became very tight when he was twisting, he was unable to sign or even give a thumbs-up. As a result, communication became a problem, so one of the nurses taught him to answer "yes" and "no" questions with his feet. He tapped his feet for "yes" and moved them side to side for "no."

Another doctor from the neurology team, whom I had never met before, came in and painted a grim picture of dystonia. He said that dystonia was very difficult to treat. He also wasn't very optimistic about TJ regaining the ability to talk. Doctors thought he had post-pump dystonia, which is very rare and almost impossible to learn about, even on the internet. Post-pump dystonia occurs months after the initial brain injury, and doctors are unsure why it happens.

After neurology left, I asked TJ if he believed he would get better. He shook his head "no" and started crying hard. I held him and consoled him, blinking back my own tears. Oh, how desperately I wanted his health restored. In order to boost his spirits and give him hope, I reassured him that Dr. Davis said rehab would help him considerably.

That night as I was leaving the hospital to walk back to RMH, I could no longer stifle the tears that had been right under the surface all day. I was so disappointed and confused. TJ had been doing so well. I didn't understand why, after all we'd been through, God would allow us to have such hope in rehab a few weeks earlier, only to have it snatched away again. It seemed cruel and unfair, and yet when I asked why, God was silent on the matter.

Earlier in the evening, I'd been craving a latte from the Caribou and planned to stop and purchase one to drink on the cold walk home. Even though I shouldn't have gone into the coffee shop in the state I was in, I really wanted a coffee. I entered and ordered my coffee with tears rolling down my cheeks, hoping that no one would notice. The clerk took my order, and after handing me the receipt, she hesitated and then inquired, "Ma'am, are you okay? Is there something I can help you with?"

Wiping back tears, I responded, "I'm sorry. I knew I shouldn't have come in here like this, but I really wanted a coffee. My son is very sick but I'll be okay. Thank you, though."

I was embarrassed that I couldn't control my emotions better but then decided that the people working in the area were probably used to it. I put it out of my mind and set out for Ronald McDonald House.

As I walked, I thought about the Lord. If I didn't know Him so well, I could easily mistake His silence as detached and unloving. However, that was *not* the God I know. Many times, during the journey, God showed me that He was with me and was walking right beside me.

I reminded myself of His promises in the scriptures:

The God I know says He loves me with an everlasting love.
(Jeremiah 31:3)

The God I know leads me in paths of righteousness.
(Psalm 23 NKJV)

The God I know sent his Son Jesus to die so I could have eternal life. (John 3:16)

The God I know calls me His child. (1 John 3:1)

The God I know says He walks beside me through the valley. (Psalm 23:4)

The God I know says His presence will go with me, and He will give me rest. (Exodus 33:14)

The God I know says He will be with me always, even to the end of the age. (Matthew 28:20 NKJV)

That is the God I know, and He is God Almighty, I thought. *What should I do when I can't feel God's presence?* I asked myself. *I will trust and believe God's Word.*

Since God says repeatedly in the scriptures that He loves me and is with me, I know now, as I did then, that I could rest assured that He would keep His promise, whether I felt His presence or not. Even Job, whom God called blameless, upright, and one who feared God and shunned evil, was struck by tragedy and unanswered questions, while God remained silent. So, if even upright and blameless Job experienced God's silence during tragedy, then I decided that I must also be prepared for that eventuality. I came to the conclusion that if I always felt God's presence and always had all the answers to my questions, my faith would never grow.

TJ's doctors decided that because of the new onset of dystonia, he needed intense therapy. Our hope was to go back to the rehab unit at Mayo for six weeks if the insurance company would authorize it. It would be our fourth visit to rehab and was a longshot. Doctors went back and forth with the insurance company for a week. Finally, we received word that TJ had been approved for six more weeks of rehab.

One evening, before we transferred to rehab, TJ's nurse was ready to go on break when another nurse came to fill in for his absence. As the nurse was leaving, the replacement asked to speak to him in the hall. I watched the men conversing back and forth through the window. Every once in a while, the replacement nurse would bend down, look at me, then resume talking. I had a feeling they were talking about me. Finally, TJ's nurse left and his replacement came in.

While looking at the floor, the replacement nurse quietly stated, "You probably don't want me as your nurse because I'm the one who accidentally pulled TJ's IV out."

I burst out laughing. "So that's what was going on in the hall!" I exclaimed. "Well, first of all, I don't even remember you pulling TJ's IV out. And second, if you knew what this kid has been through, you would understand that pulling out an IV means *nothing* to me!"

After we moved to rehab, Travis was laid off from work in November for a month, so he and Aiden began staying with me all the time. It was good for TJ to have his dad there. I was too serious and wanted him to get to work with no funny business when he was in therapy, while Travis brought lightness and fun to each day. TJ enjoyed joking around with his dad, although I thought they got out of control sometimes. They often exasperated the therapists. One afternoon, Travis was sitting on the edge of TJ's bed, and TJ jumped on his back, put him in a headlock, and fell backward onto the bed. Travis could not free himself and was turning bright red until TJ finally released him. Although I was mortified by their inappropriate behavior in a hospital setting, I realized that TJ's strength was impressive.

CaringBridge

November 18, 2013
Written by Kelly

Every night for the past few nights I have fallen into bed exhausted, but then I lay in bed for hours, unable to sleep, staring at the ceiling with thoughts racing through my head. Tonight, the insomnia has continued, so I've decided it's time for a journal update since the days are busy, and it's hard for me to find time to get on the computer.

TJ is going through a sleepy stage. We noticed on Friday that he was more tired than usual but thought it might be due to working so hard in therapy. When the weekend came, though, the sleepiness continued, and he pretty much slept the entire weekend away. Today was no different. He was able to get up and go to therapy, but he was lethargic, and it was hard for him. TJ's secretions have diminished. We've asked him several times if he is swallowing, and he says no. However, he's sleeping and wouldn't know if he was swallowing or not. Today he tried to talk to me. I saw his lips move, and I asked him if he was trying to talk. He squeezed my hand for yes. Oh, how I pray that his speech would return. Not being able to communicate is the most difficult thing about this. I miss him so much.

I've been reading a wonderful book a friend from my church sent me. It's titled *Trusting God Even When Life Hurts* by Jerry Bridges. I can't put it down, and I think about it all the time, which might explain the racing thoughts at night. It's about the sovereignty of God.

"All people—believers as well as unbelievers—experience anxiety, frustration, heartache, and disappointment...But that which should distinguish the suffering of believers from unbelievers is the confidence that our suffering is under the control of an all-powerful and all-loving God; our suffering has meaning and purpose in God's eternal plan…" (Bridges 2008, 31–32)

I may never understand this side of heaven why God allowed this to happen to us, but I do know that one of the ways this tragedy has changed me is that I have taken my eyes off this world and the emptiness it offers. I am disappointed with this life, and my plans and dreams have been shattered. My eyes have now shifted upward toward heaven, which is where God has wanted them all along. I am thinking more about what I can do to glorify my Heavenly Father, and I'm longing for the time when I'll be with Him and will have no more suffering, no more sorrow, and no more pain.

Lamentations 3:37–38

"Who can speak and have it happen if the Lord has not decreed it? Is it not from the mouth of the Most High that both calamities and good things come?"

Lamentations 3:32–33

"Though He brings grief, He will show compassion, so great is His unfailing love. For He does not willingly bring affliction or grief to anyone."

Isaiah 45:7

"I form the light and create darkness, I bring prosperity and create disaster; I, the Lord do all these things."

Travis, Aiden, and I spent Thanksgiving in Rochester. Ronald McDonald House served a wonderful meal to all the families there. I felt guilty that we were feasting while TJ couldn't eat, so I hid the reason for our exit when we left for dinner. Thanksgiving afternoon TJ was given a four-hour pass, so we took him back to our room and watched a movie together. It went very well and was good for us to brush up on our caregiving skills so we wouldn't get rusty.

After being informed that TJ would always likely need a wheelchair, Travis and I began discussing what we were going to do about our living situation at home. Our house in its present configuration would never work. Since Travis was in Rochester with TJ, I went home for a couple of days to attend my daughter Chandler's baby shower. As I was looking out the window at our backyard, a thought came to me. *Why can't we just build a bedroom and bathroom for TJ on the back of our house?* I called my dad, who was a carpenter, and asked him if it was possible to build a room addition and what it would cost. He said he would do some checking and get back to me. When I arrived back in Rochester, I told Travis and TJ my thoughts. Travis thought it might work, and TJ was very excited about the idea. If we built TJ a room, we wouldn't have the added stress of moving to another home, also probably in need of modification, on top of all the other devastating changes in our lives.

Doctors felt TJ needed cognitive testing. The afternoon of testing, I wasn't allowed in the room because they didn't want me sending hand signals to TJ. (I don't know why they didn't trust me.) TJ's nurse was in the room while the test was being administered and later said that TJ was able to answer some questions that even *he* didn't know the answer to. The nurse said the test giver was shocked at how cognitively intact TJ was. One would assume from TJ's appearance that he had cognitive deficits because generally, when someone experiences as many motor issues as TJ did, they almost always display cognitive impairment as well. However, he still seemed to be the same TJ he always was. The only difference I could see in him was that at times he had trouble controlling his emotions and impulsivity. Otherwise, he communicated and responded to questions appropriately and understood everything that was going on around him. TJ was truly unusual in many ways.

We learned that TJ was eligible for the Make-A-Wish program. This program grants wishes to children who have been diagnosed with life-threatening medical conditions. We told him to be thinking about how he wanted to use his wish. The social worker said to think big because the sky was the limit. After telling him about places other kids had chosen, like deep sea water fishing off the coast of a Caribbean island or a trip to Hawaii or Europe, we were excited to see what TJ would choose. After thinking for a bit, he finger-spelled that he wanted to go to China. *Really? China?* I thought. I was surprised by his choice. Since I had already begun imagining myself lying on a beach in Tahiti, I was a little disappointed, although I kept it to myself. He had two years to use his wish, so we decided to wait until he was healthier and better able to travel.

TJ was making small strides in rehab, but four weeks after admission, the dystonia flared up again. This time the dystonia caused his head to tilt backward, which then hindered his ability to breathe causing his respiratory rate to rise to dangerously high levels. I began to recognize the foreboding feelings of anxiety and panic.

The emergency response team was called to rehab to assist TJ. While I was standing outside of his room, I looked down the hallway to my left and saw a large group of medical staff walking toward me with Dr. Alvarez leading the pack. The cavalry was coming, and it was a beautiful sight! I was relieved to see their familiar faces. I spoke to Dr. Alvarez about TJ's present condition and felt comforted by her caring eyes and her gentle, patient demeanor.

While the emergency response team assisted TJ, the nurse commented, "You know everyone in this hospital."

"That's what happens when you've been here forever and spent time on every floor," I replied.

After troubleshooting, the decision was made to move TJ to the PICU where they pumped a "boatload" of medications into his blood stream that were soon able to calm his muscle spasms. The neurologists were perplexed as to why the muscle-contraction episode occurred because the dystonia should have been well controlled with the medications he was receiving. After much discussion, they decided the flare-up may have been the result of tapering one of his medications, so they increased the medication slightly and slowed the tapering schedule. After three days in the PICU, he was moved to the general pediatric floor.

During morning rounds, Dr. Davis told us that she was requesting two more weeks of rehab from the insurance company but was doubtful they would allow it. I prayed that they would let us finish but felt in my spirit that TJ would not be allowed back into rehab. Dr. Davis again admitted that doctors were very confused by TJ's symptoms. When I asked her what they were confused about, she said they didn't know where the uncontrolled movements were coming from. I was very relieved to hear that, as a resident had earlier told me that post-pump dystonia didn't make sense.

Friends and family had begun to suggest that I was in denial about TJ's brain injury. No one had seen how well he was doing in rehab for that short period of time before he was discharged to home and the twisting started. When I told them that he had been walking well, they looked at me like I was out of touch with reality. I asked Dr. Davis if she thought I was in denial.

"No, because we don't know what's wrong with him," she admitted. "Generally, when an insult to the brain happens, the patient is at baseline and gradually improves. For TJ, the insult happened, he awoke from surgery at his baseline, but declined rapidly. Several months later, he began to improve, only to decline again. It's unusual."

I told her I felt like there was an important piece of information missing that was preventing the doctors from being able to solve the puzzle. She agreed that something was missing. Dr. Davis's reassurance gave me peace. She cared about us and I really liked her.

Travis and Aiden had gone back to Des Moines, and I was alone again. Tired and weary, I wondered if this was ever going to end. One snowy, cold morning, I pulled the enormous black coat out of the closet that my friend Diane had graciously given me. As I put on the coat, my thoughts drifted back to the conversation I'd had the day before with the waitress at Café Presto, a restaurant across the street from the hospital, where I ate lunch frequently. After I ordered, the waitress had commented, "You've been here a *really* long time." I was surprised that she'd noticed.

Anxious to get to the hospital, I hurriedly pulled the zipper. The coat was ankle-length and had a huge, oversized hood that I had to hold up with my hands or it would flop over my face so I couldn't see. I took one last look in the mirror before leaving my room for the day. The coat was too big on me, and I decided that I looked ridiculous. However, since Minnesota winters are notoriously frigid, I didn't care one bit. I wanted to be warm.

I started making my way up the snow-covered sidewalk to the hospital. The snow was gently falling. Even though traffic was heavy that morning as people were making their morning commute, it was much quieter than usual. There was a stillness in the air and everything appeared white and beautiful.

I'd been holding up my hood with my hands as I walked along, but my arms were growing weary, so I decided to let go of the hood. Because I couldn't see, I resolved to keep my head down and watch my feet as I trudged along.

I could hear the snow crunching under my feet as I walked, and my legs felt heavier with each new step. I had just woken up but still felt very tired—and I was afraid. My mind was racing with thoughts. *What if TJ never improves? How are we going to afford an accessible van and an addition to our home? What are we going to do?*

As I kept walking, for one fleeting second, when I was in my hour of need, I felt Jesus' presence walking in step beside me. I caught my breath and abruptly stopped walking. I threw off my hood and looked beside me, but there was no one there. I was stunned. I had never had that happen before. I cried out loud, "Jesus, please stay. Please don't go." But the encounter was over. The feeling was gone. I turned and continued my walk to the hospital—but with a little lighter step because I knew that Jesus had eyes on me. I was not alone.

CaringBridge

December 15, 2013
Written by Kelly

TJ has had a quiet weekend. He's overly medicated and is very tired and lethargic. We're praying they'll get his meds adjusted so he has more energy. Travis, Chandler, Julian, and Aiden were here this weekend. Chandler is pregnant and thought she was going into labor, so she went to the ER here at St. Mary's. It ended up being a false alarm. We were hoping she would have the baby here so I could be present for the delivery, but that wasn't God's plan.

Saturday evening, I was in TJ's room, and I read a devotional about prayer. The devotional said that when we pray, we should first pray for the things that are on God's heart before we pray for ourselves. The devotional said that if we ever want to experience the Lord's power in our lives, we must put our needs last.

I was brokenhearted when I read it because I was very aware of the fact that over the last several months, I'd become self-absorbed with my son's pain and my pain and I have put little thought into anyone else's troubles or pain. I thought about all the people who have been praying for us and that I needed to be doing the same for others.

As I went down the elevator to the first floor, with tears in my eyes, I told God I would make some changes. As I was walking toward the door, a woman walked by me, and I could tell she was not okay. I felt the Lord nudge me to stop her. I stopped and turned around and looked at her. Then feeling awkward and that maybe she didn't want to be bothered, I turned back around and headed for the door.

At that moment, I remembered what I had just told God, so I abruptly stopped, turned around, and ran after her. I asked if she was okay. She had tears running down her face and said no. I asked her if there was anything I could help her with, and she said no. I then asked her what was wrong, and the floodgates opened as she told me her twelve-year-old son River was in a car accident. They had been hit by a truck and the right side of River's head had been hit hard. He was in PICU, and they told her that if he lived, he was going to be a vegetable. We hugged each other and cried, and I shared our story about TJ. I asked her if I could share River's story on TJ's CaringBridge so our prayer warriors could pray for him as well. She said yes, so I am asking everyone to please pray for River and for his precious family. They have a room at RMH, so I am hoping to see her frequently and will keep you updated.

Insurance denied TJ's admission for the two additional weeks doctors had requested in rehab. They said he wasn't making enough progress and wanted him to go to a brain injury rehab facility instead because it was far less expensive. They estimated that he would be there approximately sixty days. Travis and I expected this decision and had prepared ourselves for it. We were grateful that TJ had someplace else to go while we figured out our long-term plans. TJ, however, was not happy about it at all. He didn't want to go to another facility. When I tried to convince him that we were in a pickle and this was the best option right now, he pointed to the door. I had been banished from his room for the rest of the day, so I spent the afternoon doing laundry and twiddling my thumbs at Ronald McDonald House.

We spent the remainder of TJ's hospitalization on the general pediatric floor. Doctors were working to stabilize his medications before discharge. Even though I was thankful that he had a place to go, I had mixed feelings about leaving Mayo Clinic. On one hand, I was looking forward to being home again, surrounded by our friends and family, but on the other hand, I wanted to stay longer where I knew TJ was well cared for by doctors and staff who knew him best. I tried convincing one of the doctors to keep us longer, at least until he was off one of his medications, but to no avail.

I had decorated TJ's room for Christmas and made plans regarding how we would spend Christmas Day. When I confided to the chaplain that I was afraid TJ would be discharged before Christmas, she said, "Kelly, most people want to go home *before* Christmas." Under normal circumstances, I probably would have felt the same way, but nothing about our lives was normal anymore. As you can imagine, I was relieved when we got word that TJ would be discharged the day *after* Christmas.

Christmas morning, Travis, Aiden, and I went to the hospital to open presents with TJ. In the early afternoon, we ate Christmas dinner at Ronald McDonald House. Since TJ had been admitted to the hospital, he was unable to get a pass out, so we spent the afternoon in his room watching movies and getting packed up for the next chapter of our lives. A medical transport was leaving at 9 A.M. the following morning to drive TJ to the brain injury rehab facility that was only a half-hour away from our home. It was December 26, 2013, eight months after heart surgery.

CHAPTER 15

THE OWL

Many years prior to TJ's heart surgery, I read a story about a Christian woman who loved cardinals. At the end of the woman's life, a cardinal perched outside her window as she lay dying. The story encouraged the reader to choose an animal that is not commonly seen. In the future, whenever that animal crossed the reader's path, it was a reminder that God was nearby. So, I chose an owl, and throughout my adult years, whenever I saw an owl, I was reminded that God was very near.

When I walked into the brain injury rehab facility, the first thing I saw was a picture of an owl. I felt God's loving arms around me and was reassured that we were in the right place. We met with the staff upon our arrival and were directed to TJ's new room. It was very small but provided him with everything he needed. Immediately after walking into his room, I noticed a calendar with a picture of China, but it was open to the wrong month. China was the trip destination

TJ chose for his wish from Make-A-Wish. I once again felt the hand of God guiding us.

Psalm 34:18 says, "The Lord is close to the brokenhearted and saves those who are crushed in spirit." I knew such things were not mere coincidences but rather felt they were strategically-placed love notes from God, reassuring me that I was not alone.

Since TJ's brain injury, I had a more intimate relationship with the Lord than I had ever known. I searched for signs of His presence daily. Several times after thinking of someone I hadn't spoken to in a while, I would receive a text message from that person. I believed those incidents were God's way of soothing a mother's broken heart and reminding me of His abiding love for me.

Over the next few days, TJ had several visitors. Now that we were closer to home, we were hoping he would have more guests to encourage him, pray with him, and love him. A few teens had decorated his room and were planning on coming twice a month to have Bible studies with him. Visitors were just what he needed to encourage him and keep him moving forward.

TJ's dystonia was controlled, but the medications used to treat it made him very weak. He couldn't muster the strength to do much of anything. He couldn't even roll over in bed by himself anymore. I was perplexed and concerned about it. Just three months earlier, he was almost walking by himself, but now he was lying helpless in a bed.

It had been eight months since it all began. Travis and I were exhausted, and there was simply no end in sight. We prayed constantly for healing, wisdom, and guidance. Every moment away from TJ was spent thinking about what we could do to help him or where we could take him to get answers. When we were with TJ, we searched for any sign of improvement in his condition, no matter how small, to give us hope and keep us going.

One afternoon while TJ's nurse was present, TJ began coughing. I asked him if he needed to be suctioned. He tapped his feet for "yes," so I pulled out the suction catheters, attached them to the tubes, and began suctioning his trach. After finishing, I looked up, and the nurse was staring at me wide-eyed.

"What's wrong?" I asked. "Did I do something wrong?"

"No, I've just never had a family member do that before."

I thought her response was interesting. I immediately recalled our Mayo PICU days when I was forced to learn TJ's healthcare regimen. That was the first time I realized that the training I received at Mayo was far more thorough than what parents or caregivers usually receive from other hospitals.

I spent every day and night with TJ for the first week and a half at the new facility. Because of his inability to communicate, it was terrifying to imagine leaving him alone. In order to utilize time in between therapies and get TJ out of his room, I pushed him in his wheelchair up and down the facility halls. One afternoon, we came to the end of a hall, and as I was making a U-turn, I looked down at him sitting in his wheelchair. Because TJ could not follow a moving object visually, his pupils had slid to the corners of his eyes. Seeing his eyes in this position, along with the rest of his broken body, broke my heart. I became overwhelmed with sadness and felt physically sick to my stomach. I desperately wanted my son back.

After being given time to settle into a routine, the social worker met with me and encouraged me to think about placing TJ in a group home after he was discharged from the facility. She said I needed to get him on the list quickly because the wait was long. Because of TJ's extensive medical problems, there weren't many group homes available to him. The group home she suggested was three hours away. I told her I didn't want him in a group home and wanted him to come home because he was still a child. Coldly, she replied, "Well, he would have been leaving for college soon anyway." It was obvious by her lack of empathy that she disagreed with my decision. Leaving home for college was far different than leaving home with a severe brain injury. He was my child and I loved him. He had lost almost everything, and I wanted to make what was left of his life as comfortable as possible.

The woman continued, "I think he's going to be far too much for you to take care of at home."

"I understand that," I explained, "but TJ was doing better a few months ago. I'm hoping to get him back to that point."

She gave me a skeptical look, like she thought I was in denial, so I pulled out my phone and showed her a video of TJ walking in the courtyard at Mayo just three months earlier. "They can't explain what happened to him," I added.

Changing her tune, she said, "Ohh—then you guys need some answers."

"Yes! Yes! That's exactly what we need!" I exclaimed.

She went on to tell me that I needed to be taking care of myself and that TJ needed to become more independent. She suggested that rather than spending all my time with him, I should limit my visits to three days a week and come for either a few hours in the morning or a few hours in the afternoon. I wondered if she thought I was a helicopter mother with an unhealthy attachment to my son. Even though it may have looked that way, that wasn't the case. Our mother-son relationship was healthy before his heart surgery. Sure, he had begun to pull away from me and seek independence to start his own life, and I had allowed him that freedom. But now he was sick, totally dependent on help, and couldn't even communicate. Medical workers, no matter their training or education, didn't know or love him like I did. We'd already been victimized by their indifference. I was afraid that if I didn't stay close, TJ wouldn't receive the care he needed.

Since I previously heard wonderful things about this facility and hadn't seen anything negative, I felt comfortable, believing that TJ would be well cared for. I hesitantly agreed to limit the time I spent with him so he could become more independent. Half of me felt anxious about leaving him alone in someone else's care, but the other half felt relieved that I'd been given permission to rest. I'd been praying for rest for months. Now God had granted me rest as well as more time to spend with Aiden, who had been bounced around for months. I was happy that I could now focus on him and restore some normalcy to his routine.

TJ's therapy routine was much like his therapy at Mayo. His speech therapist began to teach him to use a loaner device that assisted communication. The device scanned the alphabet, and he squeezed a switch in his hand to select the letters he wanted. Upon first demonstrating his new device to me, his therapist asked him to spell his name. In response he typed "Krabby" because the day before I had been calling him "Crabby" all day. He used the letter "K" instead of a "C" because he missed the "C" when it was scanning. The scanning was a very slow process, but we hoped that in time, as he became more familiar with the device, spelling words would get faster.

February 5, 2014

CaringBridge
Written by Whitney (TJ's sister)

Hi Guys! This is TJ's favorite sister Whitney. TJ is starting to get comfortable again after the changes they made with his medications, and they'll start tapering him again pretty soon, but going much slower, so that TJ doesn't get too uncomfortable. I visit TJ every Saturday morning for a few hours. We had a lot of fun this past Saturday. We played the Wii (bowling) and he beat me.

I did an hour of relaxation with him. I know I sounded like such a weirdo because I'm not a therapist, but he was uncomfortable. I know he always responds well to his music therapy, so I took a shot at it, and he actually opened his mouth and was swallowing. Then he choked, was biting down on his lip, and his jaw was clamped shut so his lip was stuck between his teeth. I retired from relaxation therapy that day, but he really *is* making progress and it's good for him to feel that way.

I think he feels discouraged because it feels like it's going very slow or he makes huge progress then gets sick and has to start all over. I imagine it is so frustrating for him! We know that after he gets off these meds, he'll make huge progress. TJ's communication device will be shipped tomorrow, so that's going to be very, very nice. It will be great for him to be able to communicate and not only answer yes or no questions. This is a trial run with the device, and if it turns out to be good for him, we can get it set up so that he can text as well! I think he'll love being able to text with his friends and feel a little more connected. We know that he really misses his friends, school, and just feeling like a normal seventeen-year-old. It really lifts his spirits to have visitors, so feel free to stop by for a bit and hang out!

During that time, there was another high school senior at the facility. She had a prom coming up at her high school, so the facility held a practice prom for her. TJ invited his youth group to the practice prom. He had a great time at the dance and actually stole the show. He was in a heavy-duty walker with his therapists, but while in the center of the dance floor, he started doing his dance moves. The people at the dance surrounded him. Everyone was cheering and clapping for him. I began to cry. Part of me was crying because I was happy that he was getting to be a teenager again, while my other half wept because his previous life was a thing of the past. TJ cried all day the following day and gave me a thumbs-up when I asked him if he missed being a kid and hanging out with his friends.

I had been reading one of Max Lucado's books titled *You'll Get Through This* to TJ. The book told the story of Joseph, my favorite Old Testament story. While reading it, we learned that God chose TJ, that he was in training, and that God had a higher purpose for his life. (Lucado 2013)

For a short period of time, because TJ was angry with God about his situation, he didn't want to listen to books, the Bible, or devotionals. Once, when I began reading to him from a devotional, the brakes on his wheelchair weren't on, so he used his legs to push himself out into the hall in an attempt to escape listening to me read. I didn't let that deter me though and chased him down the hall reading the devotional the entire time I was following him. Eventually his anger wore off and he began to listen again.

During the first few weeks of rehab, he was in and out of the hospital a few times with pneumonia and abdominal pain. Because of communication problems, we never left him alone when he was in the hospital, since the staff was unfamiliar with his medical challenges. I woke up early one morning. TJ was still asleep, so I walked down to the coffee station, poured myself a cup of coffee, and then went back to a small waiting area at the end of his hall. I sat on a narrow couch facing a large window and watched the cars driving by on the freeway while the snow was gently falling. It was cold and gloomy outside, much like the way I was feeling inside.

As I stared out the window, I wondered how I would live with so much pain in my heart. A few days earlier, our attorney had used the term "catastrophic" to describe TJ's injury. The description was devastating. *What's going to happen to my son?* I asked myself. It was March, and in April we would hit the one-year anniversary of the offending surgery. The reality that this was TJ's life now was beginning to set in. Although I was still desperately hoping to get him back to the way he was when he left Mayo the first time, I had a nagging feeling that it wasn't going to happen. I didn't know how to live that way. If I stopped hoping and searching, then I feared I would become severely depressed, completely shut down, and live in a dark hole. The pain of seeing him trapped in his broken body was unbearable. He wasn't really living—and neither was I. We were trapped in a strange limbo between life and death.

The pharmacist at the hospital was concerned about the amount of medication TJ was on and felt it might be depressing his central nervous system (CNS). TJ was unable to move his left arm, which was also surprisingly cold. He was lethargic and weak, so she sent a new tapering schedule of medications back to the facility. I was relieved at the prospect of tapering because I felt he was over-medicated but was also anxious at the same time because tapering medications often made the dystonia flare.

Although TJ would have loved to visit China, he wanted to come home even more, so Travis and I suggested that he change his wish to a new handicap-accessible bedroom and bathroom at home. We told him that in a few years, when he was healthier, perhaps we could go to China. TJ liked the idea, so we relayed the news to Make-A-Wish. They agreed to grant TJ's wish and informed us that we would need to build it and they would take care of all the finishing touches, like flooring, lighting, and furniture.

Travis planned to perform most of the work on the new build himself. Since he had been around construction most of his adult life, he could do almost anything. My dad scheduled an appointment with an architect who drew up plans. Although we had no idea how we were going to pay for it, we prayed and knew God would somehow provide.

Not long after that, I received a call from TJ's former high school, Valley High. They told me the student government was hosting their second annual Tiger Run/Walk 5K to benefit TJ. I was surprised at the unexpected news and overwhelmed with gratitude at the support shown by the students and faculty. We were very excited and made plans to use the funds for the new addition. The school had no clue about our financial needs, but God did and used them to answer our prayers.

Late in April, TJ had follow-up appointments at Mayo. In between appointments, we sat down in a waiting room in the Gondola Building. I sat in a seat under the windows with TJ directly across from me. From where he sat, he could see down the hallway, but I could not. As we waited, I saw him looking intently down the hall, and then his eyes lit up. I assumed that someone he knew from the medical staff was walking toward him but couldn't see who it was. All of a sudden, I saw Janet and Tom, the mother and son who had become such dear friends on previous stays in the PICU. What a pleasant surprise that was! Neither of us knew the other had appointments that day in Rochester. We just "happened" to be there on the same day, at the same time, and in the same building. Because I don't believe in coincidences, I felt it was the love of God allowing two old buddies to see each other one more time. We visited for a while and were sad when it was time to tell our friends goodbye and go to our next appointment. It was the last time TJ ever saw Tom.

April 30, 2014

CaringBridge
Written by Kelly

TJ has been training for the upcoming 5K and is enjoying every minute of it. Last week while I was visiting, he went off to physical therapy, and I stayed in his room to catch up on returning phone calls. A while later I began to hear a lot of noise coming down the hallway outside his room, so I poked my head out to see what all the commotion was about. I was surprised to see my son riding a recumbent bike down the hallway with his therapists running beside him. What a wonderful site that was! TJ's sister Whitney is going to push him in the recumbent bike for the 5K. He's able to pedal, so that should make the job a little easier on big sis. Normally he has trouble holding his head up, and I am always on his case about it. We have noticed when he is on the bike, however, he holds it up better. Hmm—so, after seeing that, I told him he was busted and that we're all on to him. Hearing that, he started laughing.

Next Wednesday, May 7, news Channel 13 is interviewing Whitney and me and shooting some video of TJ while he is in therapy as a preview to the 5K run. I'm not sure when it's going to air, but I'll keep you all updated.

TJ has finally received his communication device. We are having a training session tomorrow morning. We're looking forward to hopefully getting text messaging and email loaded onto it soon. The other day his speech therapist asked him if he had anything pressing he needed to say or ask the nurses. Using his device, he typed, "Does Kendra (his occupational therapist) wear colored contacts?" I guess that's a pretty pressing question if you've been wondering about it for a while!

TJ's 5K story made the front page of the local newspaper and was very well received by the community. We were excited to learn that Iowa native, Kyle Korver, NBA player for the Atlanta Hawks at the time, heard about TJ's story and donated autographed items for auction.

The 5K race went very well. It was a beautiful, sunny day and there was an amazing turnout. The only glitch in the day was that the suction machine wasn't working. Generally, TJ's trach had to be suctioned every fifteen to thirty minutes. That day we were there for 2½ hours, and he didn't need suctioning once. God sure saved the day and TJ had a fantastic time. We kept asking him if he was ready to leave, and every time, he shook his head "no." We were down to twenty people left in the parking lot, but he still didn't want to leave. We finally coaxed him into packing up and going back to the facility. He enjoyed the race so much that we planned to find more races for Whitney and him to run in. In total, Valley High School raised $10,000 that we put toward his new room.

While TJ was at the facility, Travis and I were invited to a small group Bible study with our old Bible study group. It had been a very long time since we had attended church or a small group study. When we arrived, we were happy to see everyone again. As usual, we visited for a while and then went to the dining room to eat dinner together. After dinner, everyone sat around the table for a while and visited, but I was having a hard time joining the conversation. Although there was nothing wrong with the topic under discussion, I felt as if none of it mattered anymore in light of TJ's enormous challenges. It was clear that my perspective had dramatically changed. I had a very sick child, and my entire focus was on that, leaving room for nothing unnecessary. I wasn't the same person anymore. I was traumatized and heartbroken and realized that no one really understood what I was going through. Life wasn't going to pick back up where it left off the year before. I finally got up and went to the kitchen to be alone and escape the chatter. When I walked through the doorway, I saw that Travis was already sitting at the kitchen table by himself, staring out the window, so I sat down across from him. At that point, I finally understood exactly what Janet meant when she said she had trouble integrating back into society after a long hospitalization. It took several more years of adjustment before I felt like I could participate in a group without feeling like I was on the outside looking in.

Believers within TJ's social group came a couple of times to have Bible studies with TJ at the facility, but then they stopped coming. Even though we tried to prepare them for what they would see, they were unnerved by TJ's condition and a facility full of people with brain injuries. I didn't expect them to hold group Bible studies at the facility on a regular basis but had hoped that occasionally someone would come to encourage TJ, read God's Word, and pray with him. I'm sure it was incredibly difficult for them to work up the courage to step into our world. It had taken me months to adjust to our new roles, but just as quickly as they stepped in, they stepped right back out again. I wish I had been stronger, but this was agonizingly painful for us. We were at the lowest point of our lives, and when TJ needed support the most, the room was empty.

I began to feel like TJ was an unclean, unwanted leper pushed outside the city limits. I'd seen mothers distraught when their child had a falling out with *one* friend, but TJ was losing most of his friends at the same time. The pain was unbearable. I believe this was Satan's attempt to isolate us, to make us feel abandoned, to distract our focus from Jesus, and to convince us that we were alone and no one cares.

During this time, I struggled with anger and depression, but in hindsight, I wish I'd trusted God more. In time, I realized that it was God who wanted us to be alone because He was doing a work in us. He was showing His tender, loving mercy toward us; providing for us; making us totally dependent upon Him; and building our faith. He was also cutting away the sin in our lives so He could use us in even greater ways. He loved us too much to let us stay the way we were.

Even though we were much more isolated than we had ever been, we still had some wonderful friends who consistently visited. These friends had experienced tragedy themselves and understood our needs. They cried with me, encouraged me with God's Word, drank lots of coffee, and shared lots of lunches. I appreciated my friends. They were the bright, shining light in the midst of some very dark days. I specifically remember the Woolman family who often visited TJ at the facility. They would spend time reading aloud *Tom Sawyer* by Mark Twain, with the dad even adding sound effects to some of the scenes. There was much laughter when this family was around, and TJ eagerly looked forward to their visits.

While at the facility one afternoon, I heard about an issue TJ had with one of the workers. TJ was in the shower, and sometimes while showering, he became very upset. This was one of those days. The CNA was tired of him being upset and called him derogatory names. TJ reported the incident to his therapist, leading to the assistant being removed from his wing of the facility. Although I wasn't happy about the incident, I was relieved that it had been verbal and not physical abuse. Even so, I knew from that time on, I dared not leave him alone anymore. Against the social worker's recommendation, I resumed my routine of visiting all day every day.

Most of the nurses at the facility were professional and really cared about TJ, but sometimes it was a struggle getting them to understand the urgency of TJ's respiratory needs. Over time, I concluded that our clashes with staff were likely because TJ's respiratory needs were outside the norm. I once heard TJ's speech therapist at Mayo say she thought TJ's left vocal cord paralysis was causing the excessive secretion problems. Through trial and error, the nurses would eventually grasp TJ's unique respiratory needs, but it was an anxiety-ridden process for me. Although the nursing staff was good, some of the CNA staff was not. We had a few favorites, but most seemed to lack compassion for the clients with brain injuries.

The facility's initial plan was to discharge TJ after sixty days of treatment. However, doctors were tapering TJ's medication which resulted in severe twisting. Dr. Howell informed the facility that there was no place for a patient like TJ to go, so the facility agreed to keep him longer.

The twisting motions resulting from the medication tapering went on for months and were severe. It seemed like it was never going to end. When he was twisting, his hands became tight, making hand squeezing or signing to communicate impossible. We went back to the old method of going through the alphabet, using his foot to tap for the letter he wanted, but sometimes he couldn't stop tapping his feet. Communication was terribly frustrating. He used his communication device sometimes, but we hated it. It was extremely slow, and sometimes we just wanted to throw it through the window. We were told that it had improved and eased communication issues for others and were disappointed by its failure to meet TJ's needs.

Travis and I began to notice that when we stopped tapering medications, after a couple of weeks, the twisting would improve greatly. To us, TJ seemed to be hypersensitive to *all* medications. Something about the way his body processed medications didn't seem right. We were having a hard time getting medical staff to listen to us when we tried to report that something was wrong. As that process grew more difficult, Travis and I actually became obsessed with TJ's medications.

Some nights, when TJ was having a very hard night and the twisting was severe, TJ's nurse would ask me to come into the facility because she had another patient who was not doing well and she couldn't adequately care for them all. So, I would drive in and care for TJ. His bed was low, practically on the floor, to prevent him from falling out. I would lie on the floor for hours next to his bed massaging the muscles in his arms and shoulders until he finally fell asleep. It reminded me of when he was a toddler and I lay next to him caressing his face until he drifted off to sleep.

Sometimes, because TJ was so miserable, I would try to get the staff to stop tapering the meds, or at least take a break, but the head nurse told me that he couldn't live on that amount of medication, so the tapering would continue. Other times I wanted him off the medications because I was worried about the CNS depression and wanted him to be more mobile. His suffering was so severe that I would get anxious and feel sick to my stomach on the drive to the facility. Many nurses were disturbed by TJ's suffering. They told me they felt sorry for TJ and that I had to watch my darling son go through it.

During that time, TJ also contracted a severe case of MRSA—a skin infection caused by staph bacteria that allowed large, painful boils to develop all over his trunk and face. It was then that I began to realize that TJ's life was a modern-day story of Job.

The fear from the PICU days had, by now, morphed into sadness. After leaving the facility at night, the road I drove home was dark and wooded. Some nights I would have thoughts of running my car into a tree. I just wanted the emotional and mental pain to end. I clung to the verse Jeremiah 29:11, "'For I know the plans I have for you,' declares the Lord, 'plans to prosper you and not to harm you, plans to give you hope and a future.'" I continued to believe that God still had a plan for TJ's life and would use him greatly, and give him hope and a future.

A friend casually told me that TJ's life had been destroyed, but I wouldn't allow myself to believe that. If I started believing that his life was worthless, despair and hopelessness would set in, and I wouldn't be able to survive it. I had to trust God and believe that his life still had value and purpose and that God would use TJ's suffering for his good and God's glory.

One afternoon, TJ finger-spelled to me, "I can't stand this place."

My heart sank. I knew he was unhappy, but at the time our options were limited. There was no place else for him to go. Other facilities were probably worse than his current situation. Our house was a construction zone, and the showers were upstairs. There was no way I could care for him at home until the new addition was complete.

"I'm so sorry, Teej. I know you hate it here and want to come home, but the house is torn up and there's no other place for you to go. We're working hard on your room. It will be done soon. Just hold on, buddy, we're trying."

Upon waking, the first thing I did every morning was call the facility to check on him. One morning when I called, they said he was struggling with respiratory issues. Days earlier, I'd sensed that a respiratory infection was coming on, and I felt that he needed to be hospitalized. Staff always pushed back about transporting him to the hospital and said they would keep an eye on it. When I called and they said he wasn't doing well, I asked them if he could go to the hospital. They finally agreed and said they would call an ambulance. I made arrangements to meet them at the ER.

When I arrived, I stood in the hallway outside of TJ's ER room. The EMT was pacing back and forth in the hallway and was very worked up. He poked his head in the doorway, and I overheard him tell the doctor that TJ was almost in respiratory failure in the ambulance.

I frowned. "What?!"

The EMT then said to me, "I've transported TJ a few times in the past, and this time I was really worried that I would lose him."

I was very upset because the staff at the rehab facility clearly wasn't taking seriously his respiratory needs. In light of what I'd just learned, I urged the facility to pay more attention to TJ's lungs and told them that the EMT felt his life actually hung in the balance. That seemed to grab their attention, and they assured me that they would hold staff meetings and make his respiratory needs a top priority. Even so, I felt incredibly guilty that I hadn't insisted on him being taken to the ER days earlier.

My mom and stepdad Tom hosted a dinner and silent auction to raise more money to complete the room addition. They were able to raise $5,000 and also loaned us some money. We were very grateful for their help and were slowly raising the money we needed to build his room.

In mid-June we started bringing TJ home on the weekends. We would camp out in the family room. This schedule continued for several months with TJ spending his weekdays at the facility in rehab, tapering medications, twisting, and coming home on weekends.

November 21, 2014

CaringBridge
Written by Kelly

TJ's discharge date is fast approaching. His medical equipment will be delivered on Monday. His discharge party from the facility is Wednesday, and then right after that, we take him home. It sounds like everything in his room will be done on Wednesday except the floor, so we will be camping out in the family room for a bit until the floor gets done the following week.

Last night as I was driving TJ back to the facility, I was having memories of what he used to be like, and I started crying. We have our handicap van now, and he sits in his wheelchair right behind me. As I was crying, I felt TJ's hand come up over my shoulder and then grab my hand. We held hands all the way back to the facility. I have lost a lot but I have gained, too. How many mothers get to hold hands with their eighteen-year-old sons? His body is broken and beat up, but he still comforts me. He is so sweet. I have always known since he was little, that he was special.

While we were at Mayo, I asked everyone to pray for Tom, whose family we met while Tom and TJ were in PICU at Mayo, until they were both discharged from rehab in September. They were war buddies. They both fought hard to live. Janet, Tom's mother, and I became very close and have stayed in touch since their discharge. Tom has had a great year since leaving Mayo last fall, but recently they've learned that his leukemia is back and they are unable to treat it. He's not going to make it. TJ and I are both heartbroken. We made plans to drive to Wisconsin to see them once TJ improves. Tonight, TJ spelled to me, "I need to go see my boy."

Please pray for that sweet family. They've been through so much.

A month before TJ's discharge from the facility, he was so miserable that in order to solve the problem, I began bringing him home Tuesday and Thursday afternoons right after therapy until bedtime, and then Friday afternoon through Sunday until bedtime. Mondays and Wednesdays, I stayed with him at the facility all day. Because of his inability to communicate, I concluded that he was just sick of being there, so I thought coming home even more would help him get through the last little bit of remaining time. All he really had to do was sleep there, shower, go to therapy, and then he was home or I was with him. But he still wasn't happy about it.

One Sunday evening, as I was returning TJ to the facility, one of the CNAs came out to the van to help me bring in all of TJ's equipment. When we walked back into TJ's room, the man turned on TJ's shower. I heard TJ whimper. It was a noise I had never heard him make before, and it got my attention. After the man left the room to go back out to the van, I quietly asked TJ if something had happened to him. TJ stared at the floor for a while and then slowly moved his feet back and forth for "no." I was perplexed but relieved and went back to putting his things away.

The much-anticipated discharge day finally arrived. While the staff was in TJ's room preparing him to go home, I stood in the hall with one of the nurses going over discharge instructions and double-checking supply lists and equipment.

"TJ is a lot to take care of," the nurse commented. "I've been concerned that his care would be too much for you, but you really do a good job taking care of him."

"Thank you," I said, surprised by the compliment. "It's because Mayo insisted that I learn. I didn't want to learn and wanted our lives to go back to the way they were," I confessed. "But they wouldn't let me off the hook."

"Well, Kelly, your lives will never be that way again," she said, with a look of disbelief on her face that I would even think that our lives could go back to the way they were.

Her words stung like a slap in the face. I felt the old, familiar, sickening churning in my stomach. Any mother would want her son restored to health. Coming to a place of acceptance was a process that took time. I was already in a lot of pain, and the additional weight of her careless comment felt like more than I could bear. In an attempt to fight off the hopeless and discouraging feelings her words raised in me, I reminded myself, *Our lives may never be the same again, but it doesn't mean they have to be bad.*

It was tradition at the rehab facility to throw every patient a goodbye party at discharge, but TJ refused his party. The local news was planning on filming TJ's special day, but he continued to refuse and couldn't wait to get out of there. I tried coaxing him, thinking he might regret it, but he was adamant about leaving quickly. So, I gave in to his wishes. TJ spent a total of eleven months in that facility. In hindsight, if I had known why he was so anxious to leave, I would've moved him home months earlier.

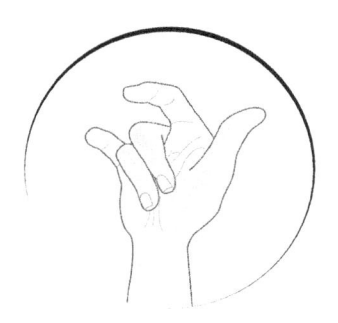

CHAPTER 16

A MAN REBORN

For TJ's revised Make-A-Wish request, he asked that his accessible bedroom and bathroom be decorated in an Iowa Hawkeye theme, so his bedroom was painted tan with a black and gold accent wall. A big, black Herky (University of Iowa's mascot) decal was placed high on the accent wall near the vaulted ceiling. The room had hardwood floors to make maneuvering his wheelchair easier, a medication cart, a hospital bed outfitted in a black Iowa Hawkeye comforter, a black entertainment center, a futon, a smart TV, and an outside door that led to a large patio. It was a dream room.

We were hopeful that this homecoming would be successful since we were better prepared and he had a space all his own on the ground floor to adequately accommodate his needs. Wells Blue Bunny funded TJ's bedroom addition and gave him a room reveal party shortly after he moved home with free ice cream for all those who stopped by. The local news aired a segment on TJ's homecoming. Many people in the community were fascinated by TJ's story. It was clear that he was becoming a local celebrity.

Shortly after arriving home, TJ had two hospitalizations, one for a staph infection caused by an enormous boil on his chin, the other for abdominal pain. By then, TJ was eighteen years old and no longer a pediatric patient, so these hospitalizations were spent on the adult floors. Other families had previously told me their transitions to the adult floors didn't go well. Thankfully, our transition was smooth, and TJ was well cared for. Unfortunately, we spent Christmas of 2014 in the hospital, but after his discharge, we settled into our new routine at home.

The routine of taking care of him at home was very demanding, but I was managing the stress of being a caregiver better than the first time he'd come home. Since I'd accepted the change in my lifestyle, I was better able to handle the demands of caregiving. In some ways, TJ living at home was less stressful. Now that we were in charge, we no longer spent time worrying whether he was getting adequate care.

February 3, 2015

CaringBridge
Written by Kelly

A couple of weeks ago, TJ's sister Chandler got married in our home. It was a special day, and I was surprised at how emotional TJ was about it. He sobbed and sobbed during the ceremony. Then afterward during pictures, he held his arms out while crying and hugged his sister. I looked around the room and everyone was wiping their eyes. It was very touching. I asked him if he was sad that the days of being kids together at home were over, and he cried even harder. I guess that hit the nail on the head. I couldn't help but think about how much he has changed. He has always been a sweet boy, but he was still a boy nonetheless. The old TJ would have been in the back of the room laughing and making fun of her.

Travis and I alternate nights sleeping in TJ's room. There's not a whole lot of sleeping that goes on when it's your night. One early morning at about 4 A.M., I was lying in bed thinking about this whole journey. Earlier that day, after talking to our attorney about TJ's situation, waves of hopelessness washed over me. I kept having thoughts about how tragic our situation was and kept asking myself, *How could this have happened? How can this ever be made right?* I was then filled with despair.

I've learned that when those thoughts creep in, I have to purposefully turn my thoughts to God's Word and focus on that instead. I will remind myself that He is in control, that anything that touches me/us comes through Him first, that there is a purpose in suffering, and that God has not forgotten us.

After wrestling with these thoughts for a while, I turned to my devotional, which began with 1 Kings 12:24, "This is my doing…" I stopped. God was speaking directly to me, and that was all the answer I needed.

Some people may think that things just randomly happen, that a loving God would never let something like this happen to one of his children. I, on the other hand, find comfort in knowing that every good and bad thing that comes into my life has been allowed by Him. The God of the universe who calls me the apple of his eye (Zech. 2:8) and tells me that I am precious and honored in His sight (Isa. 43:4) loves me and must certainly have a plan. It's my job to trust.

Initially upon his arrival home, we were still tapering medications and battling his painful muscle contractions. He started outpatient therapy three times a week. Marilyn, his new occupational therapist, suggested administering Botox shots to TJ's arms and shoulders to relax the muscles that were contracting. She said sometimes stroke patients can get into a cycle that they can't get out of and that Botox helps break the cycle. We made an appointment with a local physiatrist, a doctor who specializes in rehabilitation medicine, who administered Botox injections. The shots, coupled with intense therapy, changed the quality of his life immensely. Although the muscles in his arms and shoulders still contracted and his arms were frequently over his head, it was much less severe. He was once again able to start gaining muscle mass and wasn't in nearly as much pain.

Marilyn also told me about an occupational therapist from St. Ambrose College who installs environmental control systems for those with special needs. We decided to have the system installed in TJ's room. This system enabled him to change the channels and volume on the TV, turn the lights on and off, and sound an alarm to call us. The system consisted of a switch at the foot of TJ's bed that could be tapped in order to perform the various functions he desired. TJ was able to gain some independence as well as more control of his environment. We were thrilled with this positive change to his world.

Generally, when I slept in TJ's room, I used the TV as a night light with the volume turned down. One time, in the middle of the night, I heard the switch to TJ's environmental system click, click, click, and then the television shut off. The light from the TV had been driving him crazy the entire time I had been sleeping in his room, and I had no idea. In that instant, I received TJ's message loud and clear!

During TJ's years at home, we lived life the best we could. We often went to movies, high school basketball games, the mall, concerts, and baseball games. We tried to make life fun for him. Even though he had lost almost everything, he was still joyful. The joy of the Lord was his strength. He had changed drastically from the unforgiving, stubborn, young man he had once been and now forgave easily and quickly. Best of all, he loved me fiercely. If I was away from home for a short period of time, upon my return, he would immediately begin wailing and throw his arms around me, so happy to see me again.

I don't know how he kept his sense of humor after all he had been through, but he was always trying to make us laugh. One hot summer evening, he finger-spelled, "Mom, I'm two kinds of hot." I immediately burst out laughing and turned on the ceiling fan. I loved how he still thought of himself as a "hot" guy. He never let his loss of abilities define him.

Of course, life was still difficult for him. He was lonely and cried a lot. He tried to stay upbeat, but there were days when memories of the life he'd once known came rushing back and left him feeling depressed about his unknown future. It was difficult for me to watch him go through such grief. I cried almost every day as well. Despite TJ's sadness, his faith remained strong.

One day I became overwhelmed with grief and threw myself over him in his wheelchair, crying. "I'm so sorry this happened to you, TJ," I sobbed.

While looking at me intently, he finger-spelled, "Mom, you have to trust and have faith."

"I know, sweet boy," I replied. "I'm so sorry you have to go through this. It's not fair. I wish there was something I could do to help you. I love you, buddy."

"I love you," he signed.

Because he knew what it was like to suffer, he was very sensitive to the suffering of others. Many times, upon hearing of the hardship of others, even strangers, he would wail and sob over their situation. One dear friend of mine, Shelley, lost her son, Danny, in a car accident. Upon first seeing Shelley, with his lower lip stuck out, TJ threw his arm out to hug her. They held each other and cried together for a time.

Although TJ lost most of his former friends, Drake, a young man TJ had been friends with since he was a little boy, remained firmly present in his life. Even today, Drake's personality is very similar to TJ's—tender-hearted, gentle, and kind. Drake loved TJ and was heartbroken over his brain injury. I could see the pain in Drake's eyes as he watched TJ's suffering. Drake went away to college, but even so, he remained a faithful friend. Drake texted, regularly checked on TJ, and visited every time he came home. TJ loved Drake as well as Drake's brother Dynas, who also stayed in TJ's life and checked on him regularly. I was incredibly grateful for the friendship of these two young men.

Even though TJ couldn't talk, he and Drake figured out a way to spend time together. TJ loved watching Drake play Xbox. When TJ had gone as far in the game as his twisted hands would allow, he would then sign to me, asking if Drake could come over and continue his game. It was an activity that didn't require talking. They could just enjoy each other's company.

TJ also had many male cousins he had grown up with and was very close to: Layne, Wyatt, Logan, Seth, and Brandyn. They spent the night with TJ once in a while and entertained him by playing Xbox and their guitars. They would sometimes pick him up from his wheelchair and carry him around the house. During those times, TJ couldn't have been happier. After high school, four of the cousins went into the military but would regularly check on him. TJ loved hearing their military stories and seeing their new tattoos when they returned home on leave. He vicariously lived out his military dreams through his cousins.

Since coming home, I had begun praying about a church we could attend. We hadn't been to church in a couple of years. Although we watched it regularly on TV, we still needed fellowship with other Christians. One afternoon, my doorbell rang. I opened the door to see a pretty, blond-haired woman with a bouquet of flowers in her hand. I learned that her name was Beth and she was the coordinator of the Hand-in-Hand Ministry at Valley Evangelical Free Church. The Hand-in-Hand Ministry is a program designed to serve families of those with special needs. She told me she had heard about us and wanted to invite us to church. She explained that they would provide a buddy to teach TJ while Travis and I attended the service. I was overjoyed. It was an answer to prayer. I was thankful that even though TJ had a brain injury, somebody still cared enough to love him and teach him God's Word. We started attending church, and a man named Tom became TJ's buddy. A very close relationship developed between TJ and Tom. We were deeply grateful for Tom's servant heart.

Valley Church hosts Night to Shine, a prom for people with special needs sponsored by the Tim Tebow Foundation. When TJ first learned about the upcoming dance, initially, he did not want to attend. He hadn't adjusted to his new identity of being a person with special needs. I thought he would enjoy it, so I told him to give it a try because it might be fun and that if he didn't like it, then we would leave early. He finally agreed to go.

Parents are not allowed in the dance hall but can watch their child enjoy the evening on a monitor in another room. With tears rolling down my cheeks, I watched as TJ had a fabulous time. His buddy Tom got him out of his wheelchair so that he could dance standing up. He was surrounded by other grateful, happy people who were overjoyed to be attending an event where they were special guests of honor. They were crowned kings and queens of the prom and told that they are valuable and loved by Jesus. TJ stayed for the entire dance and spent the following day in bed because he was so sore from all of the activity. We were very thankful for Night to Shine.

In mid-August, I received word from Janet that TJ's PICU buddy, also named Tom, died on Sunday, August 9, 2015. We were heartbroken. TJ lay on the floor of our family room weeping. As I grieved Tom's death, I remembered how I felt when TJ began his downward spiral after leaving Mayo the first time and I learned that Tom was thriving. While I had been happy for Janet that Tom was improving, I had also felt a touch of jealousy that Tom was doing well and TJ was not. After learning of Tom's death, I felt deep remorse for those feelings of jealousy.

Since TJ was severely physically challenged, he was unable to do much of anything, so unfortunately, he sat in front of a TV for most of the day watching movies or playing Xbox. After he'd been at home a year and the medication tapering and severe twisting stopped, we talked to TJ about returning to school to finish his senior year. He was thrilled at the prospect of finishing his schooling, receiving his diploma, and being in the company of young people again. There was no doubt in our minds that he was mentally capable of mastering his studies. The challenge was going to be getting the information out of his brain.

TJ started school in December of 2015. Initially, because the district was unable to find a one-to-one nurse for him, I attended school as his nurse and sign-language interpreter. He took general education courses in the special-education classroom. God provided him with two special-education teachers, Mr. Welter and Mr. Hawkins, who were absolutely amazing men and exactly who TJ needed. They were both young, fun, high school baseball coaches, and each had a wonderful sense of humor. They became more than teachers to TJ. They were his friends, role models, and an excellent support system.

TJ took Government and American Literature classes in his first semester. In Government he used an automated voice that read a chapter to him. He would then answer the teacher's oral multiple-choice questions by tapping his feet for the correct answer. Listening to the material once and then immediately answering questions without the aid of a book, seemed almost impossible to me, but it wasn't hard for TJ. Over the years, I had started to notice that his memory was incredible. I believe his exceptional memory skills were because he couldn't talk and instead was always listening and studying people and situations.

June 12, 2016
CaringBridge
Written by Kelly

It's been quite a while since I've posted, and I've begun getting asked if and when I'm going to post again. Things have finally started calming down for us, so I decided it was time to get on here and give an update. It has been three years now that we have been on this journey, and it is nice to know that people still follow TJ's progress and check in on him regularly.

One of the goals of TJ's therapists at Heartland has been to have him drive his wheelchair independently. They've started trying out different driving devices that would work better for him than the joystick controller we've always used. I attached a video of TJ driving his wheelchair with the newest device, an iPad. The very first time he tried it, he did very well, but it has been somewhat hit or miss since then. His therapists have decided to try something else. Next, they're going to try a head array where he will control the chair with his head. Hopefully that will work better for him. It's very awkward for me to walk beside him and not be in control of his chair. I almost have to put my hands behind my back to prevent myself from jumping in and taking over while he is learning to drive. I really do want him to be independent, but at the same time, it's hard for me to let go.

TJ finished the year out at Valley High School. Although I haven't received his grade card yet, I believe he finished with a B in Government and an A in American Lit. We struggled a lot with illness this year, so it was decided that he would take Economics this summer to prevent him from getting behind next year so that he'll be able to graduate. He starts summer school this week and will finish it at the end of July. We are so thankful for Mr. Hawkins who is taking time out of his summer to teach TJ and will also come to our house so I don't have to get him ready and loaded up in the van.

At school we communicate with sign language because it's still the fastest way of communicating for him. I sit on a stool next to him and hold his elbow and wrist to steady his arm. Using sign language, he spells everything out, and I translate while the teacher writes it down. It's a bit tedious but we get the job done. I thought I would share one of the papers he wrote for his American Lit class on the subject of Transcendentalism. I think you will find that TJ truly is an amazing kid. (His answers are in italics.)

TJ Denham
Early American Literature
Transcendentalism

1. You are now a writer of transcendentalism. Identify five maxims that you live your life by. These are five things that you will not compromise or do away with.

    1. *The right to be stubborn*
    2. *Pursuit of happiness*
    3. *Nonconformist*
    4. *To have strong morals*
    5. *Trust in God*

2. Explain why these five maxims are important and what you do to "live" these maxims. Thoreau wrote a section in Walden titled, "Where I lived, and what I lived for." It is your turn to do the same. Describe your current life and what you live for. Examples can be what motivates you, what you stand for, what goals you have, etc.

I would have to say being stubborn is probably the best out of them all. When I was in the hospital, I already knew that the doctors were thinking, "How is this kid still alive?" I'd been sedated on so many drugs that it is amazing that I even know any of this. So, therefore, the only reason I am still alive was because I was stubborn.

What bumps straight into the next one is my own outlook on the pursuit of happiness. Before all of this happened, my outlook was to buy a nice car and, of course, have a huge house. And the biggest out of them all was coming home to Kate Upton. But now I guess I'm just happy to be alive with a mother that loves me unconditionally.

I would have to say that going by the beat of my own drum has been very important in my life. I can proudly say that I've never been the kind of kid to go out and party with my friends every Friday.

Where would I be without morals? Maybe I would have a kid or be six feet under. It is crazy to think of a world without any morals. I do believe this country is burning to the ground because we don't have any morals.

Whatever God's plan is for my life, I am ok with it. If that means sitting in a group home for a couple of years, I'm okay with it. I'm not saying I would be a happy camper, but I completely understand and trust God's plan for my life.

When TJ finger-spelled that his first maxim was "the right to be stubborn," I rolled my eyes and let out a sigh. I had been calling him stubborn all morning, so I thought he was throwing a dig at me. Then after he finished his paragraph, I had to apologize. He is on a whole different level than me and more mature than I give him credit for.

TJ's twentieth birthday is in July, so we have a big night of celebrating planned at an I-Cubs baseball game with lots of friends. We're really looking forward to that!

One more big thing coming up is senior pictures! I don't think TJ is too excited about that, but I sure am. I remember at Mayo when I discovered that he wouldn't be going back to school his senior year, I sat in a puddle of tears in the corner of his room for days. In my mind then, everything was over, senior pictures, the last homecoming, prom, visiting colleges. I never dreamed then that three years later, when he was twenty years old, we would be given another chance and would be doing senior pictures. God is so good! He is the God of second chances!

Joel 2:25–27

"I will repay you for the years the locusts have eaten—
the great locust and the young locust,
The other locusts and the locust swarm—
My great army that I sent among you.

You will have plenty to eat, until you are full,
And you will praise the name of the Lord your God,
Who has worked wonders for you;
Never again will my people be shamed.
Then you will know that I am in Israel,
That I am the Lord your God, and that there is no other;
Never again will my people be shamed."

Not long after TJ came home, Travis was laid off from his job which was our biggest source of income. I was receiving a small amount from the state for being TJ's care provider, but it wasn't much. Things looked grim. But God, who promises that He will always be with us in times of trouble, was truly with us. Altogether, Travis was laid off for two years. Looking back, I have no idea how we made it through that time, but we did and never needed for anything financially.

At times, I struggled with anger over how difficult our life was. It took two people to care for TJ, and there was no respite care provided on the brain-injury waiver. Travis and I were both exhausted, and we felt like prisoners in our own home. Others were afraid to take care of TJ, so I began praying for a nurse. No answer. So, I prayed and prayed some more. When there was still no answer, I grew even more angry. I asked myself, *Why won't God help us?* And then God took the blinders off and showed me that He *had* answered my prayer. *Travis* was the nurse. Without Travis there, I would have been caring for TJ all by myself. I soon realized that there was no one more qualified to be TJ's nurse than his dad. Travis was the best choice, and in hindsight, he is incredibly grateful that he had those two years with TJ. Despite my anger, God still provided. It took me a long time to recognize that God was providing for us because my anger created a barrier that blinded me. I learned that if I let anger and bitterness rule, then I would miss the miraculous way God was providing for us.

Once in a while, TJ's G-tube would get clogged, and I would be unable to get it cleared. We would then load up the van, go to the hospital to Interventional Radiology, sitting for hours until they removed the G-tube, put a new one in, and then x-rayed it to make sure it was in the right place. I hated going down to the hospital and sitting there all day. It was uncomfortable and hard for TJ to sit in his wheelchair that long. I decided I would just have extra G-tubes available at home and do it myself. I resolved that if I could change a trach, I could certainly change a G-tube. The only thing I couldn't do was x-ray it, but I decided we would be okay, although I figured a doctor would probably disagree with that.

A few months later, TJ had an appointment with the GI doctor. When the doctor asked me how often the G-tube got changed and inquired as to who changed it, I was afraid to tell him that it had been me and that I wasn't getting it x-rayed. I reluctantly confessed the truth and prepared myself for the scolding I was about to receive. I was so relieved when he exclaimed, "You're doing it? That's wonderful! I never see patient's families do that! You're doing a great job!" A feeling of accomplishment washed over me. I once again realized how unusual our medical knowledge was.

I again thought back to those early Mayo PICU days and how angry I had been at the doctors and nurses for pressing me to learn TJ's medical care. Since he had moved home, I'd become very grateful for the way they pushed me because our ability to take care of him meant he could live at home where he was happy, loved, and well cared for. If I could go back in time and speak to the nurse I had been frustrated with regarding TJ's site cares, I would change the whole narrative and say: "Thank you for pushing me, putting up with me, and for insisting that I learn how to care for my son. Be patient with parents because they're tired, overwhelmed, and frightened. They may resist your instruction, but stay strong because the skills you're teaching are crucial in the real world."

TJ started his last year of high school in the fall of 2016. Mr. Hawkins felt TJ needed to stop living in isolation and encouraged him to get out and connect with others again. He suggested that TJ take a literature course in a general education classroom. To my surprise, TJ agreed.

The first couple of weeks of the new school year, I accompanied TJ to train his nurse how to best care for him. A bus transported all three of us to and from school. One day I was sitting too close to the edge of the seat. My legs were crossed, and I was focused on a conversation with TJ's nurse. I was completely caught off-guard when the bus driver turned the corner. I lost my balance, fell out of my seat, and tumbled, ungracefully, down the aisle. Embarrassed, I glanced up and saw TJ throw his head back and shake it back and forth. I heard the familiar "hmmm" sound he made when he was laughing. My poor son. I can't imagine how hard it was for him to go to school with his mother, let alone watch her make a fool of herself.

Mrs. Stanfel, TJ's literature teacher, was very impressed with his writing abilities and asked if she could showcase his work in writing contests. The first contest he entered was a two-sentence horror story contest. His sentences were: "I looked down to see what was lying right below me. It was a pool of my own blood, and I explained to myself, 'It's completely normal.'"

The next contest he entered was a 2,500-word short story contest.

He wrote about his life since his heart surgery. It was interesting to hear his perspective. I learned things he experienced that I never knew. He'd been in a lot of emotional pain during the previous three years. I hoped that it was healing and cathartic for him to write about it. He titled his story *It's a Slippery Slope*. Below is the last page of his story:

"After leaving Mayo the second time, I went to a brain injury rehab facility for 11 months with minimal improvement. After leaving there, I came home and have been living at home and being taken care of by my parents for the last two years. I go to outpatient therapy three times a week and am improving, but it's very slow. I still am in a wheelchair and I cannot talk or eat. I have limited use of my arms and hands. I communicate by using sign language or a communication device. I am now twenty years old and am in high school finishing up my senior year. I am thankful for people like my best friend Drake and his brother Dynas who have stuck by my side. I am thankful for all the people who have gotten me this far like my church family, therapists, doctors, nurses, and teachers. I am especially thankful for my mom and dad for keeping me at home and helping me finish school. I am a man reborn. I was flat on my back. I could not communicate, but I learned to tap my feet to do so. I learned to use my thumbs as well. I learned sign language. I learned how to use a special computer to write, and now I can handwrite a few words. Through these abilities and resources, I have written this paper. I have grown and can see the life ahead of me. I have overcome. I will overcome. In the Bible Jeremiah 29:11 says, "For I know the plans I have for you,' declares the Lord, 'plans to prosper you and not to harm you, plans to give you hope and a future." I am still 100 percent sure that God loves me and has a plan for my life, and I still plan to pursue my dreams of becoming a doctor no matter how difficult it is."

The story took TJ many weeks to sign and was a frustrating and grueling process. Even so, he persevered until the end. I was very proud of him. He didn't win the short-story contest, but that didn't matter to me. What mattered most was helping him express his thoughts and feelings for the past three years.

A few months later, TJ finger-spelled my Mother's Day gift to me:

> "Roses are red
> Violets should be violet but instead they are blue
> Mother you are beautiful
> And I came from you
> So I think we can all agree that I'm beautiful, too."

CHAPTER 17

ADDICTED TO THE SHINDIG

The further along we progressed into our new normal, the more I became aware of the general lack of understanding in the community about the emotional pain and isolation often experienced by people with brain injuries and their families. I remember attending an event at church one evening when a woman I knew asked me how TJ was doing.

"TJ is okay, but it's hard for him because he's lonely and has lost most of his friends," I told her.

She then replied, "Yeah, but it's hard for them, too."

I was shocked and deeply hurt by her response. TJ's condition *was* difficult for his friends to handle, but, quite frankly, their "hard" paled in comparison to TJ's "hard." Their lives went on, while most days my son lived an ongoing nightmare—unable to walk or talk. When I was brave enough to be honest about the additional pain of TJ's loneliness, I was met with defensiveness instead of compassion. There was no attempt to envision life from TJ's perspective or express compassion or empathy for TJ's tragic situation. Instead, I was expected to understand how hard it was for *them*.

I wanted to get away from her as quickly as possible, so I promptly excused myself. I was unable to concentrate the remainder of the event and couldn't wait to get home. I tried to divert my thoughts from the hurtful words by focusing on Aiden, but the sick feeling the conversation gave me kept creeping into my stomach.

In the safety of my home, I threw myself into my husband's arms and sobbed.

"TJ can't walk, talk, eat, go to school without his mother along, hang out with friends all night, or drive a car. He will never get married or have children, and *I'm* supposed to be understanding of how hard it is for *them*?" I told my husband.

Travis held me tightly and then said, "I know it hurts, hon. They just don't understand."

He was right: She *couldn't* understand all we were going through. Intellectually, I knew that I needed to give grace in return for her painful words. I also realized that a seed had been planted within me, compelling me to educate others about the brain injury community. Throughout TJ's journey, a number of people we thought we could count on for support simply didn't know how to be there for us. They either stayed away or suggested that we keep our distance because TJ's condition made them uncomfortable. I can't describe the pain this response causes people with brain injuries and their families who are walking through agonizing and overwhelming challenges.

Having said that, there were also many times people showed TJ and us great love. One evening Travis, TJ, Aiden, and I attended Winter Jam, a live concert that's performed by some of the top Christian artists. Much of the music genre played was hip-hop—exactly the style of music TJ loved. Since he was a music guy and a drummer, he relished every minute of the concert. While he was focused on the stage, listening to the music, a nearby usher was watching him. She approached TJ, held his arm, and told him she was glad he was there and hoped he was enjoying the concert. TJ then became very emotional and began to cry.

Turning to me she asked, "Is he okay? Is he crying because I upset him?"

I explained, "Oh, no, he's okay. He's just grateful for your kind words and deeply touched by the music. It's been a long time since he's been able to attend something like this. He acquired a brain injury about three years ago."

"Oh, I'm so sorry," she said.

I said, "Thank you for noticing him and talking to him. He understands everything you're saying. He just can't talk."

My reply sparked something in the woman and she then went on to tell TJ that he was loved by God and that she was very glad he had come. All the while this woman spoke blessing into TJ, he sobbed at the attention and love this stranger was showing him. I never forgot the woman's kindness. I was deeply grateful that she had treated him like someone precious. When she wasn't quite sure how to handle his emotional reaction, she asked his caregiver for direction and then continued to pursue him with love.

One day after TJ returned home from a half-day of school, I parked him in his favorite La-Z-Boy chair so he could play Xbox. After getting him settled in, it was late in the afternoon when I looked at the time.

It was 3:30 P.M. Aiden would be getting off the bus in half an hour. It was school policy that kindergarteners be picked up at the bus stop by an adult.

After attempting to do a little housework before I had to leave, I heard TJ's call button sound. I strolled into his room to see what he needed and found that he had soiled himself and was very upset. I lifted him up, walked him to the bathroom, and began cleaning up the mess and doing laundry. I was so focused on TJ's needs that I lost track of time—until the phone rang. I stopped what I was doing and looked at my phone. It was the school bus calling. I quickly glanced at the clock and saw that it was 4:10 P.M. I immediately realized I had forgotten to pick up Aiden from the bus stop. Panic set in and I felt my stomach churning.

"Hello?"

"This is Lisa calling from the West Des Moines school bus. There was no one to pick up Aiden at the bus stop today, so the driver kept him on the bus. Are you home now?"

"Yes, I'm home. I'm sorry. My other son is disabled. I was in the bathroom with him and couldn't get to the bus stop. Is Aiden okay?"

"Yes, he's fine. It's no problem. The driver will keep him until the end of the route and then drop him back off at his stop. I'll let you know when he's on his way back."

"Thank you so much. I'll be there," I said and hung up the phone.

Ugh! I felt awful! All I could think of was Aiden sitting on the bus, feeling scared, with tears running down his cheeks because I had forgotten him. I quickly went back to cleaning up TJ and began a conversation with the Lord expressing my frustration with our current situation.

"I don't understand, Lord. Why would You give us this little boy when You knew TJ was going to get sick and we wouldn't be able to handle this? It isn't fair to Aiden. Please do something."

During TJ's time at Mayo, Aiden had been shuffled from house to house for months. He was too young to understand what was happening and sometimes begged his papa not to leave him. During that time, my hope was that after we came home, things would get better for Aiden and we would achieve some type of normalcy. But things hadn't gotten better. Caring for TJ still took most of our time, and Aiden was left with the scraps.

We felt like we were failing. We were juggling more balls than we could handle. Some balls were dropping. I knew deep down that it wasn't our fault, that it was out of our control and we were doing the best we could. But I still felt incredibly guilty and worried that Aiden was going to pay the price.

Months went by and nothing changed. We were still overwhelmed, and Aiden was still getting what little we had to offer after being consumed with TJ's care. However, we kept pressing on, trusting in the Lord and His promises and doing the best we could.

One day several months later, I noticed that Aiden was watching something on YouTube. Becoming concerned about what was entering his little five-year-old mind, I asked him what he was watching.

"Bible stories," he answered.

After studying what was on the screen, I noticed they weren't just children's Bible stories like *VeggieTales* or cartoons. They were adult Bible stories, like *The Ten Commandments*.

I thought, "Hmm—that's a bit unusual. What kid wants to watch adult Bible stories?"

I was intrigued and somewhat skeptical, so I sat down with him to learn more. During our conversation, I learned that he had been searching YouTube for Bible stories and had watched almost every one of them and was trying to find more. They clearly fascinated him.

I was astounded and could hardly believe it. I thought back to when I was a kid and remembered how much I disliked those movies. I thought those movies were boring and that the people on them were strangely dressed and talked funny.

After telling a friend a few months later about Aiden's incredible love of Bible stories, she commended me on our great parenting. I burst out laughing. I knew it had nothing to do with us. We had been so focused on taking care of TJ and searching for answers that would improve his quality of life that we had nothing left to invest in Aiden's spiritual education. The raw truth was that we were failing him—but God wasn't. God was instilling in his heart a love for His Word. Unbeknownst to us, God was working in Aiden's life and training him when we couldn't. God allows us to have what we cannot handle so that we'll turn to Him for help. At those times, others see that, though our own efforts are unsuccessful, God is faithful to the max.

In every hospital and care facility we were in, we met some absolutely amazing, fantastic caregivers. Several of these people came to our home to take care of TJ from time to time They were hard workers and compassionate toward the people they served. We developed deep bonds with some and still stay in touch all these years later. But, as in any profession, there were some bad apples as well—workers who shouldn't even be in the health care field, let alone taking care of helpless, defenseless people.

TJ's therapists gave him exercises to work on at home. During that time, I became very concerned about TJ's future and what would happen to him if I could no longer care for him. I pushed him to do his exercises in hopes that he would become more independent.

TJ, however, did not like doing his therapy protocol. We were always battling. One day, my urging and his resisting finally came to a head. We both exploded like two agitated pop bottles.

"TJ, why do I have to battle with you all the time over this?!" I exclaimed. "Why won't you do your therapy?! I'm so worried about what will happen to you when I can no longer care for you!"

TJ became very frustrated with my nagging and wailed loudly. Then he finger-spelled, "Because I was beat, and I just can't get motivated!"

I frowned. "What? What are you talking about?"

He then went on to sign to me that when he was at the brain injury rehab facility, the man who helped me carry his equipment in from the van used to beat him in the head. After pressing him further, he finger-spelled the entire story. I learned that the man had been taking TJ's iPad without his permission, so TJ reported it to his therapist. (Two years after the incident, when he told me all of this, I remembered how TJ always wanted his iPad in bed with him. I never understood why because, in his current state, he couldn't use it. The nurses only used it to play music for him. I was perplexed by his behavior but always did as he asked.)

Soon after TJ reported the iPad being taken, the man came into TJ's room around midnight, called him a snitch, and beat him in the head, knocking him unconscious. In the weeks that followed, this same man was rough with TJ. If he soiled himself, the man would use derogatory slurs to verbally abuse him. I remembered that this man was always right outside his room when I would visit. At the time, in my naivety, I thought, *Wow, this is great! Usually I can never find anyone, but it's nice that this employee is always right here when I need something.* Later, I realized the man was listening to see if TJ reported him to me.

When I was at the facility visiting, TJ cried all the time. I had no idea what was causing his pain because, at that time, his hands were so tight that he couldn't use sign language or squeezing to communicate with me. But the abuser knew. When I would leave at night, when the floor was quiet, he would go back in to TJ's room and would once again beat him in the head for trying to alert me through his tears. This happened four or five times. The facility was unaware that this employee was a danger to its residents.

TJ also shared with me that CNAs, specifically the one who was supposed to be removed from his hall, were disconnecting his call light. When I asked him why, he finger-spelled, "Because I was calling them too much." When I asked why he was calling them so much, he finger-spelled, "Because I needed something like suctioning or to go to the bathroom." I concluded that when he would call, they would come in, but because he was so difficult to communicate with, they wouldn't take the time to figure out what he needed. They would shut the call light off and leave. Because TJ's needs were not met, he would call them again. Instead of trying to figure out what he needed, they would just disconnect his call light from the extension. If his trach had come out while the call light was disconnected, he would have had no way of calling for help and would have suffocated to death.

I was heartbroken when I remembered back to how miserable TJ was while he was at the facility. The people who were supposed to care for him had neglected and abused him. We couldn't help but feel that we had failed him, even though we knew we had done everything we could to provide for him and get him home as quickly as possible.

It was a scary feeling to be in such dire circumstances. We didn't have adequate resources from the brain-injury waiver to successfully care for a severely compromised loved one at home, nor did we have safe placement options. Our visiting caseworker knew we needed more support, but she was unable to find programs that would provide the help we needed. She said, quite frankly, that they just don't usually see someone as compromised as TJ living at home.

We pressed charges against the man, but because it had been two years, there was no evidence, and nothing could be done about it. We were determined to keep TJ at home with us until it was absolutely impossible for us to care for him.

In the spring of 2017, after going to school for a year and a half, TJ was ready to graduate from high school. The local news did a graduation story on TJ to update the community on his achievement. During the interview, the reporter and cameraman expressed their amazement at the way TJ had learned to communicate. As TJ began signing something he wanted to share, a hush fell over the room. All eyes were on him, eagerly anticipating the profound words he would sign. As TJ finger-spelled, I spoke each letter aloud, and his teacher wrote them down:

"Can't stop addicted to the…"

"Shindig?" I asked, interrupting his finger-spelling. "Oh, my goodness, he's signing a Red-Hot-Chili-Peppers song." (Peppers 2003)

That was not at all what we were expecting, so the onlookers burst out laughing.

TJ's graduation day arrived and went exactly as I had dreamed. Travis and I walked across the stage beside him in his wheelchair. When his name was called, the room erupted into clapping and cheering, with some even giving a standing ovation. TJ deserved every bit of honor and recognition he received. Getting through high school had been grueling for him, but he persevered despite many obstacles.

While he had diligently mastered his schoolwork, he had apparently taught others as well. Later, Mr. Welter, one of TJ's special-education teachers, shared the following with me:

> "Having the opportunity to be a part of TJ's life was something I will never forget. I often talk about him with those who ask about my students because of the impact he had on us. When we first met TJ, we were immediately challenged, trying to understand his level of functioning and the supports we could provide to him. Many of the early conversations revolved around ways to keep content interesting and learn about strategies for him to communicate his level of understanding to us. It became quite clear that we had to work very hard to challenge him.
>
> TJ rolled into my room each day, oftentimes bundled up with coats and blankets as he got off the bus or out of his mom's car because it may have been 5 degrees outside, and was always prepared and willing to work with us to the best of his ability. TJ's level of education was astounding. When you looked at his seemingly failing body and learned about his mind and high levels of education, the two did not match up.
>
> It took me most of the year to realize that I was learning much more from TJ than he was from me. At times, I felt sorry for TJ and his circumstances as I learned about his active life before his medical diagnosis and complications. The faith that TJ and his family had towards each other and his situation showed up each and every day. I know that everyone has struggles, but quite honestly, some have more on their plate than others. TJ's plate was full. I may

never understand how he maintained his humor, his willingness to continue his education, and faith towards his family, his teachers, and himself. He will always be an inspiration to me and to those who hear about him and his family's story. Without knowing it, TJ empowered those around him who watched him work in the classroom. He presented lessons on humility, work ethic, and faith. These are all qualities I try to instill in my students, and without even speaking, TJ accomplished that. For that, I thank you, TJ, and I thank you for the time you spent with us."

Initially, I struggled with the idea of entering into the special-needs community, but it didn't take long until I began to fall in love with it. In this community, I learned about authenticity. No one there wore a mask. A mask would have been futile because it was impossible to hide the messy areas of our lives. This community did not judge when a child was behaving poorly or when a parent had a meltdown and felt like they couldn't persevere one more day. They understood my pain, loss, and grief at what my child would never experience. They believed that *all* human beings are precious and should be loved and accepted.

I learned about compassionate people who take care of one another and offer encouragement. There was a young woman with special needs that TJ saw frequently at therapy. She adored TJ. One day when she heard TJ crying out in pain during therapy, her sweet, young voice rang out from across the room, "TJ, are you okay?" She didn't understand that the social norm was to keep to yourself and mind your own business. What she understood was that her friend was hurting and she needed to know that he was okay. Thinking about it still brings tears to my eyes.

There were days when I was overwhelmed by how difficult our life was, like when TJ's blanket flew off in the wind and wrapped around the wheels of the wheelchair, and I couldn't get the blanket free and had to leave the wheelchair on the front porch and walk him into the house. Or like the cold, snowy day when the van's ramp broke. In manual mode, the ramp became very steep, causing us to slide off multiple times, making us late to therapy. Or like the spring day when we arrived home from therapy and TJ decided to go off-roading in his wheelchair across our muddy front lawn without my assistance. His head was thrown back, and I could hear his unmistakable, humming laughter. Gone were the days of wearing high heels, jewelry, and makeup. I had now entered into a life of wearing sweat suits and tennis shoes and sometimes unknowingly leaving the house with secretions on my shoulder or a remnant of TJ's trip to the bathroom on my sleeve. But I wouldn't have traded this new life for anything. It was a hard, stressful, painful, and agonizing life, but it was also a grace-filled, encouraging, love-filled, and beautiful life. I came to believe that this new life that I never really wanted was where true meaning was found.

CHAPTER 18

A MORNING IN THE LIFE OF TJ

Our sleeping arrangements had become rather unusual since TJ's brain injury. Because he was trached and our room was a floor above his, we didn't feel comfortable leaving him downstairs alone at night. His trach had come out by itself a few times, and I shuddered at the thought that it might happen when he was alone. I had nightmares that he might struggle to breathe and wouldn't be able to alert us.

Initially, the baby monitor we bought seemed like a good idea, but the signal proved to be unreliable. Secretly, I was happy the monitor idea didn't work because I was really afraid that we wouldn't wake up if he needed us. Not waking could have resulted in his death. The possibility of equipment failure was too great a risk for my comfort level.

The head of TJ's hospital bed was against the back wall of his bedroom. I had positioned his bed strategically so that when we were in the family room, we could look down the hall and keep an eye on him. To the left of his bed was a metal futon with a cushion for his dad or me to sleep on during the night, but it was extremely uncomfortable. After only a few uses, a deep canyon developed in the cushion where the futon folded. Why would a furniture designer think a cushion could hold its shape after repeatedly being folded and laid flat? In our opinion, it was junk.

Initially, Travis and I took turns sleeping in TJ's room. However, I tossed and turned all night, and sleep eluded me. I was always listening for him, always alert, making sure he was breathing. Most nights I spent dozing off only to jolt awake a short time later. After much frustration with my inability to rest, my sweet husband volunteered to stay in TJ's room every night so I could relax and sleep. I was relieved. However, even in the comfort of my own bed, I still didn't sleep soundly. The underlying anguish of having a chronically sick child just wouldn't allow my mind to be still. Night after night, I lay in bed for hours, mentally replaying his first week after surgery in a futile attempt to solve the mystery of what had happened to him. When I was satisfied that I couldn't make sense of it, my mind would shift, searching for ways to improve his quality of life. No matter how much I grappled with my racing thoughts, turning them off and surrendering them to God, I never succeeded at completely releasing them.

One particular morning, I went downstairs at 5 A.M. to begin TJ's morning routine while Travis rested. My hope was to get to him before he had soiled himself, although quite often he was already awake, wet, and very grouchy when I arrived. His sheets, blankets, comforter, pillows, pants, shirt, and even his hair were all soaked. In an effort to bring some levity to the situation, with a half-smile on my face, I would ask, "TJ, how on earth did you manage to get pee in your hair, buddy?" While I was only teasing, he didn't laugh or even smile at my attempt at humor. He was embarrassed and humiliated by his incontinence and would wail as I tried to wake up and make him more comfortable. I reassured him that I wasn't mad and knew he couldn't help it, but it didn't matter. He knew how hard it was on us. He felt like a burden, even though I'd told him repeatedly that he wasn't.

With his wet clothes touching my bare arms and pajamas, I wrestled him to a standing position, which wasn't an easy task, as he had no control over his 6-foot-1, lanky body. Our arms embraced one another, and he rested his chin on my shoulder. In this position, I shuffled backward toward the bathroom. Like marbles in a pinball machine, we ricocheted off walls and furniture as we awkwardly stumbled toward the doorway. I was always afraid of falling and hurting either one or both of us.

Once we arrived in the bathroom, I removed his wet clothes and set him down on the toilet. I hurriedly ran back to the bed and stripped it down. The urine odor was heavy in the room, so I quickly opened his outside door a crack to let in some fresh air. I then raced back to the bathroom, gathered his wet clothes off the floor, and added them to the wet bundle in my arms. He was still sitting there waiting for me to finish. I quickly apologized. "I'm sorry, buddy. I'm trying to hurry. Give me just a couple more minutes." I ran to the washing machine and started it as fast as I could. I had to be quick because he grew very upset when he was cold.

After returning to the bathroom and assessing the situation, I concluded that a sponge bath wasn't going to cut it. Inwardly I sighed, took a deep breath, and prepared myself for the conflict ahead. I reluctantly told him he was going to have to take a shower. As I anticipated, the wailing started up again but this time even louder. From experience, I knew he didn't want to take a shower right then. He was a grown man and despised being told what to do and when to do it by his mother. I begged and pleaded with him to stop resisting. It was early in the morning, and I was already very tired. I was well aware that I fought a losing battle. I also knew he wouldn't stop howling. The brain injury left him with an inability to control his emotions.

That morning scenario occurred quite often. However, there were other mornings when TJ would try to express himself by wailing, and I would automatically assume that he was shrieking because he didn't want to shower. Out of sheer exhaustion, I would scold him for his uncooperative behavior. In an attempt to get my attention, he would wail even louder. At times, instead of further investigating his challenging behavior to get to its source, I would respond by scolding just as loud. Our dueling voices would continue to compete until eventually we were in full-blown chaos. I would later discover that the issue had nothing at all to do with showering. I would learn that he had been cold, his trach was bothering him, the water was not the right temperature, or he was in pain. When I discovered the true cause of his outbursts, I was consumed with guilt for not being more patient with him. I felt deep regret that we had to live that way.

When TJ's emotions were elevated, he was unable to calm himself enough to finger-spell the sign language alphabet and communicate what was wrong. Unable to understand, my stress level would greatly increase as I desperately attempted to identify and correct the need of the moment. It was misery personified to be unable to communicate—a level of frustration I had never before experienced.

We diligently tried to come up with a solution to the problem, but nothing worked.

After fighting me, he eventually conceded and got into the shower. I don't know why he always resisted because he loved it once he was in the shower. The warm water loosened his tight muscles, and for a little while, his body could relax.

Taking a shower with a trach, however, was no easy task. I used a trach guard and always tried hard to make sure water didn't make contact with his trach. Still, water would creep behind it, causing him to have violent coughing spells. This would add to my feelings of guilt for not better protecting his airway. His life was incredibly hard. Sometimes we inadvertently made it even harder.

While he sat on his shower chair and soaked in the warm water, I turned my attention back to the bed. I wiped it down with disinfectant wipes and remade it as quickly as I could. I ran back to the shower, washed him up with Axe shampoo and body wash (it was his favorite because he thought the ladies liked it), then let him soak until he pounded on the wall to signal that he was ready to get out. After drying him off and wrestling with armholes and pant legs that resisted his twisted limbs, we jostled our way back to the bed. I laid him down and threw his warm comforter over him. After spending so much time in hospitals, he had grown fond of warm bedding from the blanket warmers, so I recreated the experience at home with the clothes dryer. As he nestled into his bed and felt the warmth of the comforter surrounding his body, a look of pleasure and contentment finally broke out across his face.

As he rested, I mixed his morning meds with water and administered them through his G-tube. The meds relaxed his contracting muscles. Although his muscles were much better than they had been, I still hated seeing them spasm, with his arms twisted uncomfortably over his head. Frequently, I counted the hours until it was medication time. For a short time after receiving medication, he would be completely comfortable. After finding a good show for him on TV, I was finally able to slip away for a few minutes and drink my morning coffee before returning to finish the rest of his morning care.

After rejuvenating a bit with coffee, I returned and began vest therapy and a saline nebulizer treatment for his lungs. I wrapped the vest around his chest. Two tubes were inserted into pockets on one end and connected to an air-pulse generator on the other end. When turned on, the vest inflated as the generator delivered rapid bursts of air, creating a vibration against TJ's chest wall that helped loosen the mucus. We ran three 10-minute cycles, increasing the settings with each cycle. Then we would suction any loosened mucus through his trach.

In between cycles, I cleaned out TJ's suction machine. This, understandably, was a job that no one wanted to do. While cleaning it, I looked away and thought about something else to keep myself from retching. Our new life was spent chained to that suction machine. It was used multiple times an hour, and we couldn't go anywhere without it. It was the most crucial piece of equipment we had. People were grossed out by his secretions, and he knew it. He had once been a handsome, outgoing, friendly teenager—the kind of boy any parent would want their daughter to date. Now, we were made to feel that he was an untouchable—a reject that many were uncomfortable being around.

Memories of who he used to be played in my head as I now watched him struggle every day. As I scrubbed the suction canister with bleach, I thought back to TJ's teenage years before the brain injury. He had fallen in love with the sport of paintball. He talked about it incessantly and bought a great deal of expensive equipment that he hoped would give him an edge over the competition.

One afternoon when TJ was fifteen years old and still healthy, he decided it would be funny to shoot up our backyard with paintballs. I arrived home from work one day and was irritated to find my tree trunks pink, my shed orange, and my favorite garden angel statue now painted yellow with a hole in her right shoulder and feathers from her delicate wings either broken or missing. I appeared irritated, but underneath my frown, I was trying to disguise a smile. Even though he had accidentally broken my angel statue, I secretly enjoyed the delight in his eyes and the way his shoulders bounced up and down in rhythm with the chuckle he couldn't stifle after pulling off a prank that annoyed his mother.

The backyard shoot-up had taken place five years earlier, but the broken, pockmarked angel still sat in my garden. Despite my affection for her, I had planned to replace her but hadn't gotten around to it. I had almost convinced myself that, from a distance, you could hardly tell she was broken.

Then TJ suffered his brain injury, and suddenly I saw things much differently.

How could I replace her now? I thought, as I swished water around in the canister. Her presence in the garden was tied to a memory of TJ as a healthy child. Disposing of her broken figure would be no different than tossing out great memories of the time when he was young and full of life. At that point, it was just too precious to throw away.

In order to fend off the depressing feelings that were always lurking in the back of my mind, I reminded myself of God's Word. Revelation 21:5 says, "Behold I am making all things new." I reminded myself that God was right then in the act of making all things new. He promises His people that when He finishes His work, not only will all things have been made new, but they will *stay* new. They will never break, wear out, or need to be replaced. I comforted myself with the thought that one day TJ would have a new, strong body that would never grow old. I would spend eternity enjoying his company as a healthy man, forever.

After I finished cleaning the suction machine, I forced my mind back into the present and resumed TJ's care. For breakfast, I poured his liquid food into a pouch that hung from an IV pole. The pouch was connected to his G-tube with plastic tubing. While tube feeding, his bed had to be at a thirty-degree incline. If it was lower than that, we'd run the risk of aspiration which could cause pneumonia. At the same time, sitting at that angle was very difficult for TJ because his body continually fell to the side. Multiple times during his feeding, I had to wrestle him back into a sitting position.

While he was being tube fed his breakfast, I brushed his teeth. This was the job I dreaded most. It was even worse than cleaning the suction machine. TJ had a tough time opening his mouth because his jaw was very tight, and he had little control over it. If by chance he had his mouth open, when anything like a toothbrush or suction catheter got close to it, his jaw rapidly snapped shut. Sometimes his tongue or lips were in the way and would get caught between his teeth. He would squeal in pain while I desperately tried to pry his jaws apart to release whatever was trapped. It was terribly stressful. Brushing the lower teeth was especially challenging. I had to push down very hard on his lower jaw to keep his mouth open and frantically brush that area before his mouth snapped shut, all the while worried that the toothpaste would slide down his throat into his lungs and cause an infection. I was always relieved when it was over.

By that point, Travis was awake and ready to help me tackle our very last chore of the morning routine—performing site care on his trach and G-tube and changing his trach strap. I removed the inner cannula of his trach and cleaned it with a wire brush. The skin under the actual trach was cleaned with water and Q-tips. Gauze was inserted under his trach. The skin area around the G-tube was cleaned in the same way and gauze was also applied around it.

The hardest part of his trach care was changing the strap. It required two people. A trach strap goes around the neck and holds the trach tube in place. He hated having this piece changed. He fussed, cried, wiggled, and fought, making it even more stressful. While the trach strap was being changed, Travis or I manually held the trach in place while the other one of us changed the strap. If the trach happened to dislodge, the available caregiver hurriedly inserted the obturator, which is a guide with a point at the end, into the trach, applied lubricant, and slid the trach back into his trachea. The other one of us held him down while the Velcro ties were hastily maneuvered through the tiny holes of his trach tube and put his replacement trach strap on. Whew! All done. Everyone was still alive. Mission accomplished.

Finally, it was 8 A.M., and TJ was ready for the day. I, on the other hand, was covered in secretions and urine, so I headed upstairs for a shower. Travis had left for the day, so I had to be quick. I didn't like leaving TJ downstairs alone. Just as I was preparing to get in the shower, I heard the all too familiar wailing sound coming from TJ's bedroom—the telltale sign that TJ had soiled himself again.

As days and then years went by, we accepted that this was now our life. It became increasingly more difficult to shut out the hopeless feelings. Every year life got a little darker and more challenging. We were slowly sinking under the weight of the demands incurred by the brain injury.

CHAPTER 19

POSITIVE VIBES ONLY

After TJ's high school graduation, he still planned to pursue college with the ambitious goal of becoming a doctor. I was very excited about TJ's future plans but also felt that if his communication abilities didn't improve significantly, it was going to be extremely difficult for him to manage college in his present physical condition. Due to his impaired physical abilities, his workload in high school was half that of the general education students. It took him a long time to complete an assignment. In college, there would be no breaks given to him. After graduation we decided to put college on hold and focus on improving his communication and physical abilities in therapy so he would be better prepared to meet the challenge.

In the summer of 2017, we resolved the lawsuit that we filed on TJ's behalf, and we were able to pay for in-home caregivers. Most of TJ's caregivers were young females close to his age. He was very fond of them. As soon as they entered our house to start their shifts, he was up in his wheelchair and ready to head out the door. TJ and his caregivers had a fantastic summer of movies, shopping, concerts, attending the Iowa State Fair, and running in 5K races with a local organization called Team Run Free. Team Run Free is a running program that enables those with special needs to participate in races by teaming up with able-bodied runners and "running" in a race. TJ enjoyed it immensely and never wanted to miss a race.

In late summer, doctors made a medication change, and TJ began to improve again. His arms were more relaxed and rarely over his head. In fact, I was hopeful again. He was gaining more control over his entire body. I continued to hope that he would meet therapy goals and return to the level he'd experienced before he left Mayo the first time.

Our daughter Chandler and her husband Julian had been living in Cedar Rapids, Iowa during much of TJ's illness. Although they were two hours away, they were still close enough to come home often on the weekends and spend time with family. Many times, while Chandler was living in Cedar Rapids, she mentioned that she was homesick and wanted to move back to Des Moines but was unable to make this happen due to job commitments and financial reasons. Finally, in the fall of 2017, their circumstances changed, and it was the perfect time to move back home.

At the time of their move, Julian was blessed with a work-from-home job. Chandler, however, was still searching. We asked her to be TJ's caregiver during her transition—at least until she could find a permanent job. She agreed to this arrangement and was delighted with the opportunity to spend more time with her brother. It was a win-win for all of us.

In November, a couple of days after Thanksgiving, I noticed that TJ was very lethargic and his stomach was a little fuller than usual. I couldn't help but wonder if he had a respiratory infection. The next day we noticed that he was very agitated. At one point, his lips turned blue. I hurriedly sat him up in an effort to help him breathe better. In a panic, I told Travis to call 911. Shortly after, an ambulance arrived and transported TJ to the ER. Testing showed that he had pneumonia.

After TJ was admitted, one of the pulmonologists visited with me for a while and told me that they hadn't seen TJ in the hospital since 2014. He shared that it was very unusual for a person in his condition to go that length of time without being hospitalized and commended us on the excellent care we'd been giving him. His praise boosted my spirits and encouraged me.

After a couple of days in the hospital, the internist reported that TJ could go home because his labs had returned to normal and his lungs were clear. The doctor told me they were calling it a "brief episode" and that the whole event had been really strange because it cleared up so quickly. The doctor went on to educate me that in years past, people in TJ's condition usually didn't live long so doctors were unable to study them. Because of improvements in medicine, people like TJ were now living longer, but due to the lack of studies available, doctors didn't always understand them. This was new information for me, and I appreciated his honesty.

After returning home, I noticed that TJ was still very sick with chronic diarrhea. He couldn't tolerate his feedings and was very lethargic. I was bearing all his weight getting him to the bathroom and was afraid that we were going to fall. Once, when I transferred him to the toilet, he was so weak, he fell off. I couldn't get him up off the floor and had no choice but to pull him by his arms back to the bed. Once at the bedside, it took all the strength I could muster to heave him back into the bed.

Something just wasn't right with TJ, and I was concerned. I took him back to the ER. After running tests, doctors informed us that his liver enzymes were elevated. They then performed an ultrasound of the liver that showed TJ had a fatty liver. The doctor said TJ's liver looked like an organ you would see in a fifty-year-old, which meant he had an underlying liver disease. After hearing this news, it started to make sense why he had so many problems metabolizing medications. Travis and I were devastated to hear his new diagnosis.

During the first few days of this hospital stay, TJ had a strange breathing pattern. He would breathe hard, then shallow, sometimes stop altogether, and then would return to breathing hard. The pulmonologist explained that in the presence of liver or heart failure, for reasons they don't understand, the brain sends a signal to the lungs to go into that breathing pattern. Then he added that when his liver enzymes begin to normalize, TJ would return to his regular breathing pattern.

At one point, we noticed that when suctioning TJ's trach, we removed an unusual amount of blood. Occasionally, we would be frightened by large amounts of blood flowing from his mouth. It was shocking and made it appear that TJ was at death's door. Earlier we had learned that the blood's ability to clot is impaired by the liver's inability to function properly. The doctor speculated that the bleeding was from the pneumonia. We were relieved to hear that once the liver improved, the blood would begin to clot appropriately.

Due to the liver failure, TJ was extremely weak. Using sign language to communicate was too difficult for him. We resumed asking questions that he could answer by tapping his foot. Once in a while, he could muster up enough strength to sign something, but it was a rare occurrence.

After experiencing the effects of the liver failure, TJ finger-spelled that he was anxious about the possibility of respiratory failure and kept asking to be transferred to the University of Iowa Hospital in Iowa City. After relaying TJ's fears to the doctors, they assured us that the Iowa City hospital would do nothing different. They told him that he was okay and promised that they were keeping a close eye on him to prevent another episode of respiratory failure.

At that point, TJ began retaining an enormous amount of water. His weight had ballooned from 135 to 203 pounds. Water was also accumulating around his lungs due to the pneumonia. This caused the doctors to suspect that his heart was failing. After hearing the news, Travis and I began to worry that TJ might not survive this illness. Travis began talking to TJ about heaven and making sure he was ready to meet the Lord. Travis told him that in heaven he would walk and talk again, that one day in heaven is like a thousand days on earth, and that before he could sit down for lunch, we would be there with him. TJ blinked his eyes assuring us that he was ready. TJ's sisters flew in to spend time with him.

That was not TJ's day to see heaven. Miraculously, his health took a turn for the better. After a couple of weeks, his overall health finally began to improve, but his legs were still swollen from the water retention. The added weight, along with his already frail body, made it hard for him to move. He was very frustrated about his lack of mobility. In an effort to make him laugh, I whispered in his ear, "I'm sorry, TJ, but I think you got your thighs from your mother." I had hoped for a quick and funny comeback like TJ would have doled out once upon a time. All I heard was a faint "hmm" sound. He was entirely too weak to joke back.

During this hospital stay, Chandler, Travis, and I as well as another caregiver, rotated shifts caring for TJ. Since Chandler had two little girls at home, she took the evening caregiving shift. She was wonderful at it. She took ownership of her role with TJ and having her there gave me a tremendous break. She was fiercely protective of TJ and his biggest advocate, but she also made him do things he didn't want to do. When he was young, he was very compliant in response to his older sister's wishes. Now that he was a man, he was no longer as submissive.

One morning TJ become irritated with Chandler while she was giving him a shower. When she tried to wash his right side, he moved to the left. When she tried to wash his left side, he moved to the right. After a forty-five-minute struggle, she told TJ it was time to get out. But he didn't want to get out, so he wrapped his arm around the shower bar. As she pulled and tugged on the shower chair, he held on for dear life. When she finally got his arm free, he braced his leg against the shower wall, preventing her from moving him.

My phone rang.

"Hello," I answered.

Clearly upset, Chandler said, "Mom, TJ isn't listening to me. He's been in the shower for forty-five minutes and won't get out. Therapy is coming in soon, and he needs to get ready."

"Okay, put him on speaker," I said. "TJ, knock it off! Get out of the shower *right now*. You need to listen to your sister. This is already hard enough. You don't need to make it any harder."

All it took was mom's stern voice, and he got out of the shower.

After hanging up, I chuckled for a while as I thought about Chandler and TJ's relationship. They were both adults but still reverted to acting like children and telling on one another when they were in conflict. Chandler and TJ were our two youngest children. They were three years apart and shared a close bond. Memories flooded my mind of the time when they were young. They had the typical sister-brother relationship growing up. They loved each other, they hated each other; they fought, they made up; they were embarrassed of each other, they defended each other; they told on each other and covered for each other.

TJ was the compliant younger child, and Chandler was the bossy older sister. Chandler pretended she was the mother. Being the easy-going child that he was, he did whatever she told him to do. They were the perfect match. As I mentioned earlier, she dressed him, carried him around, painted his fingernails, and styled his hair with barrettes. Other days she lined TJ and her stuffed animals up in her room and made them sit at attention while she played teacher and gave them homework. Once in a while, she even drove TJ around in her little pink motorcar.

They were the best of friends. It's hard to find a picture of them without their arms around each other. They raised hamsters together, planned practical jokes to play on their father, and made donuts in the snow on Ashworth Road as teenagers. They were definitely partners in crime.

Now that she was his caregiver, Chandler expressed frustration about TJ being in the hospital. When she moved home, she was looking forward to hanging out with her brother and doing fun things together, like going to movies, bowling, and shopping. But all they had done together was sit in a hospital room. She couldn't wait for him to get healthy again and be discharged.

As the hospitalization continued and TJ's health declined, for the first time, Chandler began to understand how stressful and exhausting it was to care for him. Many times, while on her way to the hospital, she would call crying to say that she was anxious about taking care of him. Because he was unable to talk and too weak to sign, it was impossible to know what he needed. When we couldn't figure it out, he became agitated and upset. It was miserable for both TJ and the caregiver. We felt incredibly sorry for the pain and suffering he was going through and constantly felt like we were failing him. It was a lot for a young woman in her twenties to endure.

On December 12, 2017, TJ was cleared medically to return home. However, since he was too weak and we did not have the equipment needed to care for him at home, doctors suggested that TJ either go to rehab in the hospital or be admitted temporarily into a nursing home for rehab. Because of his trach, our options were limited to a very few that could handle his level of care. None of us were keen on the idea of TJ being in a nursing home, even if it was temporary, and hoped the hospital rehab facility would accept him.

A representative visited us regarding TJ's possible admission into a nursing home. As I was talking to her, I looked over at TJ. He was doing leg lifts and sit-ups while lying in bed in an attempt to get stronger. He had heard the word "nursing home" and became so afraid of that possibility that he was doing everything he could to avoid being placed in one. After witnessing his fear, we decided that if we couldn't get him into rehab at the hospital, then we would just obtain the equipment needed to care for him at home. We were relieved when a short time later we received word that he'd been accepted into the rehab unit at the hospital.

Soon after our arrival in the rehab unit, I met with TJ's recreational therapist. We visited for a while about our goals for TJ during his time there and what his life was like at home.

"I just need TJ to be able to stand and transfer into his wheelchair before he goes home," I said.

"Okay, I think we can accomplish that. What is his life like at home?" she asked.

"Well, he goes to therapy in the mornings and then just pretty much sits in front of the TV for the rest of the day. He's lonely."

She then leaned close and said, "I have a friend whose daughter acquired a brain injury in a car accident. She said the loss of her daughter's friends and social life was the most painful part of the whole process."

As I listened, I felt tears welling up in my eyes. "It *is* the most painful part. It hurts so much. Half of me understands that his friends' lives must move on, but the other half of me is in so much pain because of it. Thank you for sharing that with me. Sometimes I just need to know that somebody else feels the same way." Finally, someone had affirmed how painful it was for TJ to lose his friends and social life. She was a gift from God. Her kind and caring words were like salve to my wounds.

While in rehab, TJ began to improve. I was optimistic that he would be restored to the level where he was before the liver failure. I was somewhat nervous about taking care of him at home in his weakened state but figured we would somehow manage. Although he was still very weak, it only took a few days of rehab before I was able to transfer and walk with him by myself. The plan was for TJ to be discharged on December 21st. We were thrilled that he would be home for Christmas.

However, the following day I noticed that TJ was breathing harder and his lips were once again turning blue. Doctors then discovered that TJ had water around his lungs as well as pneumonia, so he was transferred back to the pulmonology floor. They also found multiple blood clots in his lungs. He was started on a blood thinner. Chest tubes were inserted and moved several times to drain off the fluid. A few nights later Travis was on overnight duty when TJ began struggling to breathe, so he was moved to the ICU and placed on a ventilator.

It was policy in the intensive care unit that family members could not sleep in the patient's room, so we went home to sleep. On December 29, 2017, around midnight, the phone rang. I jolted awake because I knew it was the hospital calling.

My anxiety rose when I said, "Hello?"

"This is the intensive care unit. TJ's heart stopped, and they're doing chest compressions on him right now. You need to get down here as soon as possible."

"Oh my gosh! We're coming!"

Then he added, "Please drive carefully."

Travis, Aiden, and I quickly dressed and raced to the hospital, unaware of whether TJ would be dead or alive when we arrived. When we entered the section of the ICU where TJ's room was, a large number of people were in and around his room. Everyone turned around and stared at us as we approached, but no one said a word. While standing outside of the doorway, I became exasperated with the lack of information and demanded, "Is he alive?"

One of the residents came out of his room, and calmly said, "Yes, we got him back."

I sat down in a chair and bawled out loud.

"Did his brain get oxygen?" I asked.

The doctor said, "It's too early to tell, but we checked his blood oxygen level. It was good, so that's a good sign."

The chaplain then came to comfort us. As he was speaking to Travis, I realized that he looked familiar.

"Why do you look familiar?" I asked.

He shrugged his shoulders, as though caught off-guard by my question.

"Who *are* you?" I asked.

He answered, "Todd Smith."

I tilted my head in question. "From the church in Urbandale?"

He nodded.

I said, "Todd, that code is TJ Denham!"

Although we hadn't known the chaplain's family well, we knew the name and had seen them at church. Todd had helped out in TJ's youth group, and TJ had often mentioned his name. Todd went on to tell us that when he received the call, he had no idea that the patient coding was TJ. In fact, he told us that he wasn't even supposed to be on that shift. I knew it wasn't a coincidence. Once again, I felt the loving arms of God enveloping us.

TJ was in and out of consciousness for hours after he coded. We were told that, after trauma, the body goes into shock and shuts down for a while. Later in the morning when I walked into TJ's room, he whimpered at the sound of my voice. The nurse said people had been in and out of his room all morning. He hadn't reacted that way toward any of them. It was a good sign that he knew who I was. He started rousing around 11 A.M. and was very grouchy. Nurses told us that CPR is a very violent act and he would be quite sore for a few days afterward. When Travis asked him if he was upset with us for not being there, his feet began to tap. Although we knew it wasn't our fault that we weren't there, we still felt guilty that we hadn't been with him. We were thankful that the Lord didn't take him home while he was alone. Even so, I wondered how much more we could take.

By January 1st, TJ had improved enough to move back to the

pulmonology floor. Doctors began heavy diuretics to remove the excess fluid. TJ was storing most of the extra fluid in his legs from the knee down. They were huge, but it was better than being around his lungs. Travis, who was always looking for a way to make TJ laugh, began calling him "Mr. Kankles." Normally TJ would have thrown his head back in laughter. At that point, however, he didn't even crack a smile.

On January 3rd, TJ once again began struggling to breathe. Doctors ordered a CT scan and also performed a bronchoscopy to check on the bleeding in his lungs. After the procedure, I was in the recovery room with TJ while he was waking up. The doctor came in and sat down beside me. I was taken aback because I had never had a doctor come to me in the recovery room and actually sit with me to talk. I could tell by his demeanor that something was wrong. He said, "TJ is bleeding *everywhere* in his lungs, and some of the tissue is dying." He went on to tell me that they thought TJ had pneumonia. Nothing they were treating it with was working, so it was only getting worse. They couldn't give him blood thinners to break up the blood clots in his lungs because of the bleeding and they couldn't stop the bleeding because the clots could grow larger and be fatal.

I stared at the floor for a moment and then very quietly asked him, "Is he going to die?"

With a troubled look in his eyes, the doctor answered, "It's concerning," and immediately admitted TJ back into the ICU.

January 5, 2018

Caring Bridge
Written by Kelly

This morning's procedures went well. TJ was sedated pretty heavily and placed on a vent that they kept him on until late afternoon. His chest tube, an hour after being placed, had already drained 500 ml. I'm sure he is feeling some relief from that. He has been sleeping peacefully all day. Infectious disease said his lung cultures have yet to come back but that he's already on the strongest antibiotic available, so they'll keep him on it for a while.

A few days ago, when I realized that death was now a very real possibility, memories flooded my mind of every time I have been impatient with him or said something I would later regret. I felt like a failure as a mother. I cried and cried and told TJ how sorry I was that I didn't do better. I then sat with my dear friend Amber, and we cried together. She told me over and over to get those thoughts out of my mind because they weren't true and that we did everything for TJ and that he knew how much we loved him. Today I was given a beautiful gift from God. This morning TJ was on a ventilator because of the procedure he'd had done. Because he gets himself into weird positions, the cuff that seals his trachea while on the ventilator leaks air, and you can hear a vibrating noise sometimes as the air is coming up the trachea. Normally I think it just sounds like a bear snorting. Today as I was cupping TJ's face in my hands, I told him I loved him. As the ventilator was pushing air through his vocal cords, he looked at me very intently and then with a hoarse voice said, "I. Love. You." Travis and Chandler had been with him all morning, and he didn't do that for them, but today God and TJ knew how badly I needed to hear that, so God provided a way. We fail God but He never fails us.

> **JAMES 1:17**
>
> "Every good and perfect gift is from above, coming down from the Father of the heavenly lights, who does not change like shifting shadows."

Doctors were only giving TJ a 50 percent chance of survival. They went on to say that even if he did live, he would have chronic lung issues. The dead tissue had left his lungs with cavities that would fill with fluid and become a breeding ground for infections. Bleeding and blood clots would also be a major threat. Doctors began talking to us about placing a DNR order on TJ because they were concerned about his future quality of life.

After they left, Travis and I explained to TJ what the doctors were saying. He was peaceful and even smiling. His reaction was so unexpected, and I wished once again that he could express himself. I wanted to know what he was thinking. I wanted to talk to him about his fears. I needed him to reassure me that he was going to be okay. We asked him if he wanted to keep fighting. He tapped his feet "yes."

I was beginning to feel some pressure from the medical staff to comply with their DNR suggestion. One of the doctors commented, "I wouldn't want to live like that if I were a twenty-one-year-old man." When I told a nurse that he said he wanted to live and keep fighting, she said, "I don't think he's capable of making that decision."

Although I thought that we might be coming to the end of his life, I couldn't bring myself to place a DNR order on him. I didn't trust that we were at the point where that was necessary. When your child has special needs, you always question if people value your child just as they are. It can be difficult to trust people's decisions, so I called and spoke to Dr. Steele. I told her what was going on and that TJ said he wanted to live and keep fighting. She said, "If TJ wants to keep fighting, then that's what you do." She told me to hang a sign on his door that said "Positive vibes only." It made me smile. I was very thankful for her wisdom. Even though TJ hadn't been her patient since we left the Mayo PICU five years earlier, she still cared about him and took the time to talk with me. We were so blessed to have had her for a doctor.

CHAPTER 20

FULL CIRCLE

In late January of 2018, TJ became more stable and was taken off the ventilator. Doctors told us it would take a long time for his lungs to heal, so they suggested transferring him to a long-term acute care (LTAC) facility across town. This facility leased floor space inside the hospital where TJ's heart surgery took place. That hospital had always been a source of pain and traumatic memories for us. We typically avoided that hospital, but because all our other options were hours away, we agreed to the transfer.

To make matters worse, our caseworker said that if TJ wasn't discharged from the hospital within 90 days of his admission in November, we would lose our brain-injury waiver. The waiver compensated me for TJ's care and was a source of income for us. She said that after his discharge from the hospital, we could reapply, but the waiting list was two years long. Upon learning the news, I sank into a chair and started to laugh. It made absolutely no sense. I decided not to fret and simply trust that God would get us through.

At the beginning of TJ's stay at the LTAC facility, he began to slowly improve. We were still battling problems with his lungs, but even so, his progress made me hopeful that he might get through the illness and come home. He started rehab again and was slowly getting stronger. However, in late February, he developed pneumonia and began to decline, rapidly losing weight. He also developed a fever of 104 degrees that they were unable to bring down. Doctors informed us that his heart was failing, and we had noticed that his stomach was no longer able to digest food. He was placed back on a ventilator.

On Friday, February 23rd, one of TJ's doctors approached us in the hallway. We were fond of this doctor. He was kind and compassionate and would spend time educating our family and discussing TJ's care.

The doctor looked at me and said, "Kelly, your pastor was here this morning. Is TJ saved?"

I nodded. "Yes, TJ is saved. He's a Christian."

His face lit up and he said, "I'm a Christian, too. TJ has declined rapidly with this bout of pneumonia. I don't want to put him through any more. You need to let him go. Living on a ventilator like this isn't good. He's going to heaven. It will be better for him there, and you're going to see him again. I talked with the pulmonologists, and they also feel that it's time to let him go."

I suddenly realized why I liked this doctor so much. He was my brother in Christ. I knew he valued TJ's life exactly as it was. I knew on that specific day God had given TJ that doctor—one I could trust and feel comfortable with. He and I talked a while longer and decided that we would get through the weekend on the ventilator. On Monday we would remove life support and let TJ go. We had reached the point in his life where keeping him alive was far crueler than letting him go.

I walked back to TJ's room, bent over him, and held him in my arms as he lay in bed. While sobbing I told him, "You're dying, buddy. Doctors have done everything they can. There's nothing else they can do. You're not going to make it." He stared at the ceiling. I wondered what he was thinking. I'm sure he knew and could feel that his life was slipping away. I didn't tell him that on Monday we would be removing life support. I just couldn't bear to tell him. I didn't want him to stress all weekend, knowing that he was going to die the following week. The decision to remove life support was the most agonizing decision I've ever made. Even though I knew it was necessary, it was horrifying. I wished TJ could communicate so he could tell me it was okay and that he was ready.

That weekend, I stayed overnight with TJ at the hospital. In the middle of the night, I woke up and couldn't get back to sleep. I got up and began to walk the halls and pray. I found myself downstairs by the OR waiting room—the very waiting room where I sat during TJ's heart surgery. I sat in the same spot where I'd been sitting when Dr. Harmon came out to speak with us after the surgery. As I looked around the room, I thought, *I can't believe I'm here. We never would have chosen to come back to this hospital but for circumstances beyond our control. This is where it all began, and this is where it's going to end.* We had come full circle.

While sitting in the waiting room, I pondered why God brought us back. For five years this hospital had been a place of hurt and pain. However, during this hospitalization, we had a far more positive experience. We were surrounded by gentle, loving, caring people—some of them God's people—and we could now walk away with comforting memories, healed from past wounds. Psalm 147:3 says, "He heals the brokenhearted and binds up their wounds."

My thoughts turned toward Dr. Harmon. It was our opinion that TJ's brain injury and impending death were caused by the surgeon's mistake. For years I struggled with anger over the choices he made and the way we were treated in the days following the surgery. Over time, as I focused my eyes on the Lord, I began to find comfort in His sovereignty. The Lord could have interceded at any time before or during TJ's surgery. However, He chose not to. Over the years, I began to see the lives that could be won for Christ because of TJ's powerful story. I could also see God's presence everywhere in our lives as He lovingly carried us during our journey of suffering.

A friend of mine who is a nurse once told me, "Regarding surgeons, always listen to the recommendations of the nurses because they see the patients coming out of the OR." We chose TJ's surgeon because he was highly regarded in the medical community. We had only heard wonderful things about him. He had done a lot of good for a lot of people. In the years following TJ's surgery, I saw the shocked faces of many medical staff members upon learning the identity of TJ's surgeon. I came to the conclusion that this kind of surgical outcome was very unusual for him. Although I didn't understand it at the time, in hindsight, I can still remember the concern in his eyes that first week as TJ rapidly declined. Even though it has been a process for me, I now have compassion for him. I recently read a quote by Kimberly Drew that comforted me: "Mere men make mistakes in one moment and rise to do amazing things in the next. God is sovereign over them all." (Kimberly M. Drew 2016, 199)

I believe there were greater forces at work on that fateful surgery day in 2013. I don't understand it all, but I do believe God was in control that day. And because of the work that Christ did on the cross for me, I am forgiven. Therefore, I can be obedient to Him and live a life of forgiveness, trusting that He will make all things right in His time.

TJ was peaceful over the weekend. Many family and friends stopped by to say goodbye to TJ. The hospital set aside a room where our visitors could gather. Because TJ's room was small, they took turns visiting him. Travis and I spent our time between TJ's room and visiting with family and friends. We rarely left the hospital and spent every minute we could with him.

FEBRUARY 25, 2018

CaringBridge
Written by Kelly

I signed the DNR paper this afternoon. I'm sure it's not an easy job for doctors to tell a family that they need to let their twenty-one-year-old son die, and as I was signing the paper, I was thinking about what it must be like to be in their shoes.

Today TJ had a good day. There were a lot of family and friends around. A therapy dog came in at one point, and TJ really perked up for that.

Tomorrow will begin our very difficult journey of letting go. We will begin comfort cares which means he will get as much medication as he needs to be comfortable, and he will also be removed from life support. A nurse today thought he would live a couple of days but, of course, one never knows.

Thank you for all of your support throughout this very difficult situation. It has been a very long and agonizing journey, and I so appreciate your commitment all of these years to stay by our side and pray.

When Travis and I were finally alone with TJ, we both told him how much we loved him and how sorry we were that we couldn't make him well again. We told him we wanted him to live and we were sorry that we sometimes pushed him too hard. We apologized for any time we had hurt him. As I apologized to TJ, the thought occurred to me that TJ probably had things he wanted to say and was unable to. I asked him if he had things he wanted to apologize for. He blinked his eyes. I told him that I forgave him for anything he had done and that we couldn't have asked for a better son. I reminded him that I loved him and that he was going to heaven. I assured him that he would be okay. *We* were the ones who were going to struggle without him, but we would see each other again in heaven.

On Monday, February 26, around noon, a nurse administered the sedation drugs and another nurse removed his life support. I never did tell TJ the decision Travis and I made. I was thankful that he wasn't awake to see it happen. I was afraid that he would choke and gasp for air after the ventilator was removed because I had seen my grandma struggling to breathe when she was dying. However, the nurses had promised me they would keep him comfortable. I repeatedly prayed that God would not let him suffer because he had already suffered so much.

A nurse asked, "Do you want to donate his organs?"

Shocked, I tersely replied, "I don't know what recipients would want. Nothing is working."

"Skin and eyes," she said. "I'm sorry. I'm sorry," she apologized.

I knew she felt terrible even having to ask the question.

About 10 P.M. on Monday evening, I asked TJ's nurse what we could expect. She said she didn't think he would make it more than twelve hours. That surprised me. I thought we would have a couple of days with him. We called family to let them know they should come up early in the morning, but they decided to come back up to the hospital immediately.

A little after midnight, on Tuesday, February 27, 2018, my uncle was talking to TJ when he noticed that TJ was getting cold. I got blankets and covered him up and then sat back down. At the time, I didn't know why. Now I realize it was a bit of motherly instinct and the prompting of the Holy Spirit that caused me to get up again and go over to TJ. I started hugging and kissing him and telling him how much I loved him. With my face next to his, I heard him take two short breaths, then his heart rate plummeted and the alarm started buzzing. Travis jumped up and both of us stood over him assuring him of our love. Then he died in my arms. The mother's arms that held him when he first came into this world were the arms that held him when he was leaving this world. I was incredibly grateful that God allowed him to die peacefully in my arms.

We stayed in the hospital for a while after TJ's death and visited with family. We had spent every day in the hospital for three months. It felt strange to leave. We didn't want to be away from TJ and weren't sure what to do with ourselves. Finally, around 2 A.M., we decided it was time to go. As we were preparing to leave the LTAC floor, we realized we didn't have our wheelchair-accessible van with us and wouldn't be able to take TJ's wheelchair, so we made arrangements with the staff to pick it up the following day.

As Travis and I were driving home, my mom called and asked if we would like to meet her and my stepdad Tom at *Village Inn* for coffee. We gladly accepted. We still weren't ready to go home. As we visited, I was surprised by how calm I was. I felt numb. I couldn't cry because I was so relieved that TJ's suffering was over.

The following day, after retrieving TJ's wheelchair from the LTAC floor, I stopped by to see my friend Ginny who is a nurse on the first floor of the hospital. As I drove the chair into her department, I realized how sad it must look to see me driving the wheelchair without TJ in it. After visiting with Ginny for a few minutes, I drove the chair into the parking lot. As people walked by and glanced curiously at the woman driving an empty wheelchair, I wanted to say, "You'll never believe what just happened to me! My son died!"

In the days immediately following my sweet boy's death, I lay in my bed, smiling at the ceiling with tears rolling down my cheeks as I imagined TJ in heaven laughing, talking, and praising God. After years of confinement, he was finally free to run, jump, skip, and twirl down the streets of gold. I didn't cry tears of sadness. I cried tears of joy that he was healed, with Jesus, and no longer in pain or trapped in his broken body.

TJ's funeral was held at our church. It was the beginning of March and was supposed to be a cool, rainy day. Instead, God gave us a beautiful, sunny, tranquil day. Ashley spoke, surrounded by her three sisters. We felt blessed to see them all together, supporting one another, and honoring their brother. It was a beautiful ceremony. TJ's cousins and his best friend Drake were the pallbearers. The cousins, who were in the military, wore their uniforms. TJ would have been so proud.

We buried TJ in a cemetery not far from our home. We bought three plots. Travis and I will be buried beside him one day. The plots are on a hill that overlooks a pond with a fountain in the center. Pine trees dot the water's edge where it's serene and beautiful. We bought a headstone with a bench so we could sit and gaze at the water when we visit his grave. I've found that I am drawn to the cemetery. It's a place of peace and comfort.

Even wildlife feels at home in the cemetery. We have seen deer, raccoons, and foxes, but our favorites are the geese and ducks. Most of the time the geese are floating on the pond, but when they become hungry, they waddle to the hill where TJ is buried, scavenging for food. One day, the geese were on the hill chasing each other, squawking, and fighting. Feeling silly, I warned them that they'd better quiet down because if they woke TJ, he would be grouchy, and they would be sorry. You never wake a sleeping TJ.

I love how Jesus described those who have died as being "asleep." It gives me great comfort to know that TJ's death is not the end. His spirit is alive in heaven with Christ, while his body sleeps until the Rapture when it will rise again. I'm full of anticipation imagining the day when I step into heaven and see him again. I have my lunch order all ready.

While I'm waiting, TJ is free…

EPILOGUE

As the days and months have passed since TJ's death, his absence has become increasingly painful. I long to put my face next to his and hold him tight. I long to tell him just one more time how proud I am of him and that I love him. I miss my sweet boy terribly. Every inch of my body yearns to be reunited with my child again. I think about it often.

Because of my desperation to see him again, I began to have anxious thoughts like, *What if he wasn't saved and I never see him again? What if God isn't real and when we die there is no heaven or hell and I never see my son again?* Deep in my inner being, I know TJ was saved. I know that God is real and none of those thoughts are true. I have seen overwhelming evidence of Him throughout my lifetime. He's laughed with me through the good times, held me in His arms through the hard times, and carried me through the unbearable times. *Why am I struggling so much with doubt?* I thought to myself. I began praying for God's help to conquer the relentless thoughts that haunted me.

At the beginning of 2019, I was asked to be in a Bible study with some friends. It was a read-through-the-Bible-in-a-year study. I eagerly said yes. We started reading at the very beginning in Genesis. Shortly after, we came to the story of Joseph—my favorite story in the Bible.

Jacob was Joseph's father and he had twelve sons. Joseph was his favorite, and his brothers were extremely jealous of him. One day when Joseph was seventeen years old, his brothers decided that they'd had enough of this spoiled kid. They plotted to kill him. Reuben, one of the older brothers, did not want Joseph killed and persuaded his siblings to throw him into a pit instead. Reuben's plan was to rescue Joseph from the pit and take him back to their father. However, shortly afterward, a caravan of Ishmaelites was traveling by, and the other brothers sold Joseph to them.

Genesis 37:31–35

"Then they got Joseph's robe, slaughtered a goat and dipped the robe in the blood. They took the ornate robe back to their father and said, 'We found this. Examine it to see whether it is your son's robe.'

He recognized it and said, 'It is my son's robe! Some ferocious animal has devoured him. Joseph has surely been torn to pieces.'

Then Jacob tore his clothes, put on sackcloth and mourned for his son many days. All his sons and daughters came to comfort him, but he refused to be comforted. 'No,' he said, 'I will continue to mourn until I join my son in the grave.' So, his father wept for him."

Meanwhile, Joseph spent the next thirteen years as a slave and then as a prisoner. The entire time the Lord was with him, showed him kindness, and granted him favor. After many years of twists and turns in the story, Joseph was miraculously brought up out of prison by Pharaoh and put in charge of the whole land of Egypt. Through another series of events, Joseph and his brothers were eventually reunited and Joseph extended love and forgiveness to them. And then, the great reunion between father and son took place.

In years past, I've always been astounded by the timing of God in this story, by the patience of Joseph and his trust in God through his suffering, and by his amazing forgiveness toward his brothers. But as I was reading the story this time, a thought crossed my mind that I'd never had before, *I wonder if Jacob regretted mourning all those years when he believed Joseph to be dead. I wonder if he had regrets for not enjoying his life and his family because of his all-consuming longing to be reunited with Joseph.* The truth was that, even though Jacob didn't know it, Joseph had been alive the whole time. Sometimes it doesn't matter what the truth is because we act according to what we believe.

I pondered this more, then asked myself, *If I believe that my son is dead and in the grave and I will never see him again, then how will I live?* After thinking about this for a while, I decided that my answer would be: I will waste my life. I won't be able to get off the couch most days. I won't be effective in winning the hearts of men toward God. I won't enjoy my life or the family or friends God has blessed me with. And I will probably have many regrets.

I then asked myself, *If I believe that my son is alive with Christ in heaven like God's Word says he is and that I will see him again one day, then how will I live?* My answer: I will continue the work that God has given me to do, knowing that I will receive eternal rewards for my perseverance through suffering. I will have joy and fulfillment in Christ despite my suffering. I will enjoy all the many blessings He has given me on this earth as I eagerly look forward to heaven.

Now that TJ is with Jesus in heaven, God still has work for me to do. Even though some days I want to curl into a ball and disengage from the world, I resist the urge because I know God would not be pleased. There are people suffering who need to hear that God is good, despite their circumstances. God walks beside us. Even though we may not feel His presence in our lives while we walk through our trial, it doesn't mean He's not there. I yearn to share about God's unfailing love even during the midst of tragedy and that He has a plan for each of our lives. We are designed to bring glory and honor to the King of kings. There is no higher calling than to be a servant to The Almighty, even if that service takes us down a path we never wanted or expected to travel. I long to tell people that Christ died for them and that through Jesus they may receive eternal life. No matter what happens in this life, in Christ there is always hope.

Months after the funeral and after some of the shock had worn off, although Chandler was still incredibly sad, we began to see a beautiful spirit emerge from inside of her. In the beginning of TJ's hospitalization, she was frustrated and didn't understand why God would bring her back home to be his caregiver just to sit in a hospital day after day. After his death, she was able to look back and see God's loving hand orchestrating her move back home at just the right time so she could spend every day of his last three months with him. What a blessing she had been given from the Lord. Even though the Lord took TJ home, He held us, comforted us, and blessed us during that difficult process.

Despite what others believe, my sweet TJ's life was not wasted, even with a severely disabled body. When TJ was young, my dreams for him were to stand on a stage and preach to hundreds of people about Christ. After he was injured, he *still* spoke to hundreds of people about Christ, but he spoke to them from a hospital bed and without the ability to talk.

And now, I am his voice.

2 Corinthians 4:17–18

"For our light and momentary troubles are achieving for us an eternal glory that far outweighs them all. So, we fix our eyes not on what is seen, but on what is unseen, since what is seen is temporary, but what is unseen is eternal."

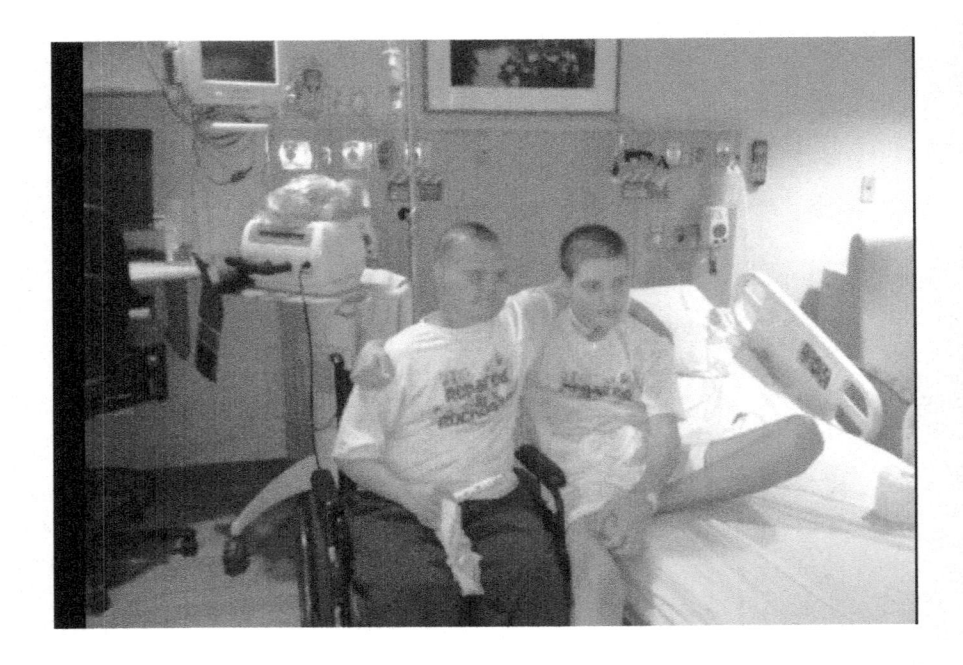

Tom & TJ in matching *Repaired in Rochester* shirts, August 2013

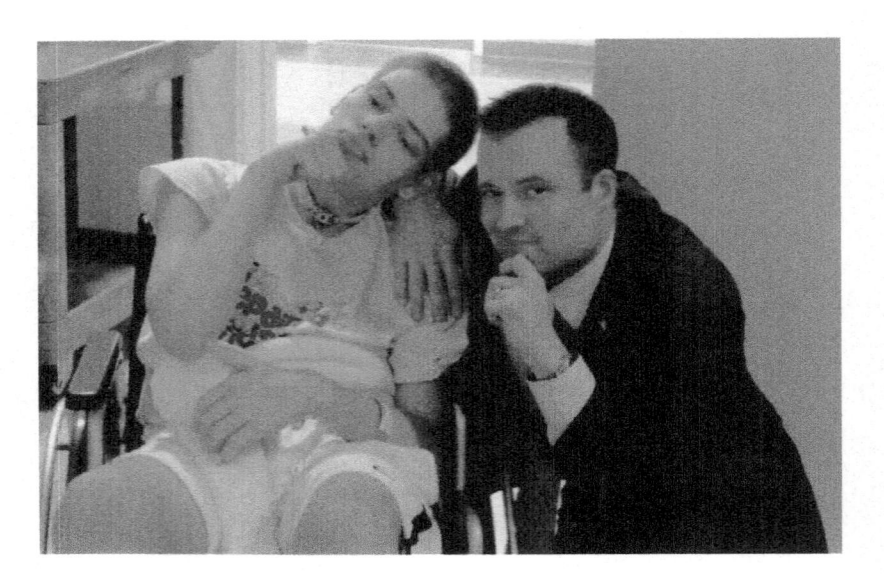

TJ & Dr. Landry, September 2013

Epilogue

TJ signing "I love you," 2015

TJ & sister Whitney at TJ's 5K, 2014

Chandler & TJ hugging after her wedding, 2015

TJ at High School Basketball State Tournament with teachers (left to right) Mr. Hawkins, Mr. Welter & school social worker, Meribeth, 2015

Drake, TJ, & Dynas at I-Cubs baseball game
for TJ's twentieth birthday, 2016

TJ with Team Run Free, Summer 2017

TJ's Senior Picture, Fall 2016

Epilogue

TJ's Senior Picture, Fall 2016

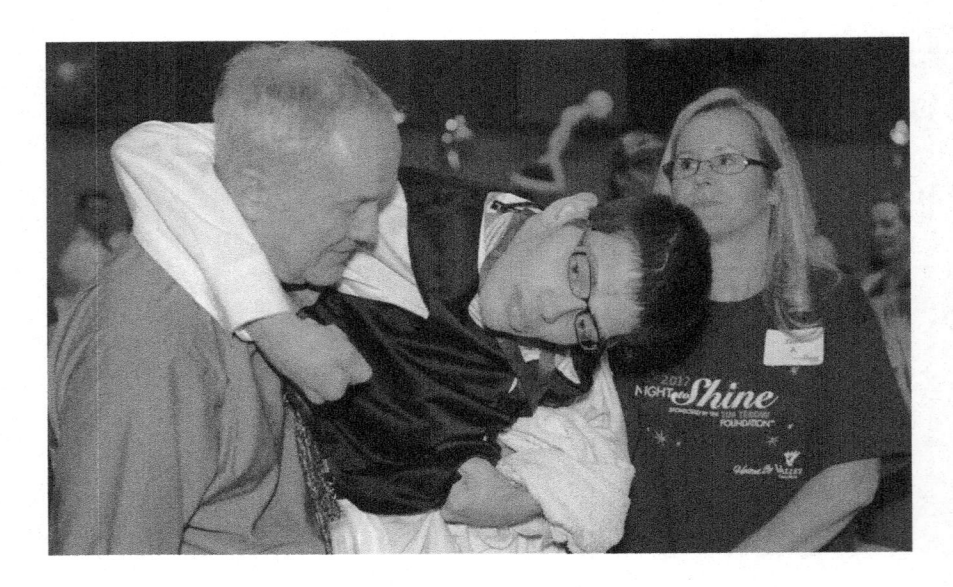

TJ with his buddy Tom at Night to Shine, 2017

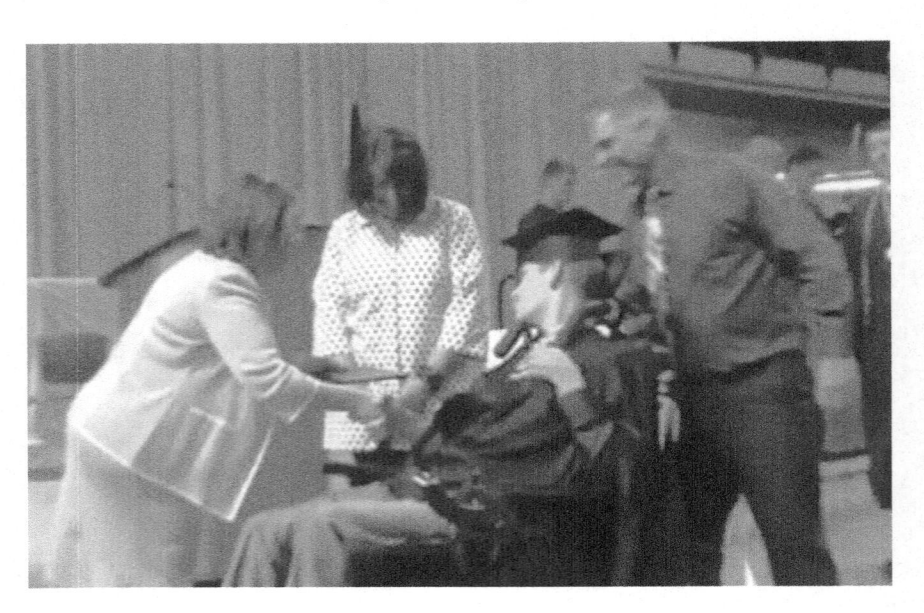

TJ receiving his high school diploma, May 2017

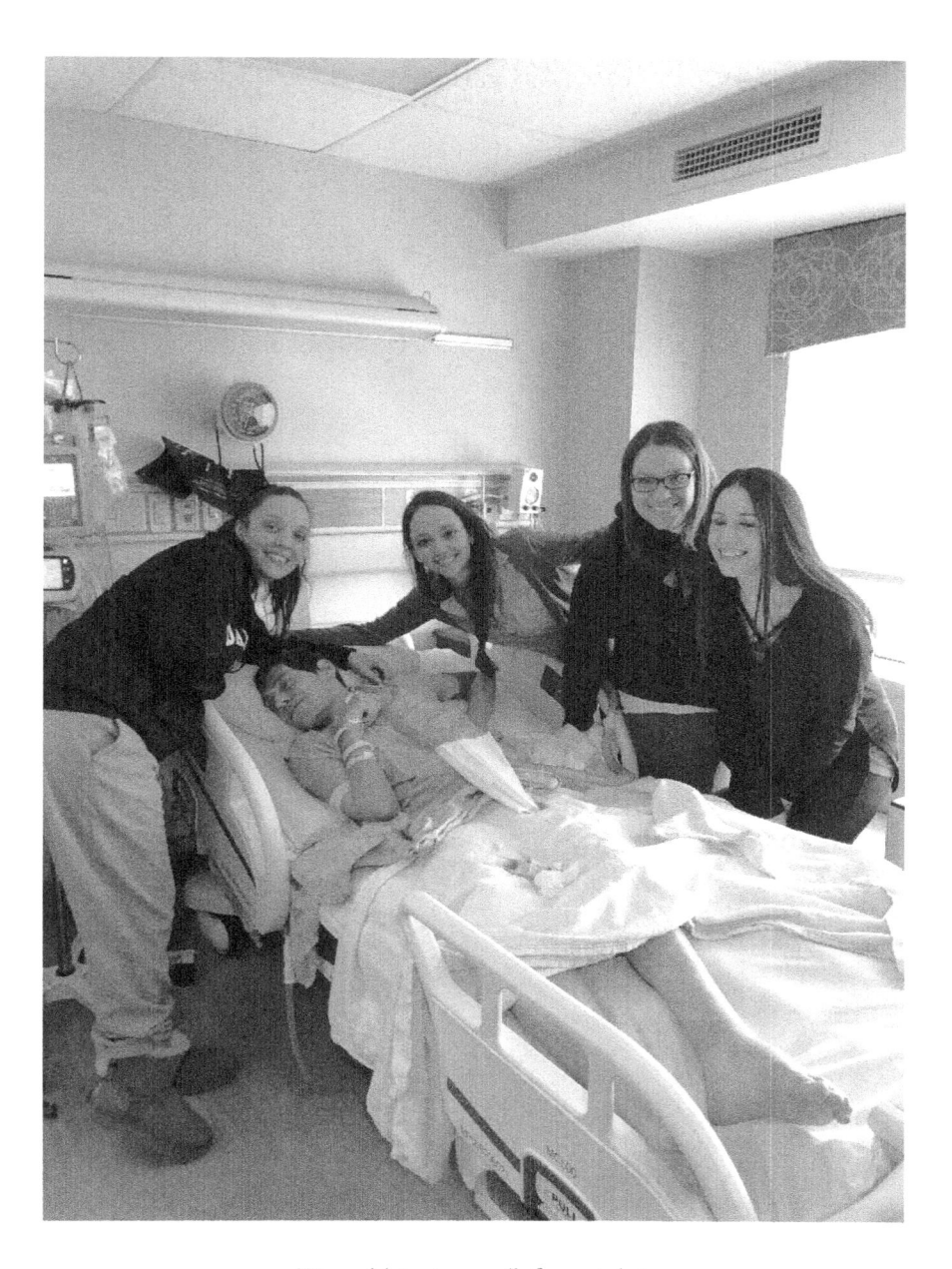

TJ and his sisters, (left to right)
Courtney, Whitney, Ashley, and Chandler,
December 2017

TJ & his cousin Brandyn a few days before death, February 2018

TJ's casket carried by his cousins and Drake

Epilogue

TJ's grave

A MESSAGE FROM KELLY

One Sunday morning during worship service, Pastor Quintin shared that his wife, Ruth, had been battling cancer. After a complicated surgery, long hospitalization, and grueling recovery, he was pleased to announce she was now cancer free. The congregation cheered, applauded, and praised the Lord. I was overjoyed that by the grace of God, Ruth had beaten cancer and her health was restored—but thoughts of doubt began to flood my mind. *Why not TJ, Lord? Why didn't You heal him? Did You not love him as much as her? Did we not pray enough? Were we not good enough Christians?* I tried to choke down the sobs that were rising in my throat, but to no avail. I finally gave up, left the worship center, and headed for the women's restroom. I spied a bench between the sinks and sat down to cry. Sometimes I just needed to let it out.

A woman entered the restroom and sat down beside me. "Is it the service that is making you cry?" she asked.

"Yeah, I'm trying to pull myself together," I answered. "My son died a year ago, and I don't understand why God didn't heal him, too. I don't know why God heals others, but He didn't heal my son."

"Are you Kelly?" she asked.

"Yeah. How do you know me?"

"I'm Sherri and I prayed for TJ," she answered.

"Oh, thank you for praying for us. I know God loved TJ. I just wish he had been healed, too. After hearing Ruth's story, I thought, *'Lord, was she a better Christian than I and that's why you healed her and not TJ?'* I know deep down that's not true, but the thought still comes into my mind."

"No, those thoughts are *not* true. God loved TJ. There are some people who will come to know the Lord from hearing stories of miracles and healings. But most people will come to know Christ through stories of pain and suffering. Most times, it is pain that brings us to the Lord—and God knew you could endure it."

❦

Luke 8:39 says, "'Return home and tell how much God has done for you.' So the man went away and told all over town how much Jesus had done for him." My hope in writing TJ's story is that many will want to know Jesus and will ask Him to be Lord of their life.

If you desire to know our Lord and Savior Jesus Christ and want the love and peace that He offers through a relationship with Him, below are verses that describe how to receive the gift of eternal life, followed by a prayer to invite Jesus into your heart:

You are a sinner – "For all have sinned and fall short of the glory of God." (Romans 3:23)

Sin's penalty is spiritual death – "For the wages of sin is death." (Romans 6:23)

Jesus died for your sins and rose again – "But God demonstrates His own love toward us, in that while we were yet sinners, Christ died for us." (Romans 5:8, 4:24–25)

You must turn from your sins – "Therefore having overlooked the times of ignorance, God is now declaring to men that all people everywhere should repent." (Acts 17:30)

You must believe in Jesus Christ the Son of God – "For God so loved the world, that He gave His only begotten Son, that whoever believes in Him shall not perish, but have eternal life." (John 3:16)

If you believe in Christ alone, repenting of your sins, God's gift to you is eternal life – "But the free gift of God is eternal life in Christ Jesus our Lord." (Romans 6:23)

Confess with your mouth that Jesus is Lord – "If you declare with your mouth, 'Jesus is Lord,' and believe in your heart that God raised him from the dead, you will be saved." (Romans 10:9)

Prayer:

Father, I am a sinner in need of a Savior. I ask that you forgive me of all my sins and cleanse me from all unrighteousness. I believe that you sent Your son, Jesus Christ, to die on a cross and that He was resurrected from the dead and is now alive with You. I invite Jesus to come into my heart and become the Lord of my life from this day forward.

Thank you for saving me.
In Jesus' name I pray, Amen.

ACKNOWLEDGEMENTS

THANK YOU TO:

First and foremost, the Lord, for the opportunity You gave me to be Your servant. My heart's desire is that You will be glorified and that others will know of Your great love for them. Thank you, Jesus, for Your constant presence, the hope You have given us, and the eternity we look forward to with You and our loved ones because of the blood You shed on the cross for us.

Jena, Katherine, Kim, Kasey, Amy, and Janice for your support, encouragement, and invaluable feedback. Many improvements were made because of your helpful suggestions.

Beth, Tom, Richard, Pastor Linton, Pastor Quintin, and Valley Church for seeking us out, loving TJ, and caring about his spiritual growth.

The many friends who stayed with TJ at the hospital, sent money, brought meals, cleaned our house, did yardwork, and prayed for years. We are very grateful for your servant hearts.

My dear friend, Melinda. What a journey we have been on together. Fifteen years ago, I never dreamed a random woman sitting next to me on a plane would become a lifelong friend. God blessed me greatly, indeed! Thank you for allowing me to lean on you the past few years. Your writing skills have been invaluable to me as I set out on this new endeavor. True to your nature, you have been patient, kind, encouraging, and always a cheerleader. I love you, dear friend.

Nancy Arant Williams for your expert editing. After searching for a professional Christian editor online, God miraculously led me to you. I never dreamed when I chose your name on the list that we would have in common my long-time friend and your cousin, Barb. Only the hand of God could orchestrate such an encounter. I now call you my friend.

The many doctors, nurses, caregivers, aides, and therapists who provided TJ with excellent medical care. You were more than a medical team to us. You were our friends, and I will forever be grateful.

Eric, Garrett, Zack, Blythe, Meribeth, Jim, David, Jannett, and the faculty at Valley High School. Thank you for helping TJ finish his schooling. The years at Valley were precious. I cannot think about the time we spent with you without tears filling my eyes. You will always hold a special place in my heart.

Brown Marketing, Consulting & PR; Creative Lunacy; Jonathan Kirsch; Galadriel; and Slater & Norris. Thank you for your expert skills, suggestions, and help with getting this book through the publishing process.

Travis, Ashley, Whitney, Courtney, Chandler, and Aiden. Thank you for the many hours you spent listening while I sorted out my thoughts, fears, and frustrations. Thank you for your encouragement, patience, love, and support in spite of my scattered brain and emotional unavailability from reliving the trauma as I wrote this book. I could not have made it through this without your support.

NOTES

Chapter 3
Beth Moore, *Believing God: Experiencing a Fresh Explosion of Faith,* (Nashville, TN: LifeWay Press, 2004).

Chapter 6
Sarah Young, *Jesus Calling,* (Nashville, TN: Thomas Nelson, 2004), 140.

Chapter 7
Beth Moore, *Believing God: Experiencing a Fresh Explosion of Faith,* (Nashville, TN: LifeWay Press, 2004).

Rick Warren, *The Purpose Driven Life: What on Earth Am I Here for,* (Place of publication not identified: Zondervan, 2007).

Chapter 9
Merriam-Webster, s.v. "deficit," accessed November 19, 2019, https://www.merriam-webster.com/dictionary/deficit.

Chapter 11
Lucy Larcom (March 5, 1824–April 17, 1893, in Boston, Massachusetts) was an American poet.

Chapter 13
Charles H. Spurgeon. *The New Park Street Pulpit: Containing Sermons Preached and Revised by the Rev. C. H. Spurgeon, Minister of the Chapel.* Vol. 5. Pasadena: Pilgrim Publications, 1991.

Chapter 14
Jerry Bridges, *Trusting God: Even When Life Hurts*,
(Colorado Springs, CO: NavPress, 2008), 18.

Chapter 15
Max Lucado, *You'll Get through This: Hope and Help for Your Turbulent Times*.
(Philadelphia, PA: Running Press, 2013).

Chapter 17
Red Hot Chili Peppers, "Can't Stop," Track #1 on *By the Way*.
Warner Bros, 2003, CD.

Chapter 20
Kimberly M. Drew and Jocelyn Green,
Refresh: Spiritual Nourishment for Parents of Children with Special Needs.
(Grand Rapids, MI.: Kregel Publications, 2016), 199.